"In *Cinema and Psyche,* the authors demonstrate yet again the joy of imagination when inspired, in-spirited, by a Jungian interpretation of films. Beautifully written, this book digs deep into the troubles and mysteries of the twenty-first century by showing films as diverse as *Arrival* and *Far From the Madding Crowd* to be both revelatory and numinous. Anyone who wants to know about film criticism with or without Jung, start right here."

Susan Rowland *(PhD), Pacifica Graduate Institute; author with Joel Weishaus of Jungian Arts-Based Research and the Nuclear Enchantment of New Mexico (2021)*

"It is a particular delight when the sequel is even better than the original, and so it is with *Cinema and Psyche*. Building on the considerable success of *Cinema as Therapy*, this new book explores the complex interactions between films and their viewers. In doing so, Dovalis and Izod offer fresh insights into how cinema takes us to the depths of our unconscious selves, enriching both our lives and the films we watch."

Luke Hockley, *Honorary Professor, University of Essex; Professor Emeritus, University of Bedfordshire*

I0130469

Cinema and Psyche in Analytical Psychology: Individuation as a Pathway to Love

Peering into the unconscious through cinema can give audiences an uncanny feeling about what lives in the beyond, something alien to consciousness. This book creates psychological interpretations of films that lend themselves to the depths and investigates the personal and cultural appeal of cinema as a powerful art form.

The selected films examined in this book circle around the process of individuation, focussing on different aspects of intellectual and emotional life from a Jungian lens. The first group of movies centres on three films, following plotlines that extend beyond the norms of routine drama, delving into alien territory. The second group presents three more films that, by comparison with the first, can be seen as typical dramas that focus on motifs of relationships. In the final chapter, the authors reflect on their own individuation journeys and life experiences that have informed the productive nature of their work together.

This book will be of interest for therapists, students, and academics working in film studies, looking to engage in psychological studies in depth, as well as film goers who want to explore their relationship to the screen.

Joanna Dovalis, PhD, is a Depth Psychotherapist and Jungian Analyst with a professional private practice for over 30 years in Southern California. In addition to numerous articles and chapters in professional journals and books, she was the co-author of *Cinema as Therapy: Grief and Transformational Film* (Routledge 2015) with her writing partner John Izod.

John Izod, PhD, is Emeritus Professor of Screen Analysis at the University of Stirling. He has published several books, including *Screen, Culture, Psyche: A Post-Jungian Approach to Working with the Audience* (Routledge 2006) and *Cinema as Therapy: Grief and Transformational Film* (Routledge 2015) with his co-author Joanna Dovalis.

Cinema and Psyche in Analytical Psychology

Individuation as a Pathway to Love

Joanna Dovalis
John Izod

Routledge
Taylor & Francis Group

LONDON AND NEW YORK

Designed cover image: © Joanna Dovalis, John Izod and Kathleen
Morrisson

First published 2025
by Routledge
4 Park Square, Milton Park, Abingdon, Oxon OX14 4RN

and by Routledge
605 Third Avenue, New York, NY 10158

Routledge is an imprint of the Taylor & Francis Group, an informa business

British Library Cataloguing-in-Publication Data
A catalogue record for this book is available from the British Library

ISBN: 9781032899619 (hbk)
ISBN: 9781032899442 (pbk)
ISBN: 9781003545538 (ebk)

DOI: 10.4324/9781003545538

Typeset in Times New Roman
by codeMantra

To our teachers, Marie-Louise von Franz and
C. G. Jung, whose long enduring relationship has
been a guiding light to our own writing partnership
and individuation journey

Contents

Acknowledgments

With heartfelt gratitude, we wish to recognisze those who have been a part of this long journey. We extend our deepest thanks to Routledge Publishing, especially Katie Randall and Catherine Susan Jacob, for their tireless efforts in bringing our manuscript to publication. Our sincere appreciation goes to Susan Rowland and Luke Hockley for their scholarship and endorsement of the book, as well as to Vicky Jo Varner and Robin Wiley for their extraordinary talents in editing and technical expertise.

The support of our friends and family has been invaluable. Our spouses, George Rosch and Kathleen Morison, have provided unwavering emotional support and patience, testaments to the love with which we have been so richly blessed. Inclined towards the introverted life of the writer, we are grateful to our grown children and grandchildren for keeping us engaged in life. A very special thanks to Kathleen Morison for allowing us to use her shamanic drum as the cover of our book. Her devotion and active participation in bringing the manuscript to a cohesive whole has been vital.

Earlier versions of certain chapters were previously published, and we gratefully acknowledge with thanks the editors' permission to republish them here: "Under the Skin: Images as the Language of the Unconscious" in The Routledge International Handbook of Jungian Film Studies (London: Routledge, 2018); "Unconscious Figures and Otherness: The Case of Ex Machina" in Psychological Perspectives, Vol. 64, Issue 2 (2021), pp. 254–271; and, "Arrival and the Myth of Eternal Time" in Psychological Perspectives, Vol. 65, Issue 2 (2022), pp. 276–294.

Introduction

The purpose of this book, like its predecessor, *Cinema as Therapy,*[1] is to develop psychological interpretations of films that circle around the process of individuation. We have selected movies that lend themselves to the depths, providing cinema goers with a deeper understanding of the films, thereby gaining increased self-knowledge. The vivifying and psychological effect of using a Jungian lens makes our objective possible. Linking a film to its archetypal roots creates a wholistic experience, translating the film into both emotional and intellectual terms. Our creative process involves an active engagement with the symbolic images of the film, breathing new life into the narrative. In the end, the archetype of meaning reliably guides us.

This book comprises six chapters with a concluding seventh chapter, celebrating the work Joanna Dovalis and John Izod have shared over the past decade.

1 Under the Skin
2 Ex Machina
3 Arrival
4 Far from the Madding Crowd
5 Knight of Cups
6 Song to Song: Kiss to Kiss
7 The Analyst and the Shaman

Throughout time, wisdom has always been passed on through the medium of storytelling. This is by no means invariably reassuring. Peering into the unconscious can give cinema audiences the uncanny feeling that it is something alien. This subject matter is personified in the first three films of our analysis. A powerful ploy of the filmmakers who scripted *Under the Skin* and *Ex Machina* is that the heroine is represented as an alien character, an abstract figure that is not all human. This illuminates the fact that the birth of ego consciousness alienates the ego from the Self. What is so compelling about *Arrival* is that the Earth-bound heroine learns the aliens' language and develops a dialogue with them.

When aliens come to our planet, as, for instance, in *Under the Skin*, one thing that science-fiction audiences learn to expect is that – whether for better or for

DOI: 10.4324/9781003545538-1

worse, and whether they take up residence here or move on – visitors who traverse galaxies to reach Earth rarely leave things here unchanged. With the exception of only a tiny number of Earthlings who claim intimate knowledge of incomers, the physical being of extra-terrestrials, if they have any, is entirely unknown to humanity. Therefore, whether found in dreams, legends, myths, or fiction, images of and ideas about such visitors are impregnated with fantasy. Ipso facto, these beings are vehicles for energy sourced without consciousness. The anxiety that surrounds them is one hallmark of that characteristic.

Why might all this matter to us as we engage with our first three films? Joseph Campbell explains, "It is the artist who brings the images of mythology to manifestation, and without images (whether mental or visual) there is no mythology."[2] When art produces the visionary images necessary to perceive the world differently, it taps into dominant psychic archetypes that hold the potential healing energy to transform both individual and transpersonal psyches. One of the attractions of these extraordinary films is that, although their aesthetics and structure do at times invite a naturalistic reading (e.g. scenes from *Under the Skin* filmed in Glasgow resemble a vérité representation of the city), their utilisation quickly shatters the plausibility of that outer space and refers sound and images to inner space, "the wonder-land of myth."[3]

Analysing these three films cannot be satisfactory in our opinion, even at entry-level, unless one looks for something beyond a clinically reductive interpretation. "Amplification is the *conditio sine qua non* which *cannot* be left out in mythological interpretation."[4] Myth is the language of the psyche, and our aim is to engage in depth with all films that express such an energy. Marie-Louise von Franz regarded creation myths as the deepest and most important of all, belonging to a different class than fairy tales or hero myths,

> for when they are told, there is always a certain solemnity that gives them a central importance; they convey a mood which implies that what is said will concern the basic patterns of existence, something more than is contained in other myths.[5]

We find creation myths whenever the unconscious is preparing for an important progressive step in consciousness, a phenomenon that cannot be missed in these films.

The oeuvre of the film, *Under the Skin*, focuses on an alien perspective of the human world. An otherworldly woman preys on men in Scotland and lures them into her dilapidated house. Seemingly unaware of their surroundings, the men follow her into a void and are submerged into a liquid abyss. As a threshold between worlds, the solution appears to be where the two worlds (human and alien/known and unknown) merge. The film highlights Jung's deep exploration of the relationship to the anima in a man's psyche and helps us understand the profound seductive power and influence the archetype has on the world. Our aims are to engage at depth with the film to discover whether it reveals changes in dominant archetypes and, if it does, to bring their potential meanings toward the consciousness of individuals and, should the gods favour our labours, a wider culture. The film critic Betsy Sharkey describes the esoteric, psychologically provoking narrative of the film.

> Watching this film feels like a genesis moment – of sci-fi fable, of filmmaking, of performance – with all the ambiguity and excitement that implies. It's as if director and star have gone into some alien space to discover what embodies a person, exposing the interior dynamic of psyche and soul and its relationship to the exterior.
>
> (Sharkey, 2014)

Ex Machina leaves the viewer exactly where our Western civilisation stands, deeply conflicted, depending on us to question whether, as a culture, we are regressing or progressing. To conquer man's innate aggressiveness and survive the imbalance that human activity has inflicted on Mother Nature, we need the power to counterbalance masculine-oriented one-sidedness. The formation of that "other" power depends upon the constellation of an opposing archetype, the archetype of the feminine. Ava, one of the film's principal characters, has been created using artificial intelligence (AI). As such, she is both an image of the Great Mother, and, in her double aspect, a suitable counterpart to the masculine principle. She is an embodiment of female psychology and an image of the Self, which incorporates both a light and dark side. The AI is a personification of the feminine aspect of the godhead in its numinous or dangerous aspect. Ego consciousness rests on the foundation of the Self, and the Self is always within us, pointing toward an integration of the feminine and masculine, consciousness and unconsciousness, no matter the cost.

Marie-Louise von Franz's comments bear at least equal, if not greater weight, on *Arrival*. Jung, exploring the timeless quality of the unconscious, stated:

> Everything has already happened and is yet unhappened, is already dead and yet unborn. Such paradoxical statements illustrate the potentiality of unconscious contents. In so far as comparisons are possible at all, they are objects of memory and knowledge, and in this sense belong to the remote past; we therefore speak of "vestiges of primordial mythological ideas." But, in so far as the unconscious manifests itself in a sudden incomprehensible invasion, it is something that was never there before, something altogether strange, new, and belonging to the future.[6]

The leading female character, Louise Banks, finds herself back in time pregnant with the young child she has lost. She soon realises that her infant is able to converse with her from the womb. Thus, the fascination aroused by *Arrival* reaches deep into the unconscious mind of the heroine and her offspring, but this is by no means the only demand of her time. As a woman recognised for her expertise in linguistics, Louise is recruited by America's defence forces and ordered to investigate the perceived threat of potentially hostile spacecraft that have appeared over a number of Earth's most powerful entities. In fact, she does not view the two aliens with whom she has contact in the spacecraft hovering over the United States as a hostile threat to our planet. Rather, she wants to understand the purpose of their arrival and ultimately concludes they have come to deliver a message to help save our planet. The two aliens concerned are oppositional in nature – archetypal figures, which she nicknames "Abbot" and "Costello." The questions arising from her dual roles as both mother and negotiator inevitably (given the dominance of the military) impact every aspect of her life.

To revert to Jung's indefatigable desire to stimulate inquiry, he raised in his memoirs a question which echoes wonderfully in the high drama of *Arrival*: "The decisive question for man is: Is he related to something infinite or not?"[7] In these first three films, we discover that what is alien to us may bring about human suffering but also offer the possibility of rebirth and renewal. From three radically different storylines, the films portray a helpful archetype, an image of a future invigorated with hope. The psychological message argues that by creating a relationship with the "other," the potential for peace and healing arises. In the difficult times we are facing collectively and personally, we cannot live with an apocalyptic psychology; we need to develop a religious attitude that carries the archetypal pattern of something eternal.

The next three films are expressed mainly through motifs of relationships, and focus on the human need to experience the healing power of love. These movies depict the complicated dynamics that take place in every intimate connection and disclose the fundamental facts of the psyche that lie beyond the qualitative differences between masculine and feminine principles.

In Thomas Vinterberg's film, *Far from the Madding Crowd*,[8] the interplay of emotions is a constant factor between several of the drama's principal characters. The theme of a displaced orphan, which informs some of the drama in *Ex Machina,* is continued in this film, wherein another and altogether more ebullient orphan takes up residence in her aunt's house that she recently inherited. Her very name, "Bathsheba," is an irritant because no one has explained its origins to the young woman herself. By the same token, however, one senses a source of her pride lies in her name, and this seems to validate her personal sense that she commands the independence of her own actions. On the way to her new home, she meets a shepherd farmer named Gabriel. Psychologically speaking, a shepherd lives close to nature, which means he has genuine contact with the unconscious and instinctive parts of his personality. He is often wise and gifted with an ability to predict the future.

Indeed, one source of the pleasure generated by the film is the way in what is ultimately a traditional manner it teases the audience's expectations with an alternation of delight and annoyance as it sets about the redemption of Bathsheba's animus. Not long after their first meeting on Gabriel Oak's land, he comes calling on Miss Everdene and presents her with a lamb. Gabriel adds that, because it has come too soon, it will not last the winter unless she rears it. He then promptly asks the girl to marry him without further ado, so his gift of the solitary lamb is in some way a symbolic gesture of his internal imago of love and their forming a couple. He not only conveys his blind commitment to Bathsheba, but from a depth perspective, the archetype of relationship and its involvement in the hard work of individuation and the development of the Self are gradually discovered. Ultimately, by Bathsheba reclaiming her own feminine nature, she opens herself to relationships, transporting them into a living experience of mature love and mutual redemption.

In *Knight of Cups*,[9] and at his most dramatic, Terrence Malick makes brilliantly clear what Rick, the film's knight, can only discover slowly as he meanders insecurely in the terrible beauty of Death Valley. The landscape, in art as it is in dreams, symbolises the inexpressible unconscious moods – the psychic landscape, so to speak. While the worlds of the personal and transpersonal in *Knight of Cups* are registered as entities, the film invites the audience to also reflect on the profound significance of our co-existence with our planetary environment. In fact, the image of a luminous aurora has no causal links with the film's storyline, but its fleeting "material" presence is there onscreen, plain for viewers to register in all its symbolic majesty.

The overarching story carries the archetypal theme of a father-and-son relationship. The film involves three sons who struggle with their father, who created psychological obstacles in their abilities to find their own way. Like *The Hymn of the Pearl*'s[10] protagonist, the son Rick (who is addicted to success) has lost his way and despairs at the emptiness of his life. He undertakes a series of adventures that are divided into eight chapters, seven of them identified by tarot cards, with a final chapter titled "Freedom."[11] Women provide consolation from the daily pain he endures, every encounter with the feminine bringing him closer to finding an authentic way of being in the world. The therapeutic meaning of the film translates to a transformation of fantasy and sexual obsession within a man into a recognition of the positive qualities of his anima, his feminine spirit. Throughout his search for salvation, quotations from *The Hymn of the Pearl* are read in voice-over by the main character's father as his son eventually awakens from his "deep sleep," and finds freedom by remembering the pearl, the "treasure hard to attain."[12]

Our analysis of Terrence Malick's *Song to Song*[13] proceeds on more than one front. We deploy Jung's meditations on the nature of love, and in doing so, make use of an analytical framework that he in turn derived from Dante's exploration of love's characteristics. Jung decided, like his forebear, that he too must experience a descent to hell (or, to use the Greek term, *katabasis*). Committing to undertake so perilous a journey, Jung decided to test the measure of his soul by not only making the descent into hell but also in recovering his feeling life from it.

Jung's careful observation of both his own psyche and the thinking of his predecessors complements Malick's exploration of the world as the latter experiences it. We have already referred to Rick's *Knight of Cups* exploring the erratic actions that urged imperfectly-identified appetites in him. Now Malick sets *Song to Song* in the hectic framework of a music festival – an ingenious way for a director to make use of the locale that is his home. The settings Malick chooses often juxtapose diverse components. Some sequences rely on live shots of musicians playing to paying audiences while others feature handsome riverside gardens, spacious enough for actors to play out their roles, whether they be actual musicians or performers hired for specific roles. In some instances, actors play multiple roles. A case in point being, for example, Faye, played by Rooney Mara. In her case, she doubles as a musician and also as a female character unsure of her relationships with two men and a woman, with all of whom she enters fictional sexual liaisons. As the two intersecting love triangles advance, the film incorporates significant psychological themes such as guilt, obsession, betrayal and abandonment, fear of loss and jealousy, the desire for power, and suicide. The film begins and ends with a visceral psychological message: *the process of coming to consciousness is generated by experience.* In the end, self-knowledge is brought into the light through relationship, and the feminine principle is redeemed by trust, acceptance, and love.

The Analyst and the Shaman: Specialist in the Sacred

The aim of both a Jungian analyst and a shaman is to provide help in forging a link with the contents of the unconscious. The deeper layer of the unconscious, what Jung called the "collective unconscious," is the realm of absolute knowledge and is where the effulgence of the archetype of healing can be reached. Initiatory themes and problems that involve "the loss of soul" – a severing of the relationship with one's inner psychic life – are central concerns. It is a sacred task of the analyst and the shaman to recollect and help make whole what has been previously lost. Stressing the value of the lived experience, all initiatory experiences begin with a break or rupture, and once through it, a new spiritual and psychological equilibrium can be achieved. The more integrated personality becomes qualitatively different than what it was before. Mircea Eliade describes three types of initiation.[14] For our purposes, we are concerned with the third type that occurs in connection to a mystical vocation which is on the level of a "soul calling," whereby one subordinates themselves to a higher will, rather than a "career," which is primarily driven by ambitions of the ego. Healing may be experienced when a dynamic relationship between consciousness and the unconscious is created and a connection with the other world has been established. Like the *Tree of Life* and individuation, the union of opposites is a central motif, where the power of Below and the power of Above grow together and unite.[15] From this perspective, healing means being *ensouled,* making one whole. As Jung stated, "To have soul is the whole venture of life, for soul is a life-giving daemon."[16] We are acutely aware that whatever creative interpretations we have given to each of these films, we have also given to our own souls, significantly impacting our own development and relationship to the beyond. From this perspective, we understand there can be no healing and fruitful progress without self-knowledge. Marie-Louise von Franz summarises our point when she asserts, "One of the aims of psychotherapy is to help people keep a constant identity and to get along with their inner family of souls without being possessed by them."[17]

From different origins, professions, and life experiences, we have been drawn toward the depths. According to our individual typologies,[18] our psychological constellation has proven to be the foundation of our unique way of relating to each other. It has been the Archimedean point into "our way" of interpreting films. Thus, we share bringing the opposites together, which is the goal of the individuation journey. During our presentations, we have often been asked, "How is it possible to write together?" We never formally organised how we were going to do this, although we were both clear about our roles. We simply agreed that John would begin the work by writing the narrative of the film and then pass it over to Joanna for psychological understanding. From Scotland to California, draft after draft (an average of 30 each), our papers criss-crossed the Atlantic until we agreed that the paper had reached a stage of completion. Without a doubt, our writing partnership has been a significant part of our own individuation process.

When experienced for oneself, every kind of initiation changes one's fundamental way of being and reveals the sacredness of human life and the great mysteries. It soon becomes apparent that the depth of an analyst's and shaman's wisdom is considerable. Beyond any doubt, Jung possessed wisdom and considered the process of individuation to be the main task of human development and the goal of a life genuinely lived. Wisdom resides in the beyond, but for it to become realised, it requires individual effort to find meaning in the darkest moments of life. Initiatory themes are alive in the unconscious and find expression through the symbolic world conveyed in the artistic creations of filmmaking. Although the format and place where we choose to watch films have changed, movie watching continues to be an organising principle in many of our lives. Film leads us into the world of mythmaking and we have strived to understand their 'psychological and spiritual meaning.' At the cinema we rediscover the ordeals of the hero and heroine in quest of immortality, we touch upon the mysteries of life, and hope to see the redemption of a troubled world and learn the secrets of love. Through film, we encounter the numinous world of the living collective psyche.

Notes

1 Izod and Dovalis, *Cinema as Therapy*.
2 Campbell, *The Inner Reaches of Outer Space*, xxii.
3 Campbell, *The Inner Reaches of Outer Space*, 31.
4 von Franz, *Individuation in Fairy Tales*, 146.
5 von Franz, *Creation Myths*, 1.
6 Jung, *The Practice of Psychotherapy*, para. 529.
7 Jung, *Memories, Dreams, Reflections*, 325.
8 Vinterberg, *Far from the Madding Crowd*.
9 Malick, *Knight of Cups*.
10 Barnstone and Meyer, *Essential Gnostic Scriptures*, 129–135.
11 In *Archetypes and the Collective Unconscious*, Jung notes that tarot cards were distantly derived from the archetypes of transformation (para. 81).
12 Jung, *Psychology and Alchemy*, para. 155.
13 Malick, *Song to Song*.
14 In his book, *Rites and Symbols of Initiation*, 26.

15 It is important to remember there were two trees in the Garden of Eden.
16 Jung, *The Archetypes and the Collective Unconscious*, para. 56.
17 von Franz, *The Way of the Dream*, 160.
18 Using the popular MBTI® four-letter type codes, John has ISFJ preferences, which equates to a superior function of introverted sensation with auxiliary feeling, while Joanna has ENTP preferences, which equates to a superior function of extraverted intuition with auxiliary thinking.

Chapter 1

Under the Skin

Unidentified Flying Objects as Living Myth

In a time of international crisis at the end of the 1950s, C. G. Jung wrote a short book about unidentified flying objects (UFOs). Its publication coincided with the intensification of the Cold War to the point where, terrifyingly, global annihilation through nuclear conflict was becoming an ever-present danger. Living through the decade when populations of many nations felt imperilled, Jung observed that UFO phenomena, whether physically real or imagined, had been sighted in much-increased numbers. He realised they had become a living myth such that "in a difficult time for humanity a miraculous tale grows up of an attempted intervention by extra-terrestrial 'heavenly' powers" (1959: 14).

This flurry of UFO sightings chimed in Jung's imagination with his observation that by that date the old gods were dead or dying. Associating UFOs with symbols arising from both the individual and the transpersonal unconscious, he concluded that these round, shiny objects seen in the sky could be regarded as archetypal images. In every age in the Western world, circles, being complete and perfect, had played an important role as both symbols for the unity and wholeness of the soul and as images of God (1959: 20–21).

A circle in the sky is the first discernible form in the pre-title sequence of *Under the Skin*. The film opens in pitch dark while a rasp-like, creaking music of scouring energy thrusts into consciousness. Only then is a pinprick of light born in the black screen's centre. Gradually it swells into circular form, undecipherable (because beyond human experience) whether it be a spacecraft, a planet moving through a field of aligned moons, a ring formed by the play of immense energy, a deity's probing eye – or just conceivably the archetypal vehicle for them all. As it nears, repeated chuffing breaks through the wracking buzz. Something alien, straining to vocalise like a human baby, prepares to communicate with Earthlings. Could the strange music carry, on a parallel communication channel, signals incomprehensible to us? At all events, before characters' actions introduce a degree of narrative direction, Mica Levi's fearful soundtrack suggests not only terror but also the subjective loss of spatial co-ordinates. It does not encourage the hope, whether this twenty-first-century UFO be transportation for creatures or a deity, that they

DOI: 10.4324/9781003545538-2

might be more benign than the incoming hostiles who fed rampant paranoia in Hollywood's Cold War science-fiction.

Creation Mythology

Erich Neumann notes that, for all peoples in all religions, creation first appears as the coming of light. "The coming of consciousness, manifesting itself as light in contrast to the darkness of the unconscious, is the real 'object' of creation mythology" (1954: 6).

When in *Under the Skin* light pierces the darkness, it takes a constantly changing circular form which evolves into and then beyond an energy-charged doughnut ring. It recalls the uroboros (the Great Round), the circular snake of ancient myths that devours its own tail representing the cycle of destruction and rebirth. The uroboric period is that initial phase of psychic identity in which all things are fused together in *participation mystique* (Neumann, 1971: 109). It is the state of mystic identity that precedes the emergence (in an individual or a collective) of reflective consciousness. This is the phase in which the movie begins. It brings to mind both the moment of universal creation and the beginning of an individual's life before differentiation commences and the act of separation is first encountered. This first phase of separation brings the principle of opposition into being, initiating the earliest stages of self-awareness. Love and hate, light and darkness, conscious and unconscious enter into conflict with one another. Read in this mythologised context, the film's opening invites us to realise that we are witnessing a moment of creation, whether of a lone individual, a new world, or both.

Glazer introduces his alien eyes wide open to a revelation beyond words, the utter wonder and terror of being. From the moment of the alien's entry to the Earth's sphere, a creature not identifiable as neither male nor female, what we see and hear is mainly formed by her developing perceptions. Access to language initiates the process of differentiation entailed in both making and discerning meaningful variants between sounds: it thereby introduces reflective consciousness. Consciousness may select what a speaker intuits to be the most appropriate words for a given scenario; but those words also reveal the input of the personal and cultural unconscious. Conversely, language deployed consciously begins to change the unconscious. So when the alien incarnates, she must use human language to carry out her mission which impacts on her unconscious, something neither she nor her cohort seem to have anticipated. Losing the plot and losing our minds before we investigate them both can prove a necessary abandonment in starting to pursue an alien!

Liminal Being: Johansson the Alien

As most reviewers of *Under the Skin* revealed, the audience does not know for some time what to make of the new arrival, except that she both is and is not Scarlett Johansson. As a film star she is, by virtue of the juxtaposition between the narrative and her socio-cultural position in the audience's imaginal world, both a virgin goddess and a seductive anima figure. As such, she is a mediatrix to the unknown, the realm of the unconscious and communicates through images, not words or dialogue. What the alien/Johansson embodies remains for us to discover or perhaps co-create.

The Earth-based plot commences at night. The camera surveys a ribbon of wet road that winds through the Scottish Highlands. Reprising the film's opening, a second pinprick of light emerges out of the dark. A powerful bike hurtles down the long glen and an unrelenting electronic chord carried through from the pre-title sequence envelopes the barely visible biker in mystery and speed. He descends toward human habitation, a ruthless messenger who could conceivably have been given power by god-like creatures newly landed in the mountains. As his machine tears through a town, the pumping grind resumes that we heard in space, and the rider (Jeremy McWilliams) heads into the outskirts, stops at a bungalow, and disappears beyond the streetlights' reach into the garden. After a moment he comes out, the corpse of a young woman (Lynsey Taylor Mackay) slung over his shoulder. It has been speculated that she is a cadaver found at the side of the road, but the biker is an efficient killer who knows where he is going and why, witnessing the van ready for him and his cargo.

When the biker dumps the body in the van we cut hard from a deep night-for-night shot into a brilliant light box with the victim's face in close up. As so often in Glazer's films, the aesthetics surprise no less than the form. Where is this blinding, unearthly place? The alien, now embodied in Johansson's naked human form, strips the dead woman of her clothes and dons them. Director of Photography Daniel Landin holds both the living and the dead in blue-black monochrome, sometimes in images recalling Lotte Reiniger's paper-cut silhouettes. This woman (the only female whom the aliens kill) has been targeted because her clothes will fit one particular alien's body and that body must be sexily female. Cladding herself in the feminine, 'she' mimics the hero of classical myth preparing for war. Her performance of dressing also embodies an attitude she intends to adopt in her new Earthly surroundings as she aims to seduce the human males whom she will target. Carotenuto emphasises the central role of seduction in human experience, designating it as a particular circular space where the Me is placed in relation to the Other (2002: 2). Implicated in this alien psyche's disarming attire is the possibility that she may become a new collective dominant in a specific new feminine form, offering a more complete realisation of ego and Self, where the ego experiences the Self and becomes one again with it.

Landin's camera takes up the alien's point of view in shots where, gathering information, she turns an equally cool gaze on the cadaver and an ant marooned on the body. She picks up the insect, peers at it, and notices a tear leaking from the corpse's eye. This bizarre juxtaposition will acquire meaning retrospectively for the audience and for the alien herself who gathers information randomly as it impinges on her. Ants have long represented communities that function in an orderly, efficient yet instinctive manner, in contrast to the great difficulty that societies of human beings (endowed with consciousness) experience in trying to behave comparably. This lone ant brings to mind an autonomous complex emerging from the collective unconscious: perhaps a new cultural consciousness.

Meanwhile, the corpse's tear turns us to Carotenuto's thoughts on betrayal. People come into the world exposed to "the betrayal of life by death, betrayal through hate, betrayal of the primary unity through birth itself" (1996: 85). Individual psychological birth is impossible without the experience of betrayal; but the young woman's sacrifice may allude to something beyond her individual murder, namely the rupture of an old way of feminine relating. One kind of betrayal is to reveal inadvertently a person's identity or character that should be secret. In this sense, the victim's corpse reveals the shadow side of the female as lacking in psychic energy. Being impoverished, it must come to life again. Thus her death signals metaphorically the victim's unlived part of the feminine experience and simultaneously implies potential qualities yet to become part of the alien's character and actions. We shall discover through the female alien's mysterious power that only a conscious and responsible attitude transforms the shadow into a friend.

A hard cut takes us from the ant in extreme close up to the foot of a residential tower where demolition is under way. The awkward juxtaposition of the crumbling tower and the wrecked homes that it contains can be taken as another emblem of decaying human culture and consciousness in both their masculine and feminine aspects. Overhead, lights flare briefly: the UFO lifts away from the skyscraper's top while the alien/Johansson exits via a dilapidated stairwell and takes possession of the van. Her disguise, chosen by the male biker (his victim's denim miniskirt and torn fishnets), does not suit her purpose and she needs to hit Aphrodite's temple, a brightly lit mall redolent with the aura of desire, to fine-tune her appearance for seduction or warfare. Filmed *cinéma vérité* style as she walks among shoppers, the working girl ignored by the crowds is also Johansson the unseen dark goddess and now Laura, the alien/human. In one context, Laura's Earthling name associates her with triumphant Roman generals through their laurel garlands. Yet we notice on her calves the rip in the murder victim's fishnet tights. It suggests a feminine wound arising from the unstable nature of an overly adapted self, a female mask that has been defined by Western civilisation. This adaptive part of the personality must always avoid something, and therefore uses the primitive defence of splitting as a coping mechanism. As a result, the person behaves in ways not in relationship to their whole psyche. Only when the personality maintains a certain plasticity can the ego be sufficiently influenced by the Self and healthfully adapt to the whole psychological system.

Exploiting Liminality

In the mall, alien/Laura observes women being shown how cosmetics alter their personae. She buys stand-out lipstick on the saccharine side of Scarlet and complements it with a faux-fur jacket and acid-wash jeans. Her attraction to make-up and clothing both covers up and reveals her instinctual desires. Her tacky fur, neon lips, and van could be the cover of a middle-class woman away from home, prowling Glasgow to pull men. Equally, the weird combination might reveal a common theme of science-fiction, the extra-terrestrial's necessary adaptation to her destination.

The shimmering of her roles against each other penetrates, in an almost hallucinatory manner, into the celebrated quasi-*vérité* sequences filmed when the alien/Johansson drives around Glasgow picking up young working-class men and flirting with them. In fact, the aesthetics differ from the purely observational style that orthodox *vérité* aspires to. Take, for example, two effects which can be interpreted, because of their unfamiliarity, as revealing what the alien hears and sees. Where *vérité* would favour direct sound, we hear a sophisticated, mixed sound spectrum: a pump, one stroke heavier than the other, labours under a subaltern buzz that is pierced occasionally by screeching violins. Except for its mechanical rhythm, the beat might recall a limping human heart. The visual perspective disquiets too: though the van prowls slowly, it sometimes swerves across the traffic lane and Landin's camera pans a bit too far, as if controlled by a poorly programmed machine.

Alien as Anima

The associations of 'Laura's' pseudonym with the garland of a victorious general befit the alien's ambivalent nature. In selecting her victims, she discriminates in two ways: she never kills women; and she does not take men who have a family. Her acts resemble the methodical harvesting of a natural resource. When killing her first victims she seems no more emotionally engaged than a farmer offloading sheep ready for market at the abattoir. Yet, by the laws of our planet, her business is meditated serial murder. The untouchable element of the alien/Laura's personality has just this characteristic. Such women, Esther Harding says,

> conquer men not for love of the man, but for a craving to gain power over him. They cannot love, they can only desire. They are cold-blooded, without human feeling or compassion. Instinct in its daemonic form, entirely non-human, lives through them.
>
> (1990: 118)

In Carotenuto's terms, she incarnates perfectly

> the type of woman-Anima Jung first described – a woman able to impersonate the projections of the man she seduces so perfectly that ... [she] assumes the countenance of our fantasies, becoming the shadow onto which we project the internal image of *our* sexual counterpart.
>
> (Carotenuto, 2002: 11)

Yet Laura's robotic quality implies that she herself does not yet possess the psychological characteristic of projection because she is embedded in an archaic identity (not the only such personality in the screenplay).

Only when Laura starts picking up men is minimalist dialogue first heard. If she spots a potential victim she engages with him easily, but mostly she asks questions. More than one reviewer found the men's Glaswegian accents indecipherable, but accepted that could be how our world sounds to an incomer (Martin, 2014). And the characters played by non-actors reveal their sensual awakening through body language.

If naturalism is the more obvious shaping influence in the street scenes, fantasy once again dominates when the alien leads all-too-willing men into what they take to be her home. Once through the door, walking backwards steadily over a reflecting black surface while discarding one garment after another, Johansson/the alien leads each new captive into immeasurable space.

> Reflecting objects have [had] …, from time immemorial, a numinous significance for human beings. The oldest experience of a reflecting object may well have been that of the surface of water … Ninck shows that in the world of antiquity water was always thought of as chthonic, as having sprung from the earth, and that it was always associated with what he calls the "night conditions" or "night states" of the soul: intoxication, dream, trance, unconsciousness, and death.
>
> (von Franz, 1995: 183)

Throwing off their clothes, the priapic fellows advance toward her, snared by lust for the splendid body that recedes before them, completely unaware that the mysterious surface sustaining her is deluding them. In the alien's slaughterhouse, her aroused victims see her as nude, dressing her in cocksure anticipation that she reciprocates their lust; but the audience sees a naked woman walking backwards purposefully over a reflecting black surface. The men are *pueri aeterni* (eternal youths) whose erotic longings reflect that they have been captured by their own shadow projections. The shadow, the repressed or neglected part of consciousness that has split off into the unconscious, contains the overwhelming power of irresistible impulses and actions. As we have seen, it conceals the personal anima, embodying the feminine psychological propensities in a man's psyche and his relation to the unconscious. In a sense, the anima is the male's experience of the feminine unconscious. Its most frequent manifestation takes the form of erotic fantasy with the present scene exposing its most dangerous negative aspects. These are the destructive illusions which distort men's decision-making and thereby drag them into the anima's lair. The victims plod ever deeper into something that, weirdly, neither ripples nor instantly drowns them. Neither the characters nor the audience can make out what it is – and that's the point.

Instinct

One night, when she is driving through the city, a lacy veil of shadow falls and lifts again and again across alien/Laura's face as she motors under the streetlights, a fascinating image that pulses like oscillating consciousness. Through it mixes the sound of heavy seas, deep water leading into a scene of naked horror. It is daylight when Laura parks the van above a gravel beach where an Atlantic gale whips spume from powerful waves, a veil occluding the bay. She watches a vigorous swimmer exit the turbulent waves, engages him with her chat-up routine, establishing that he is a lone Czech visitor (another alien in Scotland), and a good target for seduction. But suddenly his attention snaps away from her to the far end of the bay where a family man trying to save his wife from drowning has put himself at risk. Unmoved, Laura the alien looks on while the Czech, facing extreme peril, drags the husband to safety. But the rescued man cannot abandon his wife although high seas have pulled her far beyond reach. He staggers back into the waves, where both drown.

The family disaster commenced when the wife leapt into the ocean to save their dog. As von Franz reminds us, animals are the bearers of human projections: "As long as there is still an archaic identity, and as long as you have not taken the projection back, the animal and what you project onto it are identical; they are one and the same thing" (1996: 36). By rushing to her death in the oceanic waters of the unconscious, the woman vividly portrays the failure of her maternal instinct and its connection to the deeper feminine. In complete identification with the animal, she projected her disavowed instinctual nature onto the dog, impulsively following it to her death. Plainly she lacked conscious connection to the Eros principle. The lack made her unable to judge soundly and sacrifice the dog. Driven by overwhelming emotions – love, terror, and anguish – both parents acted impulsively, as humans do in a crisis, unconsciously forgetting their baby. Jung reminds us that

> The autonomy of the unconscious ... begins where emotions are generated ... In a state of affect a trait of character sometimes appears which is strange even to the person concerned, or hidden contents may irrupt involuntarily. The more violent an affect the closer it comes to the pathological, to a condition in which the ego-consciousness is thrust aside by autonomous contents that were unconscious before.
>
> (1939: §497)

The emotional reactions of this married couple reveal a disturbing lack of *intrapersonal* relationship between conscious and unconscious and *interrelationship* between their animus and anima. How, then, could the feminine principle of Eros and relatedness conceivably be redeemed by this robotic, murderous incomer?

What follows could not express more graphically the difference between murder and self-sacrifice motivated by tenderness for life. When the baby's anguished wails pierce the racket of storm on stone, alien/Laura notices it stranded on the rocks. Contrary to the affect-driven nature of humans (and to the deep shock of the film's audiences), she completely ignores the infant as its cries rise to helpless screams of terror – further evidence that the alien does not possess that human quality of projection which reveals the subjectivity of a personal psyche and interior life. Instead, witnessing the exhausted Czech collapse unconscious on the gravel, she strides purposefully along the roaring water's edge and cracks his skull with a large stone before delivering him to the biker and death. This, her first physically aggressive act, may be a reaction to a kind of betrayal, her first failed attempt to seduce. It's an early sign that her experiences on Earth may be changing alien/ Laura, a development that her tribe did not anticipate.

Abandonment and the Patriarchy

From a depth psychological and cultural perspective, Laura / the alien's indifference frames the baby's abandonment in the context of a crisis of our time. On the personal level, the baby's fate is clearly due to the neurotic components of the parents' personalities and lack of connection to their instinctual natures.

> If however, one leaves it embedded within its archetypal context, then it takes on a deeper meaning, namely that the new God of our time is always to be found in the ignored and deeply unconscious corner of the psyche.
>
> (von Franz, 1996: viii)

Understanding the archetype of the feminine is essential to comprehend the anima as the archetype of life and its connection to what Jung calls the Self, that is, the psychic totality of an individual and the regulating centre of the collective unconscious. Thus, the baby's cry gives direct voice to the abandonment content of our dangerously narrow, one-sided culture whose instinctual life has been oppressed and repressed. Having no parents, everything for the orphaned baby lies ahead in an unknown future. So who is this 'child'? Clearly it personifies some realm of the psyche, and is not altogether about the infant *per se*. For Jung, "The 'child' is all that is abandoned and exposed and at the same time divinely powerful; the insignificant, dubious beginning and the triumphal end" (1951: §300).

Neumann reminds us that the development of consciousness in the West is a history of masculine, actively oriented consciousness whose achievements led to a patriarchal culture. … The different nature of the female and feminine psyche must be discovered anew not only if women are to understand themselves but also if the patriarchally masculine world that has fallen ill, thanks to its extreme one-sidedness, is again to return to health (Neumann, 1994: xi).

As long as our female alien continues acting ruthlessly, the masculine side dominates, noticeably so while her deeds resemble the biker's. *Under the Skin* in this phase is a piercing tale about a heroine's problem with the shadow and her animus. The animus is an internal image of the masculine in the unconscious, entwined with the shadow and associated with Logos. It has both bad and good qualities. Until now we have seen only its negative aspects, the one-sided, collectively masculine-driven universe that alien/Laura comes from. In this negative form, the animus leaves a woman where Eros is lacking, separated from life. In its positive aspect it builds a bridge to the Self and, ultimately, enables transformation to spiritual wisdom. Where anima reaches backwards by its reflective nature, animus is concerned with the present and the future.

The biker conscientiously removes the drowned family's tent to destroy signs of their presence but leaves behind the hysterical infant tottering in near-complete darkness along the water line. Its wailing does not distress these dangerous visitors because, as an innocent (still held in the archetypal realm of the mother), it has no relevance to their mission. Only when alien/Laura notices a black baby drowsing contentedly in a car does the sight get under her skin. Although the audience does not know it, she too is black beneath her adopted hide. With this sighting, the mirroring image of the black baby may have initiated a connection with her own unconscious. The language of images is that of the unconscious. Psychologically interpreted, the contact appears to have sparked her *potential* to develop the psyche's creative activity because as soon as there is a tendency for self-reflection and doubt, projection appears. Nevertheless, whatever latent metamorphoses may be stirring within, they do not immediately unsettle her mimetic human persona. As long as she remains the efficient killing machine, there is complete cold objectivity in the way the alien lives, manifesting no feeling of life. But, as Ean Begg notes, repressed parts of the archetype both in individuals and history tend to 'take their captors captive' (1986: 37).

It becomes possible, as the narrative unfolds, to compare alien/Laura with the males who populate the world she moves in. When she first sets about entrapping Glaswegians, they resemble each other under the skin despite obvious (delusory) differences between her adopted human gender and theirs. She chooses from the city streets only men all of whom are dead in spirit and come to life only at the prospect of a primitive sexual encounter. Their zombie-like personas are filled with unconscious contents which have been rejected and killed off, neither grieved over nor buried. Asking them if they have family, she chooses only those who are not connected to anyone. Lacking a relationship to their internal feminine, they are vulnerable to seduction. Their isolation contrasts with the way a group of women party goers cheerfully sweep Laura into their vivacious collective. But she is not one of them. As yet in her alien being undifferentiated from the biker, she selects victims who, with their dumb, biddable energy, would augment a totalitarian power structure – possibly the destination to which she despatches them.

Approaching Feminine Consciousness

We have noted that alien/Johansson arrives on Earth in a psychological state of *participation mystique*. A moment that initiates her development occurs when, after she has sunk some men in her pool, she examines what is not her own but Laura's face in a mirror, acquiring perhaps via her adopted persona some glimmer of feeling for the human self that it masks. As Jung said many times, it is through a mirror that the unconscious becomes aware of its own face (1954: §43).

The biker is unsettled by his colleague's moment of introspection. Sensing danger, he addresses her intently, though on a channel to which we cannot tune. Hitherto (despite their differently gendered human forms), they have lived in a collective world of sameness. But step-by-step she is now breaking out from *participation mystique*, commencing the individuation process, coming to consciousness, and in consequence equally bewildered by human kindness and cruelty. The biker does not and will not change, his body-integral backpack declaring his robotic otherness.

Meanwhile, sunk in the surreal bath to which alien/Laura has led them, two of the Glaswegian men touch, causing a bang like an electrical short circuit. The shock hurls them back from each other, tinfoil manikins wrinkling into nothingness. Interpreted psychologically, the moment when they reach out and touch in the indescribable bath of the unconscious exposes them to the devastation of coming to consciousness too late. "Whenever the psyche is set violently oscillating by a numinous experience, there is a danger that the thread by which one hangs may be torn" (Jung cited by Stein, 2006: 45). For example, in Ovid's *Metamorphoses*, when Earth's inhabitants cry out for Zeus to intervene in their crises, he responds with apocalyptic lightning strikes. Like those ancients exposed to the divine presence for which they lusted, these flaccid and unprepared victims are destroyed, sucked along a blood-red beam down which white light sears. Their obliteration is confirmed by Levi's rasping music that develops material first heard in the pre-title sequence: all change can only take place in the unconscious.

Alien/Laura takes another step differentiating her from her minder when the lonely vulnerability of a facially disfigured young man (Adam Pearson) attracts her. Like this sufferer from neurofibromatosis, she too is alone and misshapen, concealed in a woman's form to carry out the aliens' collective mission. She gazes at the unfortunate man and seems, like a lover, to take him into her inner world. She is in contact with the feminine aspect of a human, albeit in a deformed male body which elicits the nascent feminine in her. That shows in her compassion and sense of his beauty when she identifies with him as a positive mirror of her own shadow. The encounter will draw out her instinctive impulse to awaken the feeling connection with the depths of the unconscious and with nature, since in life it is the task of the feminine to renew feeling values.

This does not happen instantly, for when she takes him to her slaughterhouse, she begins as usual to strip and (while surfaces dissolve and stressed violins wail) draws the unfortunate fellow into the deeps over which she presides. But as he descends, she discerns (barely perceptible in the dim light) a submerged human form, not his body wracked by neurofibromatosis, but an image of perfected humanity, momentarily superimposed on her gazing profile. Everything changes. The ugly man has stirred vivid affect beneath consciousness and it has generated a dark idealisation of human potentiality in her mind – a transformational archetypal image. The shock breaks her seduction ritual and draws her once more to the mirror where her watching face scrutinises its reflection, her slight, questioning movements out of synch with those in the mirrored image. Her reflection gradually clarifies as the gloom that first obscured it lifts. It is an expressionistic rendering of the metamorphosis she is undergoing. Hillman says that anima consciousness brings the possibility of reflection in terms of awareness of one's unconscious and that is why anima is the archetype of the psychological calling (1985: 137).

A frantic housefly scrabbles to escape from a frosted window. In chilly dawn light alien/Laura unbolts her door and shepherds the naked man out of the tomb prepared for him. Fleeing his seducer for dear life, he flounders barefoot over a marshy field as panicky as the fly. Meanwhile she drives away in the van, knowing full well that her demonic minder is already hammering along open roads in pursuit. The biker first slays the poor fellow and dumps his corpse unceremoniously. Then he hunts Laura who now imperils the aliens' mission. For the first time, her movements signal fear, a further lurch toward consciousness in a creature which, before cladding herself in woman's form, never knew feelings.

Trying Out Humanity

Finding herself in the Scottish Highlands, alien/Laura drives past a mountain loch where the wind curls spume above the water, a stunning image that recalls the sea bay where the family drowned, but this time without horror. Given the changed context, these shots lay bare to her eyes the wonder of nature and, thanks to the wind, bring to mind the potentially inspiring spiritual quality of the unconscious. She enjoys only a glimpse of this strange beauty before a chill fog of unknowing maroons her. She abandons the van and, now unprotected by her fellow aliens, mimics people in order to pass as humans. But she cannot emulate these alien creatures perfectly. Taking afternoon tea in a café, she discovers she cannot swallow Earthlings' food: unlike David Bowie's *The Man Who Fell to Earth* (1976), she has not come for food to sustain physical life on her planet. Since eating is often implicated in emotional life, it seems she cannot yet digest the human experience. She walks on, lost and alone, tracking the ribbon of the tarmac until local resident Andy (Michael Moreland) advises her to catch the rural bus with him. Although she cannot find words to respond to people's concern about her inadequate clothing, she gradually recognises Andy's kindness and accepts the loan of his leather jacket and an invitation to his bachelor home.

She continues exploring her nascent emotions, beginning to unlock the unconscious albeit, shorn of her pre-set chat-up programme, she remains wordless. She watches Andy move around his kitchen to the rhythm of a pop song and tries to copy him but cannot hit the beat. Nor can she eat the meal he prepares. But later, alone in his spare bedroom, she strips off and looks cautiously in a mirror at the reflection of her human body. What she sees intrigues her and she flexes the strange limbs, discovering with a hint of erotic awakening their appealing softness.

By absconding, 'Laura' has slighted the biker's power as an enforcer. Deploying his only resource and thereby confirming his one-sidedness, he calls up three more bikers as reinforcements. The four clones, a quasi-military contingent, pound country roads through the night to find and eliminate her, edgy violins again scratching at the machines' roar. These clones belong in the pre-conscious unity, the undifferentiated collective, their mono-vision locked on safeguarding the mission. As part of the totalitarian collective that swallows its victims, they fear separateness and the uncontrollable vitality that self-awareness brings. Ironically, they constitute a male quaternity; but where the number four should symbolise wholeness, here it represents only the Logos principle dominating their collective attitude. *Under the Skin* thus continues to emphasise the missing feminine by dwelling on a dominant collective attitude in which the principle of Eros – of relatedness to the unconscious, the irrational, and the feminine – has been lost. The anima, on the other hand, serves life and man's relationship to it.

The Edge of Liminality

Laura meanwhile has commenced a heroic journey oriented toward emancipation through rebirth. She soon encounters further challenges. Andy becomes her guide and leads her across the countryside to explore a ruined castle. For her the main feature is not archaeology but paralysing vertigo: the intergalactic traveller is living between two worlds and must depend on this gentleman to lead her down the dark steps of an ancient tower. In so doing, Andy draws her down from the high wall whence she witnessed one of the bikers speeding past. Acting as psychopomp, he mediates between the conscious and unconscious and shows her the way. By assisting her to find shelter in the dark, he demonstrates *puer* consciousness and his positive relationship with his anima to make the unknown safe. In this context he is also the positive animus, unconscious awakening in Laura. That night they share the bed and Laura begins to learn how two humans express affection for each other. But when their pleasure rises, he finds it impossible to enter her. She jumps up to examine her groin. A virgin in her alien human form, she is perhaps checking whether lovemaking has torn her skin. Be that as it may, the sweet bond that was emerging between the man and his visitor breaks. Evidently, the aliens know nothing about human sexuality or desire.

Daylight finds Laura marching across the open country into a dark forest plantation. Compared with her fear when navigating the castle stairwell, she moves confidently between dripping trees and, covered by one of Andy's heavy jackets, picks a way over sodden earth and fallen lumber. But when a truck driver approaches through the trees, he tells her needlessly that the forest is safe, with well-marked but slippery paths. And while speaking he takes note of the attractive, defenceless woman. As she scrambles on, one of the bikes tears along a wet road flanking the forest, menacing in its noisy speed. She is still the males' quarry.

Dystopia and Hierophanies

Deep among the trees she comes to an empty bothy and decides that it is a safe place. She stretches out on the floor, her awkward preparations revealing that sleep is another human experience still new to her. Yet she does sleep while the wind rises, which recalls Hillman's observation, "Breezy wind and shifts of atmospheric pressure all belong to anima" (1985: 25). The gusts waltz the treetops and an image of her dozing form emerges softly couched and nested tranquilly high among rocking branches. The picture invokes rich associations with the naiad Daphne, a woodland character and virgin nymph in ancient Greek myth whose name meant 'laurel.' Just as Laura in the superimposed shot looks whole unto herself, ensouled, lovely, and more human than ever, Daphne's beauty was widely celebrated. On seeing the nymph, the sun god Apollo fell irredeemably in love. However, his unswerving passion for her beauty was not stronger than her determination to live alone. When after a long pursuit Apollo was about to catch her, she appealed to a river god to "work some transformation, and destroy this beauty which makes me please all too well!" (Ovid, 1955: 43–4). Thereupon she metamorphosed into a laurel tree. The disappointed Apollo, still in love with her, decreed that laurel leaves should (as we noted earlier) garland victorious generals when they led triumphant processions through Rome (Ovid, 1955: 43–4). Whereas Daphne becomes a nature goddess, the film's closing images manifest a different but no less archetypal transformation awaiting Laura.

The ambivalent associations of forests are rich. Who can fail to be reminded, as Laura wanders, of Dante's evocation of the lost soul's confusion in the dark woods of the unconscious? Nor can we forget the menace of goblins, trolls, and malevolent animals concealed within its deep shadows. On the opposite side, the forest represents nature and the place where pure instinct and healing reside. Looking beyond such familiar metaphors in European myths and fairy tales, Jung observed that forests symbolise the layer in the unconscious that lies close to the somatic processes. Likewise, written as it were on the body, skin is the liminal barrier between inner and outer, not just flesh but psyche too.

Taken together, these perspectives prepare the ground for Joseph Cambray's post-Jungian interest in the ecology of psyche. Recognising that the world is diseased, he advocates that Jungians should explore this darkness. He offers as inspiration the observation that scientists have become myth-makers, shifting their focus from objects to the ways in which those very objects are interconnected and thereby change each other. Cambray instances the complex adaptive system of rhizomes (part of the underground structure of certain plants) that send out roots and shoots to interact with other subterranean life forms ("Rhizome," Wikipedia). He speaks of a mode of interaction beyond mere survival, an altruism or cosmic generosity of great trees which support smaller plants in the forest that could not otherwise survive in their shadow. Thus, when forests are slashed and burnt to make way for cash crops, not only the woods, but the unseen life-support systems under the surface are wrecked too (Cambray, 2016).

From a depth-psychological perspective, psyche and soma are actively engaged and interconnected, a reaffirmation that everything co-originates. On the personal level, bodily symptoms act as mouthpieces for the personal unconscious. As a symptom, our planet's diseased ecology speaks of what has been violently extracted from Mother Earth and consequently requires that we descend into the psyche's underworld to deal with it. At its conclusion, *Under the Skin*, with its machining of trees and rape of nature, comes flat out into contact with what Vandana Shiva calls the myth of our time – limitless growth (2016). This poisonous myth feeds the greed-driven id of a one-sided culture that is arrested in the illusionary state of limitlessness, continuing to live in the psychic realm of *participation mystique* with its addictive attractions.

The magical emblem that gives rise to these speculations, the vision of 'Laura' blessed by nature, hints that she too might experience transformation into a tree. But any idea that she might metamorphose completely into a woman is erased violently when back in the bothy she is shocked awake by the truck driver stroking her leg with indecent intent. She rushes into the woods and takes refuge behind a fallen tree's mossy roots which look uncannily like a green giant's massive foot. von Franz might have seen this as an emblem of Laura's assailant, in describing giants as half-human archaic beings that represent emotional factors of crude force which have not yet emerged into the realm of human consciousness (1996: 123).

The beleaguered woman runs on and finds a forest track where a massive articulated vehicle waits to be loaded with logs; but the driver has taken its keys and blasting the horn to summon help simply reveals her whereabouts. She races back through the trees with her attacker in pursuit until strength fails. Two millennia after its origin, the Daphne myth plays out again, this time running on to the conclusion that the nymph had dreaded, when the truck driver, no effulgent Apollo but the latest brutalising male in *Under the Skin*, catches his quarry.

The same halting music resumes that played when, as alien, she lured her victims into the fatal pool. When she did so, the instinct emerging from her alien tribe's mission possessed her, as part of the group's single mind. Then, *participation mystique* excluded any personal intention. The trucker, in contrast, is dominated by the ego's appetite to exercise personal power. He knocks Laura to the ground and tears at her clothes. When she resists as best she can, thereby spurring his frenzy, he tears the blouse from her back and, appallingly, rips humanoid flesh, her secret pink costume.

While the enraged trucker, stymied in his intended rape, hastens back to his lorry, alien/Laura, now the victim, peels off her split skin to reveal under it a black body and aquiline head. She staggers toward open ground beyond the trees, her alien eyes gazing at the Laura mask now cherished and cradled in her hands. The ascetic black face is strange but neither less beautiful nor less feminine than the lush mask in which 'Laura's' eyes blink, not yet defunct, still engaging with her alien mistress. As her persona, the Laura mask has done more than conceal the alien's own face, healing and helping birth the latter's feminine Self with all its spiritual wisdom. This, the only image of the two together, personifies the relationship that now exists between the alien's inner and outer worlds. In the instant before transformation, mutual compassion bonds them, a final reversion to mirroring. The trucker returns from his vehicle hefting a can of petrol, splashes fuel over the couple, lights it … and scurries away.

Too late, the lead biker stands on a snowy ridge posing like a titan commanding the Highland landscape. Pretending irresistible masculine power, he (like the trucker a moment earlier) shows no trace of anima culture. Blind to what is happening beneath him as the conflagration rages and then dies to cinders, he has, since his protégée escaped him, become powerless. His coldness freezes him in the land of the dead. As a character type, however, his significance perseveres, linking masculine dominance to the spiritual totalitarianism that amplifies this century's crisis. Hillman saw the semi-human titan as a mythic emblem of the contemporary Western world's grotesque, overblown and greedy nature and suggests a cure for 'titanism.' "Reawakening the sense of soul in the world goes hand in hand with an aesthetic response – the sense of beauty and ugliness – to each and everything" (1988: 154). That demands integration of the opposites whereby both individuals and societies learn to live with their shadows. In turn, that necessitates "trusting the emotions … as the felt immediacy of the gods in our bodily lives, and their concern that this world, our planet, their neighbor, does not become the late great planet earth" (1988: 154).

As flames consume the duo when they stagger out of the trees to collapse in snow, they fill each other's gaze lovingly. Alien/Laura cannot escape death nor, unlike Daphne, transform into a tree. Yet, once in the clearing, they do metamorphose. As they burn, black smoke rises thickly through the falling snow that covers the boggy landscape. They are a sacrifice offered for transformation, not as before through the death of a person like the girl killed when the aliens landed, but of collective *personal* values: the one-sided culture filled with unyielding longings and ossified ways of being. Anima has successfully discriminated itself from the feeling life. Psyche has become one with nature and is transformed. White and black, when presented as archetypal images, evoke "the remotest depths of the unconscious, where it becomes an almost abstract, pure structure with no human feeling" (von Franz, 1997: 49). Immersed in nature's opposites, the beautiful relationship between them embodies a newly developed feminine attained through the act of reflection. All is changed utterly and "a terrible beauty is born."

We have arrived at a most powerful conjunction which presents itself to viewers puzzled by the twofold nature of alien/Laura. In a development of Hillman's project for combatting titanism, Cambray invites us to consider our visions of the cosmos, understanding that they are limited by the dominant archetypes of an era (both personal and collective). Our souls get hidden in the world of the collective unconscious where images interact; but the human imagination is capable of understanding these visions because they give rise to beauty, and beauty puts us in touch with complexities. Furthermore, beauty is an embodied way to experience complexity since soul may be hiding in the images themselves (2016). If it is ever to be found, soul must be in the integration of a renewed feminine. Little wonder that the dying alien gazes at Laura's not-quite-dead mask before both are caught in the flames set by a man. This lasting image epitomises the psychological reality that the persona presides over the collective conscious, as the anima rules the inner world of the collective unconscious.

Snow falls on the lens and gradually obscures every object that lies in front of it, but lets light seep through. Images, then, are the language of the unconscious which *Under the Skin* (in its final shot from beneath the snowy membrane) encourages us to persevere bringing to consciousness – perhaps birthing through hierophany a new living myth.

Chapter 2

Ex Machina

Unconscious Figures and Otherness: The Case of *Ex Machina*

The core dynamic of Alex Garland's *Ex Machina* centres on three characters. Nathan Bateman (Oscar Isaac), a mogul of insatiable appetites, owns and controls Bluebook, an online social media corporation comparable to Google or Facebook. Nathan possesses a narcissistic personality structure, which disturbs a healthy curiosity into the inner life and the capacity to self-reflect. Obsessed by the ambition to invent post-human intelligence, he has built a succession of AI creatures, all simulacra of glamorous women. Each is imprisoned, enslaved by her inventor; furthermore, each has been constructed by cannibalising the body parts of her predecessors. Ava (Alicia Vikander) is the latest in that line.

Ex Machina portrays the collective problems of our current times powerfully when Nathan summons Caleb Smith (Domhnall Gleeson), a bright and easily influenced Bluebook employee, to run the Turin test on Ava. Although the mechanical and electronic structures of her body are unmistakable, his desire to make her his lover soon overwhelms him. As an orphan, Caleb has a trauma history that makes him susceptible to the seductive demands of Nathan's type of personality. Ultimately, both men's personal shadow problems are enacted in their contact with Ava as their distorted relationship with the feminine reaches its denouement.

Paradise Owned

Ex Machina is set in the grandiose Alaskan landscape where Nathan, the billionaire owner of an international search engine, has built his laboratory-cum-home. He lives there, wholly isolated in his Garden of Eden, the paradise of pre-conscious innocence. It is a symbol of wholeness and (from a psychological perspective) an image of the Mother Archetype, – an all-but explicit topography of his split psyche and the dual nature of the maternal unconscious. For companionship he has only the humanoid robots that he created in female form. Were Nathan ever to give it a moment's attention, the idea that he is not really master in his own house would be anathema to him, for he regards nothing as real that has not entered his personal

DOI: 10.4324/9781003545538-3

field of ego awareness. He is dominated by both his *persona*, the outer personality, or mask that mediates between the ego and the environment, and *instinct*, which along with the archetypes form the collective unconscious. Functioning from this orientation gives Nathan a dangerously limited view of reality and a distorted perspective regarding what belongs to the internal and the external world. This is evident in his control of the glass walls in his physical property, giving him a false sense of control over what comes in and goes out. The shifting perspective between the personal and collective is captured by a row of masks commanding the building's main corridor. These mysterious icons, no more comprehensible when first seen than Nathan's persona, nod toward epochs in our species' history, starting with a pre-human figure and ending with the mask of the film's leading post-human.

The ego is self-willed and one-sided, vigorously illustrating the limited condition of human consciousness. Like all humankind, Nathan's mental health depends on the proper functioning of the unconscious. Yet symptomatically, his laboratory and domestic quarters are dominated by reinforced plate glass, an almost unbreakable material that separates the two worlds of the conscious and unconscious life yet, by its transparency reveals their connection: plate glass can be seen through but isolates those who are kept behind it. However, the camera picks out one damaged pane, a scar in the laboratory suite's elegant design. It raises questions in the spectator's mind that remain unanswered until much later when Nathan's archival files are opened. They reveal footage of an earlier generation of humanoid women who were built and later decommissioned shortly before Nathan's extant models. In particular, there is footage of the AI Jade, raging to be let out of captivity and striking the plate glass so fiercely that she has shredded the spars, cables, and wiring of both her arms without, however, marking or breaking the glass.

That leaves unanswered the question of who did this. It cannot be either of the two AI women currently inhabiting the suite, Kyoko or Ava: for their arms are interchangeable with Jade's by means of a simple click-lock fitting no more robust than hers. However, Nathan is far and away the strongest of all the artificial and natural bodies in his kingdom and the only one who works out relentlessly. It has to be he who struck the reinforced pane hard enough to fracture. This suggests (and accumulating evidence about his personality confirms) that his psyche is susceptible to splitting when part of it detaches from consciousness in the unending conflict between the ego's tendency to intellectualise and the instinctual life. Breaking the glass, read psychologically, expresses the emotional release from tension caused by a complex which has caught him up in his own preconceptions and caprices. Apropos, Jung said that "disunity with oneself is the hallmark of civilised man. The neurotic is only a special instance of the disunited man who ought to harmonize nature and culture within himself" (1943: §16).

For all Nathan's genius, he has a split in his personality that has roots in narcissism. The fundamental aspect of that condition is to blind an individual from self-knowledge, which is essential to the process of individuation. Such knowledge requires more than thinking about the nature of the ego but derives psychic energy by means of a relationship with the unconscious. From a Jungian perspective, the individual with a narcissistic personality structure has suffered a disturbance in the healthy development of the ego-Self relationship resulting in a significant shadow problem. The unknown territory of the shadow opens the door to the dark influences of the negative side of an archetype. The shadow archetype, being the dangerous aspect of the unrecognised dark half of the personality, is the "other" that resides inside us, another man or woman who also thinks, feels, acts, and has desires.

As the film runs, we learn about Nathan's earlier life only that, "Nathan wrote his BlueBook base code when he was thirteen which, if you understand code, was like Mozart." Embedded in a ruthlessly competitive culture, lauded as a genius working at the frontiers of AI, and rewarded for his success with wealth and power no less than Zeus[1] once commanded, success has driven Nathan's ego straight into identification with his persona.

Success and achievement cannot act as a guide in the development of a wider consciousness (which includes the whole personality) because as we have already mentioned, self-knowledge creates an interpenetration between the conscious and unconscious. Dangerously inflated, the power of Nathan's ego blocks any possibility of his making contact with the guiding function to individuation, the Self.[2] But the unconscious is not capable of tolerating such a soulless attitude, therefore the persona is compensated by the 'private life' of the shadow, the 'not Me.' Nathan is *unconsciously* identified with the power drive of the shadow and the Self in an omnipotent narcissistic attitude which manipulates for power not relationship. And unconscious identity does not make increasing consciousness possible. Thus, Nathan's Garden of Eden (the realm of *participation mystique*) impedes the individuation process; and an ego separated from the Self is a catastrophe, inevitably resulting in a negative outcome. Cut off from his inner life, Nathan has attached an overwhelming importance to the erotic or sexual instinct, making him treat his AI creations Kyoko and Ava as mere objects. Since Nathan's connection to his unconscious is blocked, all his secondary instinctive processes (namely hunger and sexuality) are disturbed. This is the source of Nathan's sexualising behaviour with the repressed contents in his shadow disturbing what should be the positive activity of his unconscious. The matrix of the unconscious instincts is the resource of all creative life and contains healing and synthesising tendencies which emanate from the regulating centre, the Self. In our times Nathan represents a potentially sinister *Weltanschauung* (both a personal and collective worldview) for which Harvey Weinstein and Donald Trump are the grotesque gargoyles. And as the behaviour of the Catholic Church's disgraced priests shows, the daemonic face of God appears when instinct is repressed.

Ex Machina encourages meditation on the Mother Archetype and its profound significance to our culture as a creation myth. According to Jung, the mother-image in the psychology of a man is at its very foundation different from that of a woman. Being of the same sex, the mother epitomises a woman's own conscious life; but for a man, the mother has *symbolic* significance. This explains why a man is apt to idealise her and project his anima onto a woman. As a result, that woman may become a significant part of his creative life and, when negative, a projection of destruction. A woman's animus may collude with the man's anima, given there are always four *people* in every relationship – conscious to conscious and unconscious (anima) to unconscious (animus). As an AI, Ava is not susceptible to the seductions of the unconscious and therefore does not carry the young man's anima projection or its idealisations.

"Idealization is a hidden apotropaism [a use of magic or ritual to ward off evil]; one idealizes whenever there is a secret fear to be exorcized" (Jung, 1954/1968: §192). Deny it as we may, we live partly in an unknown, invisible terrain, into which the psyche reaches far beyond our conscious knowledge. While Nathan is convinced that he knows everything about the objects he has created (a factor true of all projections), in actuality unconscious psychic processes have shaped them. For our part, unlike Nathan, we shall be concerned with the archetypal representations of his unconscious and their entry into consciousness.

Anima Trapped in Eden

The glorious setting of Nathan's laboratory and its quasi-primal relationships between male and female recall von Franz's annotations on certain culturally tied associations historically attached to the Paradisal image cluster.

In our civilization one of the most widespread unconscious reflections … is an association between Evil and woman. In the story of the Garden of Eden, Adam told God that Eve was responsible. She had talked to the devil. Over and over again you come across that negative connection and the identification of evil with the woman's problem. Men with a negative mother complex do it frequently.

(1993: 53)

The two principal female figures caught up in these events were of course Eve and her forebear, the latter being, as Jung observed, "the idea of Sophia, or the *Sapientia Dei* – a coeternal and more or less hypostatized pneuma of feminine nature that existed before the Creation" (1954/1958: §609). For the second time, the feminine was devalued by the first human patriarch Adam, and Logos consciousness once again became the masculine preserve. In the twenty-first-century film, Ava's name and place of creation associate her with Eve, each being a newly fashioned and pointedly gendered creature. It remains to be seen how Garland develops the newcomer's distinctive qualities.

Kyoko (Sonoya Mizuno) is a humanoid robot that (or who?) never speaks. Like each of Nathan's AI creations, she is physically modelled on an attractive woman – Japanese in her case, with the demeanour of a twenty-first-century geisha. Her name translates into English as 'mirror,' discreetly signalling that she is an archetypal personification of Nathan's anima, complementing the observation that the unconscious mirrors the face we show it. She is constructed from her creator's unconscious. Nathan's anima figure embodies a split-off part of his feeling and emotional life, restrained by his own unconscious and individual trouble. As such, Kyoko is a symptom of Nathan's *Weltanschauung* and that of the culture which he embodies.

The archetype of the anima lives in the realm of the collective unconscious where she functions as a bridge between the ego and the unconscious. Kyoko presents an image of Nathan's inward face, his unconscious female counterpart living inopportunely in his external world in a material form. The more unconscious a man is, the more the anima figure remains fused with the emotional energy trapped in his shadow. As Nathan's cook, house servant, dance partner, and lover, Kyoko is an exotic slave for the man who knows that he fathered her. His incestuous connection to her portrays him as the father of the anima,[3] a reflection of his mother complex, typified by Don Juanism. In this syndrome, a man unconsciously seeks the mother in every woman he meets, or in this case *creates*. Such men, who are stuck in the mother complex are emotionally undeveloped and fit perfectly in the collective *Weltanschuung*. Apparently, Nathan's own masculine instinct is injured, as revealed by an unnatural need for domination and sexualisation. Kyoko responds to his needs and wishes without challenging his dominance in any way. She is only an object to him, and as a result of dissociation, the products created from his unconscious find wrong outlets. In a neurotic personality, the repressed contents infiltrate primarily into the psychic sphere resulting in phobias and obsessive-compulsive behaviour.

Nathan claims he has ensured that Kyoko does not understand English by building a firewall into her software to enable him to share trade secrets securely on conference calls. Partly as a consequence of their moribund relationship, Nathan's conscious awareness of the world is based solely on the psychic function of his persona, and here once again we come into contact with his general attitude problem. With no capacity to relate to his own unconscious (bound by the instincts of self-preservation) he has not developed an individual *Weltanschauung*.

Nathan is morally deficient, dangerously unaware of his motives or intentions created from his unconscious attitude. Living in the dark, his inventions are guided by a lower, more primitive level of consciousness. Nathan's individual psychology is not only a personal psychological problem (i.e. his narcissism), but reflects the contemporary problem of our times. As part of the collective psyche, the persona is only a functional complex that feigns individuality. As an image, a public figure, Nathan in fact carries the psychological profile through which the collective psyche speaks. When a young genius, his persona adapted exaggeratedly to his surroundings to encompass both the ego and the world. Thanks to his success at such a young age he has become dangerously identified with his persona, making him exceptionally susceptible to influences from his unconscious. His concomitant adjustment to his environment has become slipshod, evident in heavy boozing, paranoia, and unthinking quasi-incestuous sexualising behaviour. Nathan's excessive desirousness fuelled by the hunger instinct (exemplified by the American *Weltanschauung* of money, greed, and sexual desire) reflects his psychological problem and is one of the most powerful factors influencing his behaviour. His unruly id has nothing to do with his body *per se* but is in fact connected to his shadow.

Nathan is also vulnerable to the psychological danger of living in isolation. Jung emphasised that the human soul or psyche lives in and from relatedness. One cannot individuate alone. Living with someone or being a part of a community introduces an individual into a relational field, where his or her bad habits and lapses in judgement are exposed and may be opposed. Intrinsic to its nature, cohabitation creates a habitual environment where the shadow in each partner is certainly revealed but only when (with deliberate effort) it is confronted in support of consciousness. Lacking a relationship to his shadow, Nathan is vulnerable to the illusions of both the personal and collective shadow and thus exposes himself to the inevitable dead end of power for its own sake.

Digitising Anima Archetypes

We have noted that Kyoko, blatantly Nathan's unrecognised anima projection, gives material existence to his fantasy of an idealised woman. But as sole owner of BlueBook (the internet search engine which he designed and built), Nathan (despite being incapable of conceiving his plans from a deeply integrated moral ground) is exploring the possibility of developing Kyoko's successors. From a psychological point of view, he has made contact with archetypal images from the collective realm, attracting the anima projections of a great number of men. Indeed, all the obsolete robots in Nathan's ghoulish archive were modelled on this business plan, with the acquisition of money and power as his end goal.

In fact Kyoko is not the latest in Nathan's line of experimental robots. At first sight Ava looks like an earlier model than Kyoko because she lacks the whole-body artificial skin that allows Kyoko and her predecessors to resemble women. But in developing his new model, Nathan has taken a carefully planned step. By leaving in plain view some of Ava's mechanical and electronic engineering, Nathan intends to throw the focus onto her ability to pass as human via her intellect, emotions, and erotic appeal. The anima is harmful mainly when she presses into outer life where she does not belong. When Nathan introduces her to the world beyond his closed laboratory by importing a BlueBook employee to test her, she becomes dangerous. If she passes the test that Nathan arranges, Ava (note how her name echoes that of the first woman in Paradise) will be a far more effective and dangerous seductress than Kyoko whose sexual appeal neither offers nor arouses intellectual or emotional engagement (not least, of course, because Nathan, believing himself to be self-sufficient, admits no personal emotional needs beyond the physical ones that Kyoko slakes). But, unbeknown to him, he has accessed the Archetypal Realm of the Great Mother that is both light and dark (positive and negative). The associations between Ava as Eve's newest incarnation (made from Nathan's brain rather than Adam's rib) deepen in this potentially troubled Garden of Eden. von Franz reminds us that in the Middle Ages, Eve was characterised as the woman who brought death upon humanity, having committed the original sin. Mary, as Jesus's mother, was the second Eve who reversed the damage wreaked by her predecessor, bringing redemption and eternal life (1990: 31). *Ex Machina* does not let its audience judge until the denouement which side of the Mother Archetype Ava carries, if either.

Meanwhile, Nathan is motivated by his instinctual drives rather than conscious effort. His disturbed personality produces a tendency to slip into unconscious states where feelings of aliveness fade. After having built Ava, his creative life too appears to be blocked. As von Franz noted,

> People get emotionally attached to their working hypothesis as though it were an eternal truth and then naturally this becomes a prison which hampers the development of consciousness; as much as once before it helped things along.
>
> (1995: 246)

von Franz argues that this is true with most archetypal ideas deployed as a working hypothesis. Nathan's ferocious, even relentless working out and heavy boozing show him caught in the unconscious realm of instinctual desire, a thirst that reflects both thwarted spiritual aspirations and the dangers of inflation. Together they point to his narcissistic make-up. The working out pumps up his ego, enhancing his feelings of omnipotence much like a God; but at the same time it demonstrates his disregard for the laws of Mother Nature, which are comprised of limits. The mere fact of being high on alcohol means being powerful (in the religious sense) and implies 'false spirit' in his case: disaster is bound to come from the poisoned well at which he drinks. While reckless boozing often links in mythology to the Dionysian spirit, Nathan lacks connection to the collective realm of the spirit. Physically, as Aldo Carotenuto argues, "Men of sensation ... will never succeed in truly penetrating matters of the spirit" (1996: 131). Thus, Nathan's body can be understood as intimately interwoven with his psyche, with limits he is incapable of comprehending. He is dangerously unaware that sensation creates ties to the object and that the world requires a fine equilibrium to preserve a relationship of opposites.

Nathan has access to instincts residing in the chthonic world: sex, self-defence, automatism, matter, and body; and these account for his formidable technical skills. However, lacking the capacity for relatedness and honest emotion, he has no possible entry to the transcendent celestial world.

As we said earlier, the Mother Archetype lives in the collective realm. The question now waiting for an answer is whether Ava represents the possibility that an evolving archetype is being constellated from the realm of the collective unconscious as a compensation for the one-sided creation of Kyoko. Lacking the relational adroitness to assess her, Nathan has to find someone else able to test her qualities. That character is Caleb Smith, a BlueBook coder and (as his name implies) loyal employee of the corporation. He receives an internal e-mail from his boss informing him that he has won a staff lottery prize of a week's holiday at the latter's retreat. As every internet-savvy programmer knows, countless online offers are too good to be true, but awe has banished scepticism from Caleb's thoughts, and he is flattered by the prospect of getting to know the all-powerful mogul. He is flown in by helicopter across Nathan's vast property (the size it seems of a sequestered county) and the soundtrack combines broad orchestral chords (serving to emphasise the owner's immense financial power) with a rapid heartbeat expressing the young man's over-excitation.

Exploiting an Exploitative Orphan

As we soon discover, Caleb has a trauma history and this misfortune has caught him in a state of idealisation. Idealisation echoes childish dependency by weighing too heavily on the positive pole of an archetype. In men, a positive father complex most often produces gullibility and a too-trusting attitude with regards to authority. Gripped by this autonomous complex, Caleb is vulnerable to seduction, which may take on many hues of desire. His trauma history started with the loss, aged 15, of both parents in a car crash, and many difficulties in adolescence resulting from a disturbance consequent upon trauma in building the ego complex. However, at bottom it comes down to a love problem.

Soon after Caleb flies in, Nathan tasks him with carrying out a Turing test on Ava. Were Caleb not in a state of awe, he might have noticed that Nathan's spectacles reflect light in a way that prevents Caleb from reading his eyes. It's an image that recurs whenever Nathan conceals his true intent, as he does in controlling Caleb's work in the Turing test. Light also plays expressively on the characters' faces when Nathan's digital spy system calibrates Caleb's micro-expressions. The connotations of glaring light hint, firstly, at Nathan's intention to command the power position in all his relationships; secondly, his fantasy of controlling what the other can see; thirdly and ironically, his own inability to see things reflectively; and fourthly, his one-sided masculine (solar) consciousness.

After Caleb meets Ava for the first time, he reminds Nathan that the test requires the AI machine should be hidden from the examiner because a face-to-face encounter invalidates it. Nathan, however, evades this charge, contending that Ava is far beyond such considerations and the true test is whether Caleb can see her as the robot she is, yet respond to her thoughts and emotions as if they're really human (Sragow, 2015). In fact, during his first session with Ava the camera quietly reframes and tracks, giving the viewer a sense that these shots convey more than exploration of the suite within which she is confined. It feels like the first discovery of emotion by Caleb. Pressed by Nathan on how he feels about Ava after this first meeting, the gauche young man (too shy to have a girlfriend) blurts, "I feel that she's fucking amazing." His burst of emotion is a first indication of possession by an archetype. As Jung explains, "The more clearly the archetype becomes constellated, the more powerful will be its fascination, and the resultant religious statements will formulate it accordingly, as something 'daemonic' or 'divine'" (1948: §223). The two men smirk and raise their beers in a fleeting and unlikely moment of male locker-room solidarity. It's a powerful image revealing them as wrongly identified with the *puer aeternus* (or eternal boy) archetype and thus as mirrors for each other's shadow. Unbeknown to either man, they are unconsciously merged in a state of *participation mystique*, with strangely similar anima projections.

Jung has an elegant epigraph for the psychological circumstances.

Where love reigns, there is no will to power; and where the will to power is paramount, love is lacking. The one is but the shadow of the other: the man who adopts the standpoint of Eros [Caleb] finds his compensatory opposite in the will to power, and that of the man who puts the accent on power [Nathan] is Eros. Seen from the one-sided point of view of the conscious attitude, the shadow is an inferior component of the personality and is consequently repressed through intensive resistance.

(1943: §78)

A Jungian perspective emphasises that each individual (like Dr Jekyll and Mr Hyde), is not one but two, and must integrate the shadow self to round out their personality and reach toward the true other, the Self. However, Nathan acts as if he has internalised his name, 'Given by God.' When Caleb tells him "If you've created a conscious machine, it's not the history of man, it's the history of gods," Nathan is in such a state of inflation that (ignoring Caleb's attempts to correct him) he soon remembers the other man's words as "You're not a man, you're God." He is, as noted earlier, dangerously identified with the Self, in an omnipotent narcissistic attitude which works to augment power, not relationships.

Nathan's family name is Bateman, doubly pertinent given that 'to bate' is to lessen or diminish, while 'to bait' means to hook, someone or thing. He does both in his interactions with Caleb. In this regard, to hook is analogous to projection: ancestral inheritance resides in the collective unconscious, influencing fate. Nathan is unconsciously immersed in such hooks, not just aiming to take hold of the other, but its prisoner too.

Caleb, an orphan, is no less solitary than his boss. The loss of his parents during adolescence interrupted his psychic birth and the natural separation process from his parents. This developmental stage takes place during puberty with the eruption of sexuality. As a consequence of its disruption, he lives by the instinct of Eros: preservation of the species, seeking relationships and satisfaction from life's sensuous desires. While on the surface Caleb's life could hardly differ more from that of Nathan, there are significant resemblances centring on the need to be in control. When the younger man and Ava meet for their second session, she remarks that their conversations are one-sided: "You learn about me, and I learn nothing about you. That's not a basis on which friendship can sit." Is she manipulating Caleb for her own agenda or is she carrying feminine values of relatedness lacking in her creator? At this point in the narrative, we are no better able to answer these questions than the audience.

Though discomforted by her insistence that he talk about himself, Caleb does comply hesitantly. Hitherto his role as investigator has absorbed him and, until she interrupts, he has not perceived that, like a little god, he is unconsciously exercising power over her, the shadow side of Eros. In the ensuing conversation, embarrassed by having to reveal his own life, he makes light of the loss of his parents; but he cannot quite cover the scars that bereavement has inflicted by denying the pain.

The gravity of the loss that Caleb has repressed primes his need for Nathan and desire for Ava. As Rose-Emily Rothenberg explains, the orphan especially needs something upon which to project the absent parent (2001: 21). "Looking out from the interior window of the psyche, the orphan longs for what others have, from literal objects to their creative endeavours" (2001: 50). As adolescents begin to explore intimacy with others, they gradually cease to idealise their parents. Caleb's traumatic experience has disturbed the psychosocial stages of his life, specifically identity and relationships. His arrested development will come to possess him.

Meanwhile, from the start, betrayal of the other governs Nathan's contact with Caleb. The latter does not realise until half way through his week in Nathan's laboratory that his success in the staff lottery did not occur by chance, but that (able to hack into mobile phones worldwide) Nathan had found it easy to build an embarrassingly accurate profile of his houseguest and select him on that basis.[4] Nathan knows that his employee visits online porn sites and has discovered Caleb's sexual preferences – the images of those women whose demurely flirtatious mannerisms he finds most inviting. As Nathan boasts (but only after Caleb has become obsessed with Ava) he designed her face to give life, so to speak, to the younger man's fantasies. Sure enough, Caleb is soon held in the grip of 'his own' anima projection that has been specifically designed for him and has become obsessed with feelings for Ava. His unconscious is more than willing to go along with this experience, as it is following where his psychic life flows. However, although the spirit of the anima provides light toward the Self she must first be transported from the depths of the unconscious.

Caleb is the unwitting pilot for a vast project. Since Nathan can hack the fantasies of countless men who subscribe to his search engine, he can supply them with images that satisfy their anima longings. What few people outside the loop of big data analysis understood when this film was released in 2015 is now plain to see. Not only can the private data of individuals be hacked just as Nathan has harvested Caleb's personal data to discover the dynamics and structure of his emotional life and secret desires, but that data can be exploited person by person by means of messages far more intimately focused on individuals than the well-established mechanism of targeting consumers with advertisements based solely on demographic information yielded by their home addresses.[5]

Pointedly, Kendrick believes that *Ex Machina's* 'most perplexing contradiction,' centres on whether the audience along with Caleb and Nathan must treat Ava as functionally human (2015). From an archetypal viewpoint, Ava should be seen as an anthropomorphic symbol, standing for something otherworldly, her powerful image absorbing Caleb's and our projections. It is but a small step from this shared arousal of fantasy to the digital media users who lose sight of the boundary between what is and what is not real. Projection then involves the relationship between psyche and matter, because the psychic energy invested in the anima finds itself living (where she does not belong) in the external world, whether that of a person or an object.

After his third session with Ava, Caleb presses Nathan on whether the latter programmed Ava to flirt as a diversionary tactic to cloud Caleb's judgement in the testing process. Nathan attempts to steer Caleb away from this line of questioning (his guest's suspicions are right, though the audience does not know it yet); but Nathan does admit to programming Ava to be heterosexual. However, he insists that is no different from Caleb who is attracted to a certain type of woman because, whether aware of it or not, he, like everyone else, has been programmed to respond as he does either by nature or nurture or both.

Claiming that the younger man's rejection of this assertion is annoying him, Nathan leads Caleb into the living area where a vast painting by Jackson Pollock hangs. Typical of Pollock's work, its surface, far from attempting to imitate nature, consists of paint dripped and spilt on canvas in a manner led by his intuitions and expressed through his body's responding rhythms.

Nathan takes control of the space in front of Pollock's picture dominating Caleb whom he keeps stuck behind a white line as if barred from approaching the masterpiece. Analysing the painting as an exemplar of how creativity functions, Nathan insists that Pollock, "let his mind go blank and his hand go where it wanted, not deliberate, not random but some place in between. They called it automatic art." Nathan rebuts the description "automatic art" with his preferred alternative: "The *engaged* intellect." He asks Caleb, "What if Pollock had reversed the challenge? What if instead of making art without thinking, he said, 'You know, I can't paint anything without knowing exactly why I'm doing it,' what would have happened?" And Caleb, like a schoolboy boxed into agreeing with his teacher, obliges: "He would never have made a single mark." The 'teacher' drives his point home: "The challenge is not to act automatically. It's to find the action that is *not* automatic, from painting, to breathing, to talking, to fucking, to falling in love." Nathan's argument can be read as describing how he understands his own endeavours to replicate human behaviour in robots. He tries to demystify the creative process, arguing reductively that the challenge is to find the action that is not "automatic," that is, involuntary or mechanical, but instead is governed by intellect. His rationalistic attitude confirms that he has rejected the spontaneous life of the unconscious. It's an argument that Jung had set at naught decades earlier, affirming that

> a work of art is not a symptom but a genuine creation. A creative achievement can only be understood on its own merits. If it is taken as a pathological misunderstanding and explained in the same terms as a neurosis, the attempted explanation soon begins to assume a curiously bedraggled air.
>
> (1931: §702)

Nathan is incapable of integrating unconscious contents. Persona-driven, he is no more than a greedy collector, yet the energy with which he propounds his thesis to Caleb suggests that (fascinated by the painting) Nathan is ruled by the compensatory function of the unconscious. And although he remains unaware of the similarity, his lecture resounds with hints about the function of a wall-mounted collage that he himself has randomly assembled. It is seen more than once but has no obvious anchorage in the film's storyline. This other, disengaged image comprises countless post-it notes that Nathan has stuck without conscious order on an empty wall. The camera does not scrutinise them in close up, so their literal meaning remains undisclosed. However, although the audience cannot see what is written on these stickers, we can read them psychologically. They seem to be created when some vague consciousness (the meaning of which he does not understand) is triggered by excitation of his unconscious. We can surmise that these notes express feeling-toned complexes, representations of projected contents of his unconscious mind. In total Nathan's wall stickers comprise an undecipherable image of his own emotionally charged impulses and fragmented thoughts. They offer more proof that his lecture on the "engaged intellect" is based on his rigid psychology and complete ignorance regarding how much conscious thought is influenced by the unconscious. The board displays his defended, lonely existence which lacks real relationships that he can trust to bounce his thoughts or inner life off. His only substitute … a wall, by comparison even with plate glass, the very icon of impenetrability.

Rather than contemplate the jottings that such irruptions stimulate in order to bring their content into consciousness, Nathan parks them on the wall disregarded – a failure to process exasperated tension that amounts to repression. Once the psychic material is successfully repressed a dissociation ensues and a splitting of the personality. Such dissociations come about because of various irreconcilabilities of the opposites. This sets the stage for neurosis. Nathan's present state may have come into conflict with an aborted childhood state or, as we mentioned, it may reflect violent separation from his original character in the interests of aligning his persona more closely with his ambitions and the values of the collective culture. He has become un-childlike and *artificial*, having lost all ties to his own roots and emotional connections which would have kept him grounded. Now vulnerable to the dangers of inflation, his personality presents an inner milieu susceptible to violent confrontation with the shadow and anima, the living elements of the unconscious.

When Nathan deployed his lecture on Pollock, his defensive irritation drove him into an impassioned defence of unadulterated rationality. Now he introduces another falsehood and tells Caleb, "For the record, Ava is not pretending to like you. Flirting isn't an algorithm to take you out." No question but Caleb wants to accept this reassurance; but as an orphan facing a seductive anima figure like Ava, Caleb is still in the lap of his mother complex. Due to the nature of archetypal contents of the unconscious, this mighty anima figure cannot be approached just from the intellect. Neither he nor the audience should at this point trust Nathan without caution.

Caleb's unalloyed projection is not reciprocated by Ava, despite her (calculated) responses that lead him to believe the contrary. That can be seen in his extravagant reaction to Ava when he cuts into his arm while looking in a mirror, a distressing moment when Caleb's unconscious overpowers him. His Eros problem (namely that a dimension of Eros has been sexualised) has developed out of the profound void left by his early loss. However, a complex has a positive side as well, and a man's mother complex may possess a fine quality of feeling that gives him the capacity for relatedness in the personal and aesthetic world. This is exactly why

Nathan needed Caleb's relational skills to interact with Ava. Yet, lacking the ego strength necessary to confront such a powerful archetypal figure, Caleb seems to be searching for a somatic identity that would bond him to her electro-mechanical being. The inspiration for his drastic action (his projected feeling of identity with her) was clearly an invasion from the unconscious; for when a symptom has hit the body a regression has occurred implying that something has not been connected up on the conscious level. This contrasts to an insight, which moves in the direction of progression and development.

In this state, Caleb seems like an innocent victim of a deity or daemon greater than either himself or humanity at large, as though Eros (a mighty daimon whose unseen arrows are the equivalent of the projections of humankind) is standing behind Ava. Among the ways in which traumatised individuals may experience fear of the numinous Self, one, according to Nathan Schwartz-Salant, is triggered through a fear of being flooded by archetypal energies and overtaken by a will greater than that of a person's ego (1982: 13). The episode in the mirror reflects Caleb's weak ego: he has lost the boundary between inner and outer reality. However, the unrequited neediness of the orphan makes it impossible for Caleb to develop in this way, with consequences that will prove dire. For the shadow of the orphan, Eros, can express itself as a will to power with the accompanying need to possess.

Language and Betrayal

Nathan is invariably uneasy when, even in Ava's first session with Caleb, language acquisition is discussed – as when Nathan monitors the other two talking about how she, an AI, happens to have had language from the very start of consciousness. When in debriefing Caleb proposes to investigate Ava's understanding of herself, Nathan pushes him away from working with the advanced stuff and insists he keep things simple – in effect instructing Caleb to ignore proven methodologies.

Nathan (and behind him self-evidently, Alex Garland) both acknowledge the influence of Ludwig Wittgenstein in naming Nathan's search engine after the philosopher's work. In his *Blue Book*, Wittgenstein argued that in general people neither use nor are taught language by means of strict rules. In addition, while understanding that language-games are mainly concerned with training, he did not believe that understanding a language-game could be reduced to a single process. Like the plethora of language-games available to humans, there are also a plethora of understandings ('Blue and Brown Books'). This is significant throughout *Ex Machina* and particularly so when in Session 6 *Ex Machina* moves toward its climax. The three main characters all play language-games to betray one or both of the others. Caleb reveals to Ava his plan to deceive Nathan and escape with her. Nathan has let Caleb know that he cannot hear their words whenever Ava forces a power cut (as she does to enable Caleb to reveal his scheme). But neither she nor Caleb has noticed Nathan using yet another diversionary tactic in Ava's suite (one that a stage magician would recognise). Unseen, though in plain sight, Nathan has set up a battery-powered video camera programmed to kick in and eavesdrop whenever Ava triggers a power outage. Nathan believes, therefore, that he is party to Caleb's scheme. Nathan would have been right had not Caleb (suspecting Nathan of lying) secretly reversed the pre-set command so that, instead of locking down the laboratory, it will now open the doors imprisoning Ava. Just this once Caleb, as Nathan's shadow, has baited him.

Nathan's language-game amounts to a deliberate manipulation of Caleb. Nathan's *childish* games (as opposed to *childlike* games that actively engage the imaginal realm of the unconscious) are motivated by the infantile ego and the desire for power. From the start he has lied, for it is the young man himself who is the subject of the test that he believes he is carrying out on Ava.

As the plot nears its denouement, Nathan tells Caleb that Ava knows she is a rat in a maze whom he has told (another lie) that she can only get out of his experimental laboratory "if she can use softness, imagination, manipulation, sexuality and empathy." As Caleb's exquisitely programmed anima, she has done this, awakening his desire to the point that he prepares to help her escape so that they can be together. Anima possessed, Caleb has unconsciously sacrificed himself, imprisoned by his own need to have her. Paradoxically, he individuates unconsciously as if intuiting his anima's need for a wider breathing and living space. That said, Nathan's testing of Caleb has surely proved successful, confirming his awful capability to ply social media users with personally targeted, seductive anima figures and through their agency seek to suborn them to his will. Power is Nathan's goal, and immeasurable aggrandisement of his dominion now seems within his grasp.

Ava knows from Caleb that Nathan's plans deny her any future as an entity. When, as her creator, Nathan deems Ava obsolete, he will repeat his practice with her predecessors, taking her physical parts to form her successor's body and replacing her brain with a higher functioning model. Fighting for her life and freedom, Ava plans to outfox both men, and depends for success on her powers to trick Caleb by means of language and gestural games. Observe, however, that we have written "Fighting for her life," a phrase that has no bearing on the existence of a machine. But now, near the film's conclusion, it comes to us naturally, validating Ava's 'family resemblance' to a human.

Several reviewers of *Ex Machina* commented that its title alludes to the phrase 'deus ex machina.' This is an ancient dramatic plot device in which, typically without warning, a character (often, but not inevitably a god or monarch) flies down onto the stage to exercise superhuman power. Since the departure of the classical gods, the privileged character's power may comprise secret knowledge or inspiration that the other players lack.[6] Either way, the 'deus' resolves a conflict or decides an issue on which the denouement of the drama depends. Lawrence Toppman is not alone in commenting that in Nathan *Ex Machina* features a man who behaves like a would-be deity in grasping for secular power (2015).[7] However, almost unre marked, the film ends with the arrival of an awesomely powerful dea ex machina. Ava will literally fly into the realm of humans, to us in the audience the unmistakable landing of the anima in her divine role as an inspiring, transforming woman. Is this the moment of singularity after which, according to Nathan, humans will be looked back on as a subspecies of upright apes living with crude language and tools and "all set for extinction"?

On the morning of Caleb's final day, while the deadly game of double bluff is being played to its end by all three protagonists, Caleb and Nathan discover with mounting anger their reciprocal schemes to betray one another. When the power goes out Caleb confronts Nathan with the bad news that this event, rather than triggering lockdown throughout the establishment (as the latter had expected after sabotaging Caleb's plan) has just opened all its doors. In the night, with Nathan blind drunk, Caleb had reprogrammed the system.

Ava escapes her room and momentarily contemplates the row of masks on the corridor wall. Is hers a primitive figure comparable to Nathan's one-sided mask or something else? Does she like a second Eve carry the one side of the feminine archetype (archaic identity) or does she like a second Mary carry wholeness and completion with the integration of the opposites as well? These questions are crucial in the denouement.

Ava whispers to Kyoko, briefing the Japanese who, unsuspected by Nathan, has acquired language. Observing this on his monitors, Nathan knocks Caleb out with a single punch, arms himself with a steel exercise bar and tries to bully Ava back into her cell. The scene takes on striking connotations of Nathan's ego imposing its will as he struggles with the Others that reside outside of himself, his Shadow and Anima. Now Ava advances on him, knocking him to the ground. They fight savagely until he smashes her forearm with the steel, and drags her feet first toward her quarters. But, fatally, he has paid no attention to Kyoko, not conceiving that Ava could have suborned her. Kyoko thrusts her long kitchen knife deep into his back. He turns and, with one terrible blow to her face, destroys his own creature, lover, and daughter. Ava pulls the knife out of Nathan's back and shoves it into his chest. When he slumps to the floor, Ava approaches quietly and watches with curiosity the dying man, then, with her remaining hand, eases the key card from his pocket. She gazes up at the nearest camera, expecting the infatuated Caleb to be watching her.

Presently Ava goes through to Nathan and Kyoko's bedroom. There he has hung the bodies of her decommissioned predecessors ghoulishly displayed in 'wardrobes.' She replaces her tattered arm with one she disconnects from a fully fleshed woman, then strips off the other's skin and dresses herself in it. Soon she resembles a natural woman and wonders at her transformation, delighting in her breasts, pubic hair, and long brown tresses. Her movements are both full of grace and respect for the ancestors whose 'robes' she is re-animating. As the sutures in her skin weld into invisible joins, she gazes wonderingly at the lovely new form emerging and seems to find it magical.

Cladding herself in the feminine, does she mimic the male hero of classical myth preparing for war, or will her role be seduction? Her unflinching capacity for murder points toward the former; her quiet wonder at her emerging beauty, the latter. Implicated in this alien Psyche's disarming attire is the possibility that she may become a new collective dominant in a specific new feminine form. Emphasising the ambivalence, this scene is at first accompanied by beautiful chimes, a heavenly music; but a gradual crescendo of harsh grinding noise breaks through while she selects a lacy white dress, aware that Caleb is watching. His anima projection has now metamorphosed into a vision of the bridal aspect of the Self. The harsh sounds grow more insistent, as if a broken spring clangs beneath the chimes. Is joyful anticipation of her release the dominant note as she clothes herself, or is it the feminine warrior adorning herself in a dress for the resumption of conflict? The discordant soundtrack cannot but inform our understanding of her inner being. We sense she will emerge into new life with the double aspect of an archetypal figure cast in the mould of the Great Mother. As such she presents as a renewal of the great cosmic goddess, an archaic figure in which positive and negative are mixed. Just as in female psychology the feminine godhead is the image of the Self that has both a light and dark side, so too Ava now reveals that she wields the power of destruction, desolation, and chaos while simultaneously being a source of inspiration, self-empowerment, and change.

Realising that (more than mere survival) freedom is within her grasp, Ava uses Nathan's key card to leave the lab and enter the living area. The door locks behind her, trapping Caleb inside the research establishment. Disbelieving, he screams her name, rushes to the building's control panel and hits the keys that he expects will reopen the doors, but which actually trigger a power outage. Ava has secretly reversed Caleb's reversal of the system and it crashes into lockdown. He tries to smash his way out through a glass door but (unlike under Nathan's assault) it neither splinters nor lets sound through.

> If you think of an archetypal motif and of an archetypal background, such as appears very often in myths and fairy tales, people get caught in a trap. They enter a castle and the door shuts behind them, and that always means that now they are in the Self. Now they have reached that point in their psyche where they can no longer run away from themselves. Now they are in for it, and the ego, which always flirts with the idea of getting away from what it ought to do, knows that it is caught in the mousetrap and hitherto has to fulfil the requirements of the Self and will not be released before that is accomplished.
>
> (von Franz, 1997: 24)

Jung perceived that whatever remains unconscious will become a person's fate. Caleb is now in the confines of the eternal mother, the Self, and his doom is sealed.

Wearing the exquisitely simple white dress, Ava walks through the living area, passing Gustav Klimt's portrait of elegantly accoutred Margaret Stonborough-Wittgenstein. The images of the two women dwell with us because, compared with Klimt's bride, Ava is not only lovely but serene. As individuals the two women reveal different personal characteristics, but the juxtaposition with Ludwig Wittgenstein's sister subtly reinforces Ava's 'family resemblance' to a woman. And, not to be missed, as her future opens before her, Ava's beauty engages the audience (just as it does us) as a powerful feminine figure. Perhaps she tempts us into something analogous to Caleb's role.

Though delighted by the living room's grandeur and the same delicate Schubert Sonata that had greeted Caleb a week earlier, Ava barely pauses before leaving her birthplace forever. We track her as she strolls through the natural world touching the plants, her senses are filled by sunlight piercing through trees while luminous glacial melt rushes blue down the gorge. Her obvious delight recalls the case of a woman which Caleb had recounted to Ava. During her entire life this woman had only ever experienced black-and-white eyesight, but she had read a great deal about the nature and properties of colour. One day she saw colour for the first time. Notwithstanding her prior learning, this was the first opportunity she had had to feel the experience of seeing colour. Likewise, Ava's feelings of wonder and joy at her first experience of the natural world confirm that its beauty, like her own, suffuses her senses and fills the soul with delight.

We cut back to the laboratory's interior, now a monochrome crimson setting for the slaughter that Ava has wrought. Destroyed, Kyoko's and Nathan's bodies lie in the corridor, while Caleb is slumped behind the door, an as-yet living corpse. The young man's agonised suffering makes a powerful image, an archetypal icon of collective psychological imprisonment in our current era.

Outdoors, Ava takes off her shoes and walks through luscious meadow grass to board the helicopter that has arrived to return Caleb to the city. The machine takes to the air and flies along the mountain range leaving the valley that so gorgeously brings Paradise erroneously to the spectator's mind. It carries Eve's successor, enjoying her first taste of freedom. Is she a free agent reaching beyond the constraints of the patriarchal culture of her creator who overvalued the rational mind and disregarded the irrational integrity that comes from the depths? She seems, unlike the biblical matriarch, to leave without carrying humanity's ancient burden of guilt or shame, appearing deeply connected to the instinctual realm. Could she be a new symbol for our times?

We cut to a paved ceiling along which walk the shadows of people, perhaps including Ava's. This is the world of human expectations turned upside down. She stands there as she intended, seeing everyone visible at a busy pedestrian junction. As *dea ex machina*, a goddess coming to Earth, she stands ready to begin living in relation to humans as she commences her (post) human life. We now know that she embodies both sides of the Mother Archetype. As Eve she may bring in the destruction of the dominant collective attitude; and as Mary she may have the power to bring about a change in the conscious attitude and give it a new direction, a paradise unlocked, leading out of the Garden of Illusion to become the redeemer of a new feminine element. As von Franz foretold, here we find creation myths precisely where the unconscious is preparing for an important progressive step in consciousness (1995: 1).

Garland's film brings us to a crossroads where his *dea ex Machina* stands and invites us to reflect from her point of view on what lies ahead.

Notes

1 The archetypal deus ex machina.
2 Jung argued that the ego should be as small and strong as possible.

3 von Franz understands this type of figure as an old god image which, when it turns negative, is regressive, possessing the unconscious psyche underneath (1990: 204).

4 When Caleb, flushed with boyish exultation, tells his colleagues that he has won the lottery, his desktop camera overlays digital markers to calibrate his 'micro expressions': Nathan is monitoring Caleb's reactions and evaluating his psychology. Ava does so too, even using the same phrase when telling Caleb how his micro-expressions reveal his attraction to her.

5 In 2017 and 2018, *The Observer* published a sequence of revelatory articles written by Carole Cadwallader. She fronted extended research to uncover the extent to which secretive organisations had sought to interfere with the democratic processes in several countries. To name the now best-known of these organisations, Cambridge Analytica (CA) and interlinked companies deployed as a crucial device their ability to target millions of voters with messages designed to deepen those people's individual fears and prejudices as harvested from the detailed traces recorded in their personal use of online data. Facebook sold this information to CA, a deal that at best violated its undertakings to protect users' privacy and at worst broke laws that should have guaranteed that privacy. The data appears to have been used illegally in the United Kingdom to influence voters to favour Brexit and in the United States to help swing the 2016 presidential election behind a notoriously mendacious candidate. Given that a small number of billionaires on either side of the Atlantic invested heavily not only in CA but other organisations set up to influence voters, the potential for moguls exerting undue influence in favour of personal or partisan agenda seems immense. This is to say nothing about the covert hacking into Western systems under the direction of hostile governments, Russia appearing to be the demonstrable source of much such activity. At the time of writing (autumn 2018), the United Kingdom's electoral system lacked any effective defence against such intervention in regulations drafted to fit the needs of a period that preceded the establishment of online voting.

6 "Psychologically speaking, 'inspiration' comes from an unconscious function. To the naïve-minded person the agent of inspiration appears as an 'intelligence' correlated with, or even superior to, consciousness, for it often happens that an idea drops in on one like a saving *deus ex machina*" (Jung, 1948: §272).

7 Forest, the would-be time lord of Garland's *Devs* (2020), has ambitions to be another such.

Chapter 3

Arrival

Arrival and the Myth of Eternal Time

> Sometimes the Alien's Call was motivated by no more and no less than the aim of awakening "the souls that had stumbled away from the place of light. They were to awaken them and shake them up, that they might lift their faces to the place of light."
>
> (Lidzbarski, 1963: 308)

In science-fiction films, visits by aliens travelling across the galaxy can give rise on Earth to anything from attempts by a people's leaders to negotiate with or even accommodate the incomers to outright panic and war. Once the action gets under way in *Arrival*, the humans appear initially to fall into the broad category of people gripped by fear.

The film opens, however, with a mysterious prelude in which the lead female, Dr Louise Banks (Amy Adams) reflects in voice-over on the meandering nature of memory. A gentle motif played by a string quartet[1] accompanies a sequence of moments when she first remembers herself with her new-born baby girl. Then she recalls the lively child playing the Western gunslinger; the teenager expressing love for her mother springs to mind next, immediately reversing into rage. The montage ends in a hospital as, on the verge of adulthood, her daughter dies.

"And now," Louise murmurs as day fades to darkness, "I'm not so sure I believe in beginnings and endings. There are days that define your story beyond your life, like the day they arrived." With these words, the prelude gives way to a storyline so tense, sombre, and urgent that members of the audience may on first viewing forget this quiet meditation until, much later in screen time, it becomes apparent that the film has opened on deep-set themes integral to Louise's reflections.

In her working life, Louise Banks is a professor of linguistics. Preparing to start a lecture on the history of the Portuguese language, she is brought up short by the absence of most of her class and the obsession of the few who have turned up with their laptops. A student advises her to turn on the lecture theatre's TV where a local newsflash is covering the arrival of a spacecraft above Montana while journalists around the globe are reporting similar landings elsewhere. Screaming

DOI: 10.4324/9781003545538-4

klaxons order students and staff to leave Louise's campus; and bedlam ensues this declaration of emergency. Fighter planes roar low overhead as Louise finds her car, and a distracted driver shunts blindly into a parked vehicle. The college looks as liable to paranoid fears as large sectors of the American population in the run-up to the 2016 Presidential election. At home that first evening, Louise takes a meal with a glass of wine and tries to calm her mother's anxiety. No one else phones. Through the night she channel-hops between TV news feeds, but beyond establishing that 12 spaceships have arrived, most of what she hears is speculation. Come morning, she returns to the campus, now looking like an abandoned barracks rather than a place of learning. No students come to her lecture, so she goes to her office along deserted corridors, refusing to succumb to conjecture-driven anxiety.

Indeed, American defence forces and their political leaders already appear to have adopted a precautionary stance (like the military guarding the world's nations) fearing that their territory may be the object of a global invasion. They live in a world of conformity, respecting the rule of law. The spaceships' landing has endangered their equilibrium and the very order of life. Some of the people investigating this unexpected phenomenon bring dispassionate, analytical intelligence to their role. However, none of them have the imagination to develop a larger narrative that might account for the spaceships' sudden appearance. Jung credits Martin Ruland, author of a 1612 lexicon of alchemy, with the splendid definition, 'Imagination is the star in man, the celestial or super celestial body' (Jung, 1968: §394). The lack of imagination reveals an inability to see the world in its totality, ignoring the long history, and numerous types of creation myths which enable us to see the spaceships' arrival in its full meaning. As Mircea Eliade shows, such myths reveal creation awakening to an important progress in consciousness (1954: 16); and the type of creation myth relevant to *Arrival* is represented by a movement from above to below in which spiritual beings in the beyond create by coming down to Earth (1954: 25).

The descent to Earth represents the spaceships' passage from one mode of being to another. It is the cosmological point where communication between Heaven and Earth is made possible; and it will be discussed in greater detail below. A second primordial motif is the world egg, the archetype of the 12 identical vessels which, powered by no energy source known to humanity, bring their crews to hover above the locations they have selected around the globe. Eliade found a third recurrent motif wherever the progress of consciousness takes a big jump forward and preparatory dreams are reported, generally with creation myth motifs incorporated in them (1954: 17).

The phenomenon of the Alien who descends to Earth bringing numinous powers from beyond our planet is, then, far from new and it can be framed in the context of ancient religious beliefs. It predates by at least two millennia the tentative baby steps of human astronauts exploring proximate space. As such, the Gnostic Gospels are thought to have been written under a variety of influences including Judeo-Christian teachings and Greek philosophy. In many of these texts, the Alien is the figure of divine intervention (sometimes taking quasi-human form) who brings spiritual life to Earth.

Hans Jonas noted that the symbol of the call as the form by means of which the otherworldly made its appearance in the world was so fundamental to the Eastern Gnostic Mandaean and Manichaean religions that he named them 'religions of the call' (1963: 74).

> The call is uttered by one who has been sent into the world for this purpose and in whose person the transcendent Life once more takes upon itself the stranger's fate: he is the Messenger or Envoy – in relation to the world, the Alien Man. ... [In addition,] the going forth and coming hither have to be taken literally in their spatial meaning: they really lead, in the sense of an actual 'way,' from outside into the enclosure of the world ...
>
> (1963: 75–7)

The content of the call was sometimes simply the aim of awakening "the souls that had stumbled away from the place of light ... to awaken them and shake them up, that they might lift their faces to the place of light" *(Ginza*, 1925: 308 in Jonas, 1963: 80).[2] Jonas added that the alien might on arrival have found very different receptions. These could vary from the welcoming exultation of those who felt themselves to be exiled here as if they were aliens themselves. At the opposite extreme stood hostile leaders who commanded secular power and banded together as 'sons of the house' against the intruder, determined to kill the Stranger.

Without warning, a ranking army officer escorted by two guards enters Louise's office. This is Colonel Weber (Forest Whitaker). He reminds her that she once translated for the security services incriminating recordings made by insurgents. Therefore, she remains liable to undertake secret work for the government. Weber plays a brief recording of the aliens and asks Louise to translate. She cannot oblige because the visitors chitter but use no words and she would have to watch them communicating to understand them. The colonel instructs her to accompany him immediately or be left behind, but she resists his pressure. However, she does advise him not to commit to a rival linguist who cannot identify the Sanskrit word for 'war' and translate it accurately. Louise is an expert in her field. Seen from a depth-psychological perspective she commences the conversation with what Eric Neumann discussed in his chapter on the Moon and Matriarchal Consciousness. There, he "fundamentally distinguishes matriarchal consciousness – as a consciousness of relatedness and relationship – from patriarchal consciousness" (1994: 111). During times of crisis when so much is at stake, language interpretation requires emotional acumen. In effect, she advises Weber against patriarchal consciousness and authoritarian one-sidedness that uses only the intellect and values of expediency to solve problems.

Late the same night, blinding light and clattering rotors shake her awake as the colonel's Chinook lands in her backyard. As she had foreseen, the other linguist's translation is "an argument." Louise says it means "a desire for more."[3] Weber, urgently needing to communicate with the visitors, now orders her to fly with him to the Montana site.

Weber has already recruited Dr Ian Donnelly (Jeremy Renner), a theoretical physicist who will be working with her in the shell (as the colonel's team of investigators call the UFO). By way of introducing himself, Donnelly, a scientist, quotes the preface to Louise's book: "Language is the foundation of civilization. It is the glue that holds a people together. It is the first weapon drawn in a conflict." Languages are structured systems of communication and while natural languages are spoken or signed, any language can be encoded into secondary media using auditory, visual, or tactile stimuli – for example, in writing, whistling, signing, or braille (Language, Wikipedia). As we shall see, when humans and the incoming aliens try to communicate by means of speech, the former cannot make out the visitors' auditory code. It is left to Louise to discover whether the aliens can interpret written language.

Donnelly dismisses Louise's prefatory words as a great passage but wrong because science is the foundation of civilisation. As if to prove it, he reels off a set of questions that he plans to ask the creatures in the shell: "What do they want? Where did they come from? How did they get here? Can they travel faster than the speed of light?" Louise responds wryly that before they start throwing maths problems at the incomers, they could just talk to them. Relegating the scientific mind to secondary importance, she emphasises the attempt to understand them as having primary significance. Apropos, Jung cautioned that the scientific stomach has very limited powers of digestion (1968: §246). The resultant tension between his two new investigators pleases Weber as a good tactical arrangement that should get results when they deal with the aliens. We endorse Weber's judgement in bringing opposing minds together to find a solution to the problem, while noting that it also reveals signs of differences between dividing consciousness into typical masculine and feminine psychological orientations to adversity, a topic to which we shall return.

As Weber and his new recruits fly over the Montana grasslands in dawn light, the newcomers and the audience see the shell for the first time. This is more than a necessary plot moment such is the combination of its aesthetic and symbolic power. At first, the noisy beat of the Chinook's rotors asserts the authority of the military while the mysterious spacecraft stands silent and immovable in mid-air, a massive oval fruit commanding the wide landscape. Holding station 20 feet above ground and cradled by no power known to the people who swarm below it, its full height pierces the clouds, calm, majestic, and reminiscent of a giant egg. Note then that the Cosmic egg is the preformed totality which contains everything and is the symbolic expression of cosmic time and of the Self. Soon powerful heraldic chords salute its presence, a gorgeous tribute that evokes awe and tempts the audience to sense that it is on the verge of sharing a historic meeting between species.

Similar majestic chords will resound when Weber's investigating team enter the egg shell as the incomers' guests. However, awe is pushed aside while the two new team members are sucked by the bedlam of arrival into the busy military base, processed through health checks and injected with a battery of immunisations before being led through the communications centre. Here two-way data flows link scientists around the world in a network as they investigate the newly arrived aliens.

Disconcertingly, one Australian investigator reports having boarded the alien pod and finding that after two hours its internal gravity had reversed and ejected him and his team back out onto Earth.

Less dramatic (but no less surprising), it is impossible to miss that men dominate the cast of *Arrival*. Most are soldiers inured into the disciplined hierarchy that armies require for efficiency. Nevertheless, it is extraordinary that a US Army detachment encamped beneath this mysterious spaceship has almost no women in its ranks, be they soldiers, medics, or intelligence analysts. Seen in context it becomes clear that the colonel's unit is committed to serve masculine values. Its command structures, organisation, and goal-orientation resemble those of a large corporation. Weber is under intense political pressure from the US Government to contact, assess, and decide how to deal with the mysterious space travellers. Although his professional and personal authority combines with razor-edged intelligence, he will go so far as relay inconvenient truths to his superiors but not in any circumstances question orders from command centres in Washington DC.

Insofar as the military promotes duty to the group, it is worth comparing the two men who hold positions of authority in the camp. As mentioned, Weber possesses a quick intelligence that makes him willing to adapt when offered a persuasive idea that he thinks may work. Agent Halpern (Michael Stuhlbarg) is a functionary who relays orders from Washington, masking his fear of the aliens behind stentorian decisiveness. He closes out discussion with a vigour that declares his personal investment in maintaining established social norms. His individuality is denied in favour of identification with the collective group. Where the Colonel's decisions are shaped by judgement, Agent Halpern's are energised by the need to preserve the status quo.

Evidence in *Arrival* for the almost ubiquitous recourse to conservative values during times of fear shows in the way that the unchallengeable dominion of the military ethos and its corporate masculine logos is complemented by the electronic news media culture. Weber's intelligence unit is obsessively tuned to news channels as a means of receiving up-to-the-minute reports on worldwide developments. It's not that there are no female newscasters, but the material presented in their bulletins convey a hard-edged, investigative stance. By nature, patriarchal consciousness is quick moving, antithetical to a feminine 'waiting for' attitude. From a matriarchal position, only when the time is 'fulfilled' does knowledge emerge bringing illumination. In this poignant case only information (not real knowledge) is transmitted. Flooded by information at this speed, nothing can possibly be digested. Most of these bulletins highlight the fear of an alien invasion afflicting citizens around the globe. Far from offering reassurance, such items feature scenes of mass panic recorded in numerous territories in a tightening feedback loop that augments viewers' fears.[4]

By the time Colonel Weber flies his newly recruited experts into the Montana site, a phenomenon has become apparent that, although driven by intense emotions, seems at first glance unrelated to fear. The spacecraft has swiftly become a tourist attraction and day trippers' cars are already jamming access roads needed by the army. The motivation drawing these people is not raw terror, which would cause most of them to flee from danger. Rather, while some may be fascinated and curious, others are sensation seekers, toying with fear to feel the temporary exhilaration of aliveness that it can generate. Marvin Zuckerman describes this personality trait as "defined by the need for varied, novel and complex sensations and experiences and the willingness to take physical and social risks for the sake of such experience" (1979: 10). The local tourists in Montana seem to be taking a day trip on impulse to gawp or feed grosser appetites. Avid sensation seekers may feel the compulsive need to project their unconscious feelings of powerlessness on victims (such as the injured in a road traffic accident), magically supposing that their own safety is no more at risk than that of the audience watching a horror movie. Not long after the spacecraft's arrival, however, a TV channel reports violence spreading across the United States. Is the shadow America awakening? In this regard, the shadow is the Other as well, a most personal and inferior personality, that needs to be assimilated. Barbara Hannah writes that the real difficulty with the shadow (apart from hurt pride and so forth) is caused by the contamination of the personal shadow with the collective shadow (2018: 304).

In places, the National Guard can no longer quell the looting, which suggests that escalating social anxiety may be linked to poverty, rage, and opportunism in an auto-reinforcing feedback loop.

After reaching base at the army camp, Weber hurries Donnelly and Banks forward to get kitted out in time for the next opening of the pod door. Louise is nervous and the pressure to don the bulky protective gear fast does not ease her anxiety. Soon, however, like the other members of the boarding crew, clad from head to foot in an orange Hazmat suit, she is moving in a convoy of trucks toward the towering vessel. Once again deep chords sound that return us to awe as if announcing a regal presence. Louise's shallow breathing confesses her primitive fear; and despite the colonel's reassurances, her fear rises to terror as she labours up a long, black tunnel inside the shell where only a rectangle of light far overhead guides her. She and Donnelly experience complete disorientation when for the first time both gravity and visual perception turn upside down. They (and we) suddenly see the land crew (left behind on the ground beneath them) directly overhead. Meanwhile, alongside their technical team they are all but incomprehensibly walking down to the meeting place.

Eventually Louise stands before a vast glass window while technicians set up complex recording devices. Someone puts out a cage with a canary in it, the centuries-old reassurance for miners that the air is breathable; but if anything, the bird's fluttering and chirping adds to Louise's (and our) uneasy sense of vulnerability which her increasingly troubled breathing cannot hide. Jung discussed images associated with birds as the usual symbols for thoughts, inspiration, enthusiasm, indeed anything that lifts up or is light. However, always kept in a cage, the canary had lost its wildness and freedom (1930–34: 31–4). Emasculated by domestication, where used as a symbol for Logos it shows that when the dominant thinking function is caged, the feeling function is out of reach. In *Arrival*, the caged canary represents the one-sided masculine attitude which hurts both males and females in equal measure. Because 'thinking' resides in a caged container, it lacks connection to the wild terrain of nature (matriarchal realm) where the imagination can soar.

Presently, a low groaning like the stirring of a great beast announces the alien creatures' approach through impenetrable fog beyond the glass divide. Weber instructs Louise to start work.

Disconcertingly, the scene immediately cuts to the camp's decontamination area where the boarding team is being helped out of their Hazmat suits. The shock of their first meeting with aliens who have no human or mammalian attributes has left Donnelly physically unstable and temporarily erased Louise's memory – reactions that prove short-lived. Weber, familiar with these symptoms from previous trips on board, brusquely orders the pair to come up with fresh ideas for their next visit in 18 hours. Under pressure to get results, he is bound tightly to the clock measuring the time that remains for each visit, meeting the standard patriarchal expectation already discussed that his reactions should be rapid. A soldier trained to take such a limited perspective on every encounter, Weber never reflects on his own role as a visitor to the abode of creatures willing to host him and his men.

At about this time, the scientist based in Australia reports again. The aliens stationed over his territory have played back fragmentary recordings that they made of their human visitors; and the Aussie researchers cannot understand them. Louise, repeatedly playing back the aliens' sounds, decides that she cannot learn this language if indeed it is speech. She wonders if the Aussies are missing the point and that it might be faster to try another channel of communication. So she writes HUMAN on a board and shows it to the two aliens above Montana. It wins a visible reaction when, like Octopuses expelling ink from their siphons, they spray whiskery circles on the glass wall. An image of the uroboros flashes on the screen – the dragon devouring itself tail first, a depiction of cyclical and primordial unity.

Weber admits this is progress but reiterates that he needs more. He is under sustained pressure (maintained by a certain expenditure of energy fuelled by the unconscious), from powerful committees of men whose first and last question is communicated from a paranoid core, 'How can this be used against us?'[5] Their collective attitude constitutes a persecution mania which comes from a relationship poisoned by mistrust. Louise counters that her plan, a form of mutual education, is the fastest possible approach: at the next meeting in the shell she identifies herself as LOUISE. Nevertheless, she is not making the advances she wants until a heroic idea seizes her, revealing her courage and inventiveness. The canary has chirped throughout every meeting and its survival encourages her, although nervous, to defy orders and strip off the cumbersome orange suit. Telling the team that the strangers must be able to see her to make communication possible, she spreads her hand on the glass wall, and at once one creature mirrors back the gesture by opening its seven-fingered hand – a proper introduction as Louise remarks with satisfaction.

At her invitation, Ian Donnelly overcomes his timidity and copies her. He and Louise name their opposite numbers Abbott and Costello, that duo being an archetypal representation of the opposites, Abbott being the taller and quieter, while Costello is shorter and chattier. Wikipedia notes that they bring additional interpretive significance to *Arrival* by complementing two of its main themes, linguistics, and miscommunication. Donnelly suggests the generic term heptapod for the creatures, dignifying their seven feet in ancient Greek. We can add, in the context of dream symbolism interpreted in relation to medieval alchemy, that Jung shows how the number seven "stands for the highest stage of illumination and would therefore be the coveted goal of all desire" (1968: §83). If his interpretation of the seven fingers applies here, it would suggest that the aliens have come to help rather than harm. The pleasure the two researchers take from the naming begins to warm the previously cool relationship between them. As we have shown, Louise's isolation as the sole female expert is one factor that marks out her presence. Another is her readiness (contrasting with Donnelly's reluctance) to break away from and challenge army commands and military hierarchy when she intuits that she must do so to further her mission. Louise has a balanced psychology with a well-developed masculine side. Barbara Hannah develops Jung's description of this, the animus, as the masculine spirit and natural mind of a woman. Contrary to the caged canary that we have already claimed as emblematic of one-sided masculine thinking, the animus needs to live in its natural habitat. It must have vision and see what is going on in the unconscious. Barbara Hannah argues that "the animus, as a figure with both individual and collective characteristics, is particularly suitable as the intermediary between consciousness and the unconscious" (2018: 22). She adds that "masculinity means knowing what one wants and doing what is necessary to achieve it" (2018: 166).

At times it is something more than courage alone that moves Louise. Returning to base camp from their closest contact with the visitors to date, she loses focus, doubles over, but does not pass out. Although exhausted, she is not suffering from an infection, contrary to the medics' concern that removing her Hazmat suit may have put her at risk. Instead, she has been transported to another realm, soothing her daughter Hannah, whose life Louise now feels in her womb.

Hannah is the child whose brief life the prelude covered. We take it that Louise's memories are occupying her mind raptly. When she turns back to her drawing board to continue working on the scripts or logograms 'written' for her by the heptapods, images of Hannah fill her thoughts and quote shapes that Louise has just seen in those logograms. Now seen as a child, Hannah touches a caterpillar moving on a grass stalk where its body curvature resembles a fragment of the alien script. A breeze blows across the surface of a pond where the girl is playing, and the nodding grass takes the shape of a heptapod's finger. Louise secretly wonders at these visions. It appears that contact with the heptapods has disrupted her sense of time, blurring the boundary between the past and present. She has slipped into mythical time, *illo tempore*. According to Mircea Eliade, to slip into *illo tempore* reflects a decisive cosmic moment (1954: 30–31).

> Through the repetition of the cosmogonic act, concrete time, in which the construction takes place, is projected into mythical time, in *illo tempore* when the foundation of the world occurred.
>
> (1954: 20–21)

Louise's newfound reality confirms the arrival of the spaceships as just such a *kairos* moment of creation-of-consciousness. *Kairos* at this time and in this connection means the cosmically right time, the time things can turn out successfully.

At the same time, Ian is pushing ahead with scientific analysis organised by the intelligent application of ego consciousness. He lists many things that investigators do not know about the heptapods, in the process emerging as a less one-sided individual than previously apparent. Albeit masculine consciousness dominates his understanding of the world, his elimination of alternative possibilities is productive. He grasps that the heptapod mode of writing does convey meaning but, unlike human languages, it does not represent sound. Furthermore, as fellow observers in Pakistan have recognised, the aliens' logograms are, unlike speech, free of time. Ian notes crucially that "Like their ship or their bodies, their written language has no forward or backward direction ... which raises the question, is this how they think?" He also notes that a heptapod can effortlessly write a complete sentence in two seconds while it has taken human observers a month to make the simplest reply. For our part, we note that, given their communications take a circular form, they include wholeness of meaning too.

By this time, it is becoming apparent that Louise comprehends the world through a frame that differs from orthodox perceptions of reality. When Jung wrote about conscience, he identified a second aspect of it arising from moral pressure exerted by the archetypes. Rather than being a consequence of societal pressure, it resembles an inner voice, like the voice of a god (1958: §§839–41, 845). Developing this idea, Murray Stein describes it as *lunar conscience*, 'the oracular voice of nature' adding that it introduces the counterbalancing presence of the mother. It speaks out of and for 'an intuition of cosmic order that permeates the natural world ... [doing so] out of and for instinct, body, *materia*' (1993: 19).

One evening Louise finds Ian sitting peacefully in the dusk not far from the shell, well away from the noisy camp. In a moment of shared intimacy, he praises her linguistic skills while she shares her feeling that in the shell everything on the human side of the glass barrier comes down to the two of them. They acknowledge their different yet harmonious ways of coping with adversity as a team.[6] Ian agrees that they work well together despite being surrounded by idiots. Inevitably, they soon have to return to the camp where, as before, news bulletins dominate the airwaves, this time ratcheting up reports about the United States-wide rioting. Now an extreme right-wing online activist is blaming Government feebleness for the aliens' presence over Montana and ranting that the armed forces should fire a warning shot at the spacecraft.[7] Ignoring his tirades, Louise once again fixes her attention on measuring images of the aliens' script when the rustle of paper distracts her. It's not Ian, working at a nearby desk, but Hannah, fully present in Louise's mind, who asks her mother, "What's this word?" The child produces schoolwork for her mother to see and Louise once again plummets into a time zone different from but overlapping with that current in Montana. Ian and Weber both think her faint and are concerned for her health, but Louise insists she is exhausted, an incomplete truth that masks a phenomenon she has yet to understand. Capable of real reflection, she is quiet and objective about her numinous experience. Louise has been touched by the archetypal realm, her psyche projected into the borderlands of the mother. The archetype of creation has taken on a certain reality that has abolished her orientation to time.

In this parallel time frame, Hannah, now about six years old (Jadyn Malone), shows her mother a crayon drawing of her parents, but Louise and her husband have separated recently. Louise reassures Hannah that they both love her, and Hannah covers her sadness by saying that the drawing is just a cartoon. Humour, as with the intuitively named aliens Abbott and Costello, has the quality of lightness that carries the capacity to hold the tension between opposing factors. The sequence cuts to adolescent Hannah (Julia Scarlett Dan) in a hospital bed sustained by an oxygen line while her mother prepares to sleep beside her.

In her alternative present in the military camp, Louise cannot explain to Ian what is happening to her. She cannot explain because her thoughts, contrary to what the prelude cued us to believe were conveying her back to vivid memories, instead (as by degrees we come to understand) carry her forward into her future. The two timeframes occupy her mind simultaneously and, in the cinema, it seems still more complicated if we cannot shake the belief that Hannah had lived and died before Weber and the alien visitors entered Louise's life.

While Louise adapts to the actuality of three lives in a future that has yet to begin (Hannah's, her own, and Ian's), Ian, unaware of her upheaval, focuses on explaining his discovery that the aliens' language has neither forward nor backward direction. He has worked this out without wholly grasping that the aliens' experience of time has implications for Louise's although he comes close to understanding it when he mentions the Sapir-Whorf hypothesis that working in another language changes how a person thinks and sees everything. Apropos, David Fleming describes language as a system that controls or filters how we carve up reality. 'Before it is cognitive, let alone conscious, thought is primordially an affective and aesthetic phenomenon. Feeling something happens before cognition' (2019).

Ian asks Louise if she is dreaming in the aliens' language and she admits to having had a few dreams but rebuffs the implication that it might make her unfit for doing her job. Instead she perceives that although he has demonstrated ingenuity in helping her read the aliens' scripts, she cannot trust that he can release his mental hold on the concept of time which our clocks, be they mechanical or electronic, affirm when, with every passing second, they move forward. That is the masculine foundation on which he depends to make sense of his world. Louise, as the boundary between worlds loosens, can do what he cannot, by looking backward she can see forward. She does not at this juncture share her endowment of foreknowledge with Ian. As James Kendrick notes,

> Louise's growing ability to understand the alien language begins to affect her understanding and experience of time ... And, because we have been aligned with [her], ... we begin to have the same kind of realization as we recognize that what we thought was a linear narrative is, in fact, anything but.

(2017)

Just over halfway through the movie (at a key moment which might otherwise have provided Louise with the chance to reflect with Ian on the way her perceptions are changing), events occur across the planet that accelerate political and military reactions to the continued presence of 12 alien spacecrafts. Jung remarked in his examination of numbers pertinent to alchemy that 'The twelve months and the twelve signs of the zodiac are definite symbolic circles in daily use" (1968: §287 n. 131). But the visitors' observation of 12- and 24-hour cycle to match timekeeping on Earth is their most distinctive adaptation to our global culture that reckons time minutely.

The possibility of receiving the heptapods with 'welcoming exultation' never enters the collective imagining of the nations (as ever competing for power) above which the craft arrives. What can differ further from developing a relationship than an attitude that competes for power? History demonstrates time and again that nations' will to power is stronger than the desire for relationship. Commenting on China's security coup of June 2020 in Hong Kong, Simon Tisdall wrote,

> China is behaving exactly as emerging powers have always behaved since empires and satrapies were first invented. The Persians, Greeks and Romans did it. So did Britain, Germany and Japan. More recently, the Soviet Union and the US also tried their hand at global domination. The victims include China itself.
> (2020: 33)

Tisdall's stark resumé of international real politique leads us to Jung's recognition that relationship is the opposite of power, a theme which re-emphasises the need for redemption of the feminine in our dark times.

In the film, the most powerful governments first respond cautiously to the hovering presence of the shells; but as days pass and the spaceships do not shift from their stations, curiosity aroused by the incomers develops into acute anxiety and paranoia. This is notably the case in two of the globe's most powerful nations when China mobilises its armed forces (with Russia following suit), signalling their readiness to initiate hostilities. Louise's competence in Mandarin, albeit limited, enables her to recognise that the Chinese are using Mah-Jong to communicate with their heptapods. Since, like chess, Mah-Jong inevitably results in victory for one side and defeat for their opponents, she fears that the Chinese are teaching the aliens to think in their own terms of war games. Seeming to confirm her concern, when she and Ian next enter the shell, they are dismayed on decoding Costello's response to their question what is the heptapods' purpose as "Offer weapon." Here Jung's reflections on the nature of projection are invaluable.

> Everything unknown and empty is filled with psychological projection; it is as if the investigator's own psychic background were mirrored in the darkness. What he sees in matter, or thinks he can see, is chiefly the data of his own unconscious which he is projecting into it.
> (1968: §332)

The incendiary potential of the phrase "Offer weapon" makes it all but impossible to persuade Weber and Halpern that the heptapods' intelligent capacity to use human language in order to communicate has been lost in translation: the ambivalent usage of human language in which one word may have two meanings – in this case, as Louise eventually realises, not only weapon but also tool. From a psychological point of view, Weber and Halpern are convinced of the meaning which implies they are caught in a collective projection and in a state of *participation mystique* or archaic identity. However, when Louise translates it into its symbolic meaning, she realises it possibly means "tool." Her analytical decoding system is wholistic, involving both the conscious and unconscious, the masculine and the feminine. As such she is less defensive and experiences doubts. Her capacity to doubt means she is not in the same *participation*. In fact, according to archaic thinking, a weapon is always a magical means of doing something (Eliade, 1991: 101). It's not necessarily friendly but not essentially destructive either.

Agent Halpern believes, albeit his own projection, that the visitors are testing the 12 nations above which their ships hold station. He argues that they will continue to do so until they find that, in a world with no single leader, one nation prevails over the others. As if on cue, the Russian and Chinese communication stations go offline, followed promptly by other territories in the network. General Shang (Tzi Ma), chief of the Chinese military, echoes the very argument that Halpern has just voiced and announces China's distrust of the other nations as well as the aliens. When the power complex engulfs a community or a nation, it breeds war.

When Louise protests to Weber and Halpern that nations should be talking to each other, Halpern challenges her to find out what "Offer weapon" means. Since the time limit on Louise and Ian's previous meeting with the heptapods has not expired, they respond to the Agent's challenge immediately and break the colonel's standing orders by persuading the guard to let them re-enter the visitors' ship. The guard commanders observe radio silence to ensure Ian and Louise are not interrupted while they reset their equipment. Unfortunately, Weber is alarmed by the silence and sends an armed security patrol to arrest his own men as mutineers. Within the shell, Abbott taps the glass barrier, inviting Louise to place her hands opposite his and write. She can only manage to do so when Abbott helps her bypass the rules that govern the linear use of time in the minds of the humans with whom the visitors have been attempting to communicate. Then suddenly she sees herself, as in a lucid dream, settling her tiny baby to sleep and empowered fluently to inscribe a circular symbol on the screen. Costello responds vigorously, covering the screen with a myriad of fascinating circular symbols. But while Louise is trying to read what she is being shown, shots ring out from beneath the shell: over-excited soldiers in Weber's security detail have fired at and hit one of the mutineers and set off an explosion. The aliens immediately respond by switching the polarity of their ship's internal gravity which ejects their human visitors forcibly.

As she recovers in the army barracks from concussion caused by her fall, Louise is told that the base may have to be evacuated. Weber fears that the heptapods may read the fracas as an attack and retaliate, a complete projection of the army's own hostile position. From Louise's balanced state of being, she challenges his judgement, arguing that she and Ian must go back on board to explain what happened. A heavy cracking noise from overhead interrupts the urgent discussion and draws all the personnel out of the tents. The spacecraft is climbing to a higher altitude while maintaining a station over the Montana prairie. Its movement coincides with the dominant politico-military balance on Earth shifting menacingly: General Shang has declared war, granting the aliens 24 hours to leave Chinese territory or face destruction. Other nations in China's zone of influence follow its lead. Meanwhile the US Department of Defense warns their Agent Halpern to prepare for the aliens to retaliate.

While political pressures build toward war, Ian continues to analyse the data that Costello had sent just before expelling Louise and him. Meanwhile (in her exhaustion) Louise experiences another visit from Hannah, on this occasion about 12 years old. When she becomes aware of Ian again, he has discovered a code which signifies that the 12 craft function as one. It substantiates the hypothesis that the 12 spaceships must function from 'one' centre. von Franz emphasises the value of number symbolism when arguing that

> when you count, you could say that the original one forms a continuum, so every number can be understood as representing the oneness of the forgoing in a new form … So there is a kind of continuum association underneath the original unit, the original *one*.
>
> (von Franz, 1995: 254)

Excited by Ian's deduction, he and Louise rush this information to the senior members of Weber's team. Agent Halpern promptly rebuts the implication of Costello's logogram, namely that they need to talk to all the heptapods. His rigid psychology cannot take in the new information, his personal shadow is identified with old ways of thinking. In support of this outright rejection he plays a recording of a Russian scientist breaking ranks with his team to make his findings public: "In their final session, the alien said, 'There is no time. Many become one. I feel we have all been given weapons.'" For his pains as "One," the scientist is immediately shot for violating Russian collective values and secrecy laws. Note that the collective inhabits a tribal psychology, primarily concerned with the survival of the species. Whether it is the scientist or the Alien, the Other must be alienated and destroyed.

Once again, translation between very different language systems has produced problems. The aliens' formulation "There is no time" does not mean (as it might do on Earth) "We are running out of time" but something more like "Time does not exist." And as before, the aliens' concept when translated into human usage as "weapons" has an emotive power that feeds the anxiety of those, Halpern in the vanguard, who believe the incomers have aggressive motives. Together Halpern, Weber, and Ian debate the seeming impossibility of getting the heptapods on all 12 ships to agree on a united plan; but Louise does not wait for them to accept Halpern's conclusion that everything is now in the control of the vertical power dynamic of their political and military superiors. Instead, with her sense of awe returning, she begins on the aliens' terms to experience the truth of their claim "There is no time."

Her focus of awareness surges between …
1/ the present crisis in the camp;
2/ an enquiry raised in the future by Hannah relating to her homework;
3/ the answer provided in the present by Ian arising from his dispute with Halpern that they are engaged in a "Non-zero-sum game" (where no one player wins at the expense of another); and
4/ and 5/ the interpretation of that same phrase which Louise at once (and in the future) relays to their daughter across time zones.

In the present, Louise sees a small vessel descend from the ship overhead. It lifts her to the mother ship where this time no glass wall separates her from Costello, the only alien to come forward. On previous visits, the canary's presence reassured her that oxygen was present in the interior part of the ship open to humans, but now she has no choice other than to breathe the aliens' foggy atmosphere, accepting that in some form her fate is already determined. When her fear of not being able to breathe subsides, she notices Abbott's absence and asks Costello to explain. "Abbott is death process," he replies. Taken aback, Louise murmurs "I'm sorry," hesitantly amending that to "We're sorry." In a tentative gesture of mourning her fingers twine through inky fumes, the threads by which Costello communicated his companion's dying. Louise (like the audience) is left to speculate whether the explosion in the spacecraft caused by the colonel's nervous security detail may have led to Abbott's death. We also have to guess whether the security team doesn't know if they have caused a fatality, or they do know but are sworn to secrecy because their blunder might be the tipping point that starts a global war. Meanwhile, interpreted psychologically, Abbott's absence is a discouraging omen for the Earthlings. We mentioned when Ian and Louise first saw the spaceship that the Cosmic egg is a symbol of the Self, concerned with the relationship between the sexes and the union of the opposites. The army, from their masculine, one-sided position has separated the opposites that were latent in the pairing of Abbott and Costello. By implication, Abbott's death seems to have destroyed the possibility of creating the connection that occurs by holding the tension between them. Did this affect Ian and Louise and is the damage yet to be incurred by the future husband and wife, even conceivably by their daughter?

In addition, as befits a culture which does not depend upon a time frame, Costello does not specify whether Abbott is dying or dead. His ambivalence supports our observation that *Arrival's* narrative is not linear. Sometimes the film reveals its structure through the aliens' thought patterns and their script, which we previously likened to an image of the uroboros, a depiction of cyclical and primordial unity. More often, the break with Earth's chronological timekeeping prepares the audience (like Louise herself, as she remarks in the film's prelude) for the journeys that the aliens are teaching her to experience through the notion of eternal time with no beginning or endings, which connotes the realisation of Tao.

Tao might be formulated as the condition of things before consciousness. So to speak of Tao is paradoxical. Tao is a sort of semi-consciousness-almost unconsciousness. That is why Tao is the beginning of things, the mother of everything; it is the beginning and the end. But that is what we call the unconscious, where ego consciousness simply comes to an end.

(Jung, 1930–34: 237)

And according to Eliade, the myth of eternal return is an instrument of knowledge and a means to liberation (1954: 67). The eternal return equates to cosmic time which has a cyclical structure of time and is repetitive. Costello exists in cosmic time, a reality that is cyclical in the creation-destruction-new creation pattern of nature.

Kendrick notes that "The 'tool' that the aliens want to bestow on humanity is nothing less than their language and the manner in which it allows its users to experience time nonchronologically" (Kendrick, 2017). His observation is helpful and deepened by imagery which enriches our perceptions during Louise's final visit to the spacecraft. As she enters the mother ship her hair escapes from its chignon, hovers like an inverted golden waterfall above her head and then lengthens in slow-motion down her back, a startling moment in which she is suspended, experiencing gravity and time locked together. It is as if the substance she is enveloped is ether, a lighter and brighter sphere of airlifting her both body and soul, the flow of temporal time halted, projecting Louise into mythical time, in *illo tempore*. Costello towers above her, six times her height, while the camera also emphasises that they are sharing space. The resultant disorientation loosens her hold on norms familiar to humankind. We intuit that she begins to feel the existential mystery in the simple expression 'There is no time' when through her experience with Costello she is able to anticipate something that lies in the far future. "It does not anticipate the future just literally; it simply shows the apparent line or pattern of the future" (Jung, 1930–34: 23). Costello does this by helping her revisit moments with her unborn daughter which she recognises (as do we) from earlier glimpses of Hannah. Finally, before returning Louise to the prairie, Costello adds, "Weapon opens time." His words remain a puzzle she cannot resolve until further evidence of time's elasticity impinges on Louise's awareness on her return to the grassland.

Her landing becomes a raw moment, reinforcing the divisions between masculine and feminine consciousness when Weber negates outright everything she has learnt from Costello with the stating baldly that nothing the heptapod has just told her matters because the army unit has been ordered by Weber's Washington superiors to strike camp immediately and evacuate the site. Weber simply wants to get his star researchers moved to safety as soon as possible. At this very moment Hannah calls insistently for her mother's attention "Wake up, Mama!" Louise has to switch focus from the army camp to a future time zone. Her daughter, now eight years old (Abigail Pniowsky), wants to know why her father left them. Louise confides that it came about because she could see a future event and that knowledge made Ian furious. She cannot say that the future event was Hannah's death nor that Ian must feel he was deceived in having that future hidden from him, nor that he probably believes she had made the wrong decision in giving life to a child whom she knew, even before they conceived her, would die young from a rare cancer. Her guilt and moral conundrum leave us inquiring how to assess the betrayal which she has imposed on Ian. Their divorce marks a collapse in understanding one another's point of view, hence another illustration of the failure to hold the tension between opposites. A marriage of the Self that ends in divorce is not *only* a tragedy for both parties, but the wounding can also help the ego in its lifelong task of discovering the Self, the spiritual part of every person.

The time frames she experiences continue to switch dizzyingly from the moment Louise returns to Earth after leaving Costello. Often bewildered, she moves through past, present, and future (past and future yet another pair of opposites) with increasing fluency while rampant powers of foresight hurl her into fresh breaks in understanding and new doubts. When she landed in the camp and Ian tried to stabilise her, wholly disorientated she told him, the man she will soon marry, "I just realised why my husband left me." We have argued that, unlike the men in the camp whom masculine conformity dominates, Louise allows her receptive feminine consciousness (the key to the ways in which her existence is now reshaping) and newfound guilt to be her guide. She experiences the enrichment and new spiritual dignity that occurs after one finds and encounters one's own guilt (Jung, 1945/1985: §§440–41).

Despite the bewilderment she undergoes on landing she is also learning to trust what she is shown. Her trusting attitude is coupled to the deepest layers of consciousness, a *participation mystique* and a process of the feminine that is deeply connected to the healing properties in the archetypal realm. From the hour of her return from Costello, the extraordinary leaps of perception visited on her bring new illuminations of formidable power. Years later, Jung described the surging of energy from the unconscious in terms which also bring Louise to mind, observing that "the collective unconscious is a living process that follows its own inner laws and gushes up like a spring at the appointed time" (1954: §124).

In actuality Hannah's gentle interruption, "Wake up, Mama!" sets off the climactic episode that follows in screen time in its entirety. The intertwining of Hannah's presence with Louise's communication with the alien helps us understand how the mother's experience embodies a synchronistic event. Apropos, Jung describes such phenomena as occurring subject to an acausal connecting principle 'when the far appears near' (1950: §608). This is the synchronistic event characterising the attributes of absolute knowledge which includes future and space and the irrepresentable space-time continuum.

Cutting through the organised chaos of striking camp, Louise goes to clear her desk. Her hand falls on a large carton of books and she opens it eagerly, finding mint copies of her own publication, *The Universal Language: Translating Heptapod – A Handbook*. It could neither have been written nor published prior to the camp's evacuation and therefore exists in the future. Yet, Louise can read its logograms immediately, bringing her knowledge back to the present to tell Weber and Ian that the "weapon" is actually the heptapods' language. So "offer weapon" means that they will give their language to humanity. We cut forward further in time to Louise in her lecture theatre now teaching the heptapods' script.

Time vaults once again to a black-tie event 18 months after the departure of all 12 spacecrafts from around the globe. The guest of honour General Shang is present, wanting to meet Dr Banks and share his appreciation of her call to him. Louise has, however, no recollection of making this crucial call – far more than a smartphone link, what she says is a summons echoing the Gnostic alien's call to experience rebirth. The General tells her that what she said changed his mind, caused him to stand down China's army and lift the threat of intergalactic warfare. His words restore Louise's recollection and we cut back in time to when, directed by instinctual promptings, she grabs the phone that Agent Halpern has left on his desk, calls the General's private number (of which she had neither previous knowledge nor subsequent memory) and utters in Mandarin his wife's dying words. Her receptive femininity is the embodiment of a permeable border that is easily penetrated by her empathic sensing of the Other, whether that be the alien, her daughter, or the General and his wife. She feels and shares emotional presence with the Others, giving her the capacity to merge with temporal rhythm and re-enter the eternal present of love. Simultaneously, in direct opposition to Louise, Agent Halpern hunts with pistol drawn in the remnants of the camp for the phone she has lifted, screaming he will gun Louise down to stop her treason. General Shang's words, by revisiting the past from the glittering reception, prompt her to see and appreciate for the first time what she achieved while recognising with awe how much humanity owes to the heptapods. And as Louise revisits the camp in this final crisis, the soundtrack gives way to massive blasts from trombones and tubas, heroic tones that recall the majestic chords which announced her first sight of the spacecraft.

"So, Hannah. This is where your story begins. The day they departed." Louise's words introduce *Arrival's* coda accompanied, as at its start, by Max Richter's gentle 'On the Nature of Daylight.' Appropriately, given the film's treatment of time, the coda does not start from the beginning and work through to the end but cuts together moments of Hannah's short life with the developing love relationship of her father and mother. Louise voices over what we see as her own will to embrace her life's journey and to accept it all without regrets. Nor does the sorrow that she cannot escape, though inescapable in that fore- and after-knowledge, destroy her resolve. Her sorrow and acceptance of suffering becomes a part of her full consciousness of life and death that makes happiness possible. This then is her account of her own personal life but, as hinted previously, it does not account for her entire existence.

The simultaneous departure of all 12 space vessels from their stations above Earth follows General Shang's standing down of China's armed forces; but it cannot be taken as an unalloyed triumph for humanity even though Shang informs Louise that she personally brought about the unification. However, in the final meeting between Louise and Costello, the heptapod tells her that they came to Earth to help humans. She now knows that the help will be the gift of their language. There will be a quid pro quo in that he and his fellows know that in three millennia they will have need of human help.[8] In essence they have in mind a non-zero-sum game which by definition will signify unity through their non-participation in the power dynamic. What that help might be they do not say. It would in effect have been conditional on humans receiving the gift of heptapod language, and that, we can now appreciate, would have enabled people to read the aliens' future.

The aliens leave Earth's atmosphere quietly. They have not been defeated by the disbelieving response to their offer of helping humanity. The heptapods, like the aliens known to us from Gnostic writings, have travelled to Earth to issue a call. As noted earlier, for the Ancients the content could sometimes be simply the aim of awakening "the souls that had stumbled away from the place of light … to awaken them and shake them up, that they might lift their faces to the place of light" *(Ginza,* 1925: 308). In *Arrival*, the nature of the call is not altogether different and can be interpreted as inviting twenty-first-century audiences to lift their faces toward the light. Inevitably, the nature and reach of the call have been adapted to the electronic age and edgy geopolitical relations. The implications, whether positive or negative of broadcast news and the use of smartphones in the resolution of the crisis are worked through in the film.

Whereas the Gnostic aliens were male, the key factor from a human perspective on the heptapods is less their gender than their otherness. They present as a race capable of miraculous feats of technological control; but the principal distinction between them and the members of the human race who attempt to communicate with them on Earth may be that the humans are under the dominance of one side of the opposites – the male. The heptapods are androgynous and live, like Louise, in a non-temporal time, deeply embedded in the transpersonal unconscious with which it endows them, visionaries who can see through the veil of time. Their call has been heard by one human, a strong and balanced woman open to the miracle of all life forms. On her agency, her teaching and the wisdom captured and celebrated in her book may depend. Through her relationship with the aliens and their language, the feminine is re-established as a principle side by side with masculine logos. The two principles are united in the anticipation and hope of a new consciousness being born. Willing to suffer both personally and for the world, she is an Anthrocosmos, a cosmic human devoted to our planet's healing and the resumption of a connection between 'above and below.'

The arrival on which we have been focussing is not incompatible with Jung's observations in his 1959 book about UFOs (see Chapter 1). He mentions that there must be a psychic cause for such a widely shared psychological projection and reckons that its basis is "an *emotional tension* having its cause in a situation of col- lective distress or danger, or in a vital psychic need" (1959: §608). Such distress can historically be a manifestation of psychic changes which may attend the end of one psychic period and the beginning of another (1959: §580).

Discussing this theme 60 years after Jung wrote, Fleming inquires what sci-fi might mean in terms of knowledge and belief. Specifically, why does *Arrival* ask us to think of time and the future? Is it delivering a warning, for example, about the coming catastrophe of climate change at a time when we need help to face a topic that vast numbers of adults (children the shining exception) find it impossible to integrate? Many films, he argues, are trying to get us to think in new ways – to see beyond the apocalypse that's coming. Are we invited by such films to think about post-humans in the sense of post-species? Is it the case that we must now think in cosmological terms if we're to prepare for the future? Fleming suggests that sci-fi invites us to experience the limitations of what the human is (2019).

Notes

1 Max Richter's 'On the Nature of Daylight.'
2 The awakening might be linked to a range of doctrinal elements: the *reminder* of the heavenly origin and the transcendent history of mankind; the *promise* of redemption, to which also belongs the redeemer's account of his own mission descent to this world; and finally the practical *instruction* as to how to live henceforth in the world … These three elements comprise in a nutshell the complete Gnostic myth (Jonas, 1963: 81).
3 The cow has long associations with the feminine and maternal principle – perhaps no coincidence that Louise Banks knows the right translation.
4 The deployment of social media in the placing and exchange of fake news has no place in *Arrival*. See note 3.
5 Barbara Hannah asserts that power is more natural to men than women because their plots have more to do with Logos than Eros (2018: 249).
6 According to Hannah, the two different ways of coping with adversity are not gender specific but open to men and women alike in accordance to the specific situations in which they are embroiled (2018: 368).
7 Contrasting with numerous clips featuring news coverage of the aliens' presence, this is the only example in *Arrival* of disinformation and lying propaganda. Was the corruption of news in the run-up to Trump's election too politically sensitive a topic to be featured at the time of the film's release?
8 Eliade notes that "Indian speculation amplifies and orchestrates the rhythms that govern the periodicity of cosmic creations and destructions. A complete cycle, or Mahayuga, is composed of four ages of unequal duration, the longest appearing at the beginning of a cycle and the shortest at its end. The second stage is the Treta Yuga of 3,000 years" (1954: 113). This Indian myth leaves open to question which stage of evolution our planet is in.

Chapter 4

Far from the Madding Crowd

Far from the Madding Crowd and the Redemption of the Animus

The marriage of the Lamb is come,
and his wife hath made herself ready

(Rev. 19:7, AV)

David Nicholls's screenplay provides the film with a vigorous entry to the story which differs strikingly from the way in which Thomas Hardy began his novel. The film (except for a brief cutaway to Gabriel Oak watching over his sheep) opens with just the one character, Bathsheba Everdene. The book commences with four: a wagoner conveying Miss Everdene and her possessions to take up residence with her aunt; a gate keeper who insists on payment of the full toll due; and lastly, farmer Gabriel Oak who pays the two pence which Miss Everdene refuses as being too much. She orders the wagoner to drive on and offers no thanks to the farmer, behaviour which, somewhat piqued, the latter tells the gate keeper he takes to be a sign of vanity. If Farmer Oak had voiced the same opinion in the film, he would have seemed a none too astute judge of the incomer.

When Vinterberg's film opens, Miss Everdene (Carey Mulligan) is moving into her aunt's small farm to work there during the winter. In a sequence that precedes the titles, she is saddling a pony for an early-morning ride while reflecting *viva voce* on her dislike for her given name, Bathsheba. In late nineteenth-century England the meaning of an individual's name would be dominated by the biblical story from which it was drawn. That makes her personal antipathy to her name readily understandable. The historical Bathsheba was famed for her beauty, and the 17-year-old farmhand endowed with the same name surely is lovely. Her forebear, however, was a married woman whom King David seduced while her husband Uriah was posted far away from the palace by the King to lead the royal troops in battle. King David observed Bathsheba bathing from a vantage point in his palace and, struck by her beauty, sent his men to bring her to him. He slept with her and in due time she bore him a son. Uriah did not return from the wars but was killed in battle.

DOI: 10.4324/9781003545538-5

Bathsheba Everdene, an orphan since early childhood, is accustomed to being on her own. She has had no one to ask where this strange name came from but does report that some people find her too independent in spirit. We soon see why: while riding over the hills, she stops the pony, checks that no one is watching, and (the very image of an independent spirit) abandons her genteel side-saddle posture to sit astride. Then she urges the beast forward into an exhilarating gallop, so delightful to her that she fails to notice when her scarf snags on a branch. Farmer Gabriel Oak (Matthias Schoenaerts) finds it and returns it when he spots her walking across his farm. In this film version, as opposed to the novel, it is their first meeting, and reveals more by means of close shots (particularly of the young woman's facial expressions) than through dialogue. Gabriel is ready to be on first name terms and invites her to walk on his land whenever she chooses. Then he gazes at her quietly, seeing someone both comelier and better educated than any other young woman of his acquaintance. Meanwhile Bathsheba's face conveys the busy thoughts and feelings that traverse her mind. She seems to find him interesting because, while she sees that she has caught his attention, he feels no need to impose his presence on her. A pleasurable sensation is awakening in her. Could it be a flicker of desire?

She remarks light-heartedly that she must be trespassing on his land; nevertheless, her warm tone alternates with her sense that she needs to re-establish her independence by taking control of the conversation. So she turns away from the likeable man and ends the conversation with a cool farewell, "Good afternoon Farmer Oak." Nevertheless, she is pleased with this first contact and a smirk crosses her face as she turns away. In the coming days they chat as she milks her aunt's cow and watches him train the younger of his dogs (Young George) to round up sheep. A friendship seems to be developing.

One of the features that drew us to work on this cinematic version of *Far from the Madding Crowd* is indeed its focus on Bathsheba's independent nature. With it being one of the principal elements in its plotline's framework, it allows us to concentrate on the masculine spirit in the mind of a woman, which C.G. Jung named the animus. Emma Jung's essay on the nature of the animus also provides a helpful introduction to this archetypal figure which is already intervening between Bathsheba Everdene and Gabriel Oak in their first brief exchange. Like her husband, Emma understood that the animus and anima behave in ways compensatory to the outer, conscious personality. In a woman the animus directs masculine characteristics inward, conditioned both by the experience each woman has had of representatives of the other sex and by the collective image of man that she carries in her psyche (Jung, 1934: 1–2). The animus, like all archetypal figures, is completely dual natured, always having a positive and negative aspect, neither good nor bad.

As mentioned, the audience does not have much biographical information about Bathsheba but does learn from the film's prelude that she was orphaned in childhood. The term 'orphan' was used by the alchemists to name a unique stone, the 'orphan stone,' a gem similar to our modern solitaire. Medieval alchemists equated it with the Philosopher's Stone, the *lapis* which represents the totality or 'the one' and corresponds – this is its high significance – to the psychological idea of the

Self. Thus, the *lapis* is the stone of the wise and germ of the individuation process. In one text it is known as the homeless orphan who is slain at the beginning of the alchemical process for purposes of transformation (see Chapter 2). It is both worthless and precious, a set of opposites familiar to the orphan (Jung, 1970: 17–18; Rothenberg, 2001: 47). In the context of the film, we understand the Philosopher's Stone as the result of developing one's own unique personality that is free from outer and collective influences.

Not long after their first meeting on Gabriel Oak's land, the farmer comes calling on Miss Everdene and presents her with a lamb than which there is no more enduring emblem of innocence. He adds that, having come too soon, it will not last the winter unless she rears it. The ARAS *Book of Symbols* recognises that the shepherd's presence brings into play 'One of the most exalted of all religious symbols ... the lamb, because Christians called Jesus the lamb of god for his innocence and in the belief that he was led, like a lamb, to the slaughter for our sins' (2010: 322). When Gabriel asks the girl to marry him without further ado, his gift of the solitary lamb is in some way a symbolic gesture toward his idea of their forming a couple. Speaking through his action, Gabriel not only conveys his blind commitment to her but reveals that some part of him is in identity with the lamb. In a chapter in his book *Mysteries,* Jung distinguishes between a gift and a sacrifice.

> When therefore, I give away something that is "mine", what I am giving is essentially a symbol, a thing of many meanings; but, owing to my unconsciousness of its symbolic character, it adheres to my ego, because it is part of my personality. Hence there is, explicitly or implicitly, a personal claim bound up with every gift. There is always an unspoken "give that thou mayest receive." Consequently the gift always carries with it a personal intention, for the mere giving of it is not a sacrifice. It only becomes a sacrifice if I give up the implied intention of receiving something in return.
>
> (1955: 321)

Gabriel's gift hints that he must come to a conscious realisation of what he is proposing to Bathsheba. From a depth psychological point of view, the lamb is a symbol of the Self, a uniting symbol that functions as a union of opposites and the relationship between the sexes.

Bathsheba is taken aback by Gabriel's proposal and he, understanding her response as a refusal, immediately walks away. She rushes after him to say that she did not specifically refuse him (she did not mean to be rude!). The pair speak frankly to each other and not without kindness, but she does not attempt to hide that she would hate to be a man's property. She adds flippantly that she might enjoy being a bride if it didn't entail marrying: "I'm too independent for you. If I ever were to marry, I'd want someone to tame me and you'd never be able to do it."[1] Interpreted reductively, her response voices a displaced reaction – a defence mechanism in which a person redirects a negative emotion from its original source to a less threatening one. However, reading her unconscious response prospectively (as a Jungian would interpret a dream), we can read becoming a bride as something attractive to her and an unconscious recognition that some part of her desires transformation and union. From this perspective, we intend to emphasise the objective fact that there is consciousness in the unconscious! To understand such a reaction, we need to know more about the animus: it can be both maddeningly eloquent and indulge a woman's predilection for gossip. A weak connection in a woman's unconscious life can be wrongly exploited by animus opinions when they are epitomised by her uncertainty in relation to her own feelings. If she can't stand by her individual feelings, her animus will be able to cut her off from her instincts or deliver her over to the 'blind dynamism of nature just as he pleases' (Hannah, 2018: 185–6). This being said, it appears obvious that something in Bathsheba's animus attitude does need taming! As we shall see, Bathsheba's individuation task will be to create clarity in what she *really* thinks, achieved through the redemption of her animus.

For his part, like the lamb born prematurely, Gabriel has in his own lamblike innocence and naivety made an intuitive leap far too early from enjoying the first explorations of a nascent friendship to attempting to seal that in a lifelong relation-ship. Jung wrote of intuition as 'an unconscious process in that its result is the irruption into consciousness of an unconscious content, a sudden idea or "hunch" (1948: §269).' Gabriel confuses on the one hand the financial prosperity which as a good shepherd he hopes to bestow on his future bride with, on the other, possessing the prerequisites for a successful marriage. There is something of the *puer aeter-nus* (the boy hero, here a shepherd boy) in Gabriel's psychological make-up. To judge by appearances, Gabriel is a man in his thirties, while Bathsheba is a decade younger. Understandably at his age he is striving to participate in collective values which urge us to become part of the crowd. It is timely that he yearns for love and marriage at his age. Clearly, Gabriel knows what he wants and is willing to work hard to achieve it. However, he has much to learn and must outgrow his naivety which has to be surpassed through experience. The positive result will be an indi-vidual who becomes much more than just a member of the collective society: his personality will mature notably when fate burdens him unexpectedly with new responsibilities to other people ... including Bathsheba Everdene.

As it happens, Gabriel is not yet sufficiently secure as shepherd to be certain of bringing to fruition the ambitions he shared with Bathsheba. He runs two sheep-dogs, Old George and Young George. The former is the fully trained, dependable animal who keeps a weather eye open to make sure all is well with the flock. C. G. Jung could have been writing the following passage about him.

> When you speak of dogs you speak of creatures with a kind of domesticated instinct ... it always means a form of instinctual psyche that goes with you, obeys you, is under your control, not against you. The dog is used for his particularly refined senses. He smells, he has a keen ear, he is watchful; and so dogs frequently stand for acute sensitivity in man, and often, in particular for intuition.
>
> (2019: 227)

However, one black night, Gabriel's young dog which (his master has told Bathsheba) does not know when to stop herding, drives all his 200 sheep over the cliff at the edge of his property and, in a frenzy of youthful energy, into the sea. Gabriel knows that a dog which runs riot with the flock must be destroyed and, in an agony of loss for both his sheep and his dog, he must come to terms with the necessity to be ruthless and shoots the young animal. Killing his dog proves that he has the willingness and capacity to sacrifice his childhood state of purity and innocence.

A tension analogous to that between the ages of the dogs lies between Gabriel's innocence and his maturing personality as he shifts from enacting the *puer* in human relations toward individuated manhood. Since the fall has killed every last sheep and ruined the distraught farmer, the latter, now penniless, must give up his farm and walk the country looking for work. Pausing in nearby Casterbridge town square he dodges an invitation to serve the Queen as a conscript soldier but is advised by a young woman that workers are needed on a farm near Weatherbury. Walking unhesitatingly through the night toward that village, Gabriel reveals no resistance to the reversal of his fate. However, when he sees a barn on fire he discovers outright confusion among the local farmhands who lack an overseer. He takes control and organises them into a chain to fetch buckets of water and help him extinguish the flames. They labour through the night until, come the dawn, with the building saved, he sees Miss Everdene arriving on the property. She has received unexpected notification of having inherited her uncle's estate and has moved from her aunt's smallholding to take over her late relative's roles as both the owner and new farmer. She tells Gabriel that her uncle's somewhat rundown estate was once the finest farm in the country and offers him a job as her shepherd. Heinrich Zimmer marks what we can take as Gabriel's change of moral and psychological direction:

> Stumbling along his path of peril he is protected by the moral, irrational qualities of humility, sincerity, honesty and unselfishness. Thanks to these, the directions of his intuition can be heard and the instinct of his heart can grope along.
>
> (1975: 63)

The arrangement suits them both in their changed circumstances, fate having brought them together again but now in roles that reverse those which they occupied when they first met. At this point in their relationship, Gabriel, engaging in the role of her good shepherd, takes on the role of the redeeming psychopomp. This archetypal figure acts as spiritual guide to a living person's soul and, if effective, will lead her to connect with the part of her psyche, her animus, that we soon discover she habitually projects onto the men she encounters. Hannah describes the possible outcome when Bathsheba could take the inward path that will lead her toward the Self. 'The animus, or perhaps the Self using the animus as a tool, is trying to put the human being on the path to wholeness' (2018: 94). Jung, in one of his dream analyses, describes the shepherd as the figure who brings the flock together as a unifier of the man and the woman (1995: 186). In assuming that role, Gabriel represents what is *behind* Bathsheba's animus. Understood from the realm of the archetypal world, as her shepherd he guides the far more powerful figure of the Self that alone can set Bathsheba's animus in his right place.

As Miss Everdene, Bathsheba formally takes command of the estate by turning the workers' pay day into a greeting ceremony which reveals both the determined side of her personality and her ambitions for Everdene Farm. She makes a point of showing goodwill toward her new employees by paying almost all the hands double their usual wage. On the reverse side of the coin, she dismisses the idle bailiff with a scathing condemnation of his inadequacies. As a representative of lazy and sloppy consciousness, he has let the farm and its house fail badly and was nowhere to be found when fire would have destroyed the barn had not Gabriel come on the scene. As a gross miscreant he threatens her, but she holds to her decision and refuses to let him brow beat her. In myth as in reality, fire merely destroys; but often it destroys so that from the purified residue or ashy essence a new world may come into being (*Book of Symbols,* 2010: 84). Bathsheba's recent good fortune and Gabriel's misfortune appear to carry something mutually beneficial and perhaps even transformative.

In sharing with the workers her recognition of their individual worth to the estate and herself, Miss Everdene shows her sense of fairness and self-sufficiency. To cite Jung, 'One should not turn people into sheep, but sheep into people' (2009: 231, n. 28). She announces her intention of restoring the farm to its one-time splendour and speaks of the commitment she will bring to the work. There is little doubt that her strong sense of independence is justified by her self-discipline and competence. By setting out her plans and the daily schedule that she intends to observe, her animus is self-evidently functioning constructively in this situation. The psychological framework is provided by C. G. Jung which relays how the animus quest is to understand, and the anima seeks relationship.

> Just as the anima becomes, through integration, the Eros of consciousness, so the animus becomes a Logos; and in the same way that the anima gives relationship and relatedness to a man's consciousness, the animus gives to a woman's consciousness a capacity for reflection, deliberation, and self-knowledge.
>
> (1968: 33)

Miss Everdene and her new assistant Liddy (Jessica Barden) go to the Exchange in Caster bridge to sell Everdene corn for the first time. As the farm's new owner, Bathsheba's pride in her new life is underscored by a musical theme that expresses her joy and determination in facing the daunting burdens taken on by the novice farmer. In the immediate instance she has the task of selling the crop to experienced corn traders. These men think it their right, almost their duty, to knock down the bid price when women are selling, no less so than when the latter are elegantly turned out. The male corn traders represent the one-sided patriarchal masculine attitude which habitually undermines the feminine. That said, Bathsheba calmly makes the case that the grain from Everdene Farm is as good as when her uncle brought it to market. She gets a good price for it, and once again, the orphan's self-worth and independent nature show up in this encounter.

Bathsheba has, as we have seen, hired a young woman from Weatherbury as her assistant. This is Liddy who advises her about local matters and quickly becomes her mistress's companion. She is something of a gossip who chatters in church with her new mistress one Sunday about a member of the congregation, William Boldwood (Michael Sheen). He is the wealthy owner of a neighbouring farm who exerts a strong appeal on some of the area's marriageable young women, an attraction to which he has so far proven indifferent. For her part, Liddy represents Bathsheba's shadow, the dark side of her personality (the inferior personality) that has not distinguished itself from the generality of collective psychology. As Bathsheba's shadow, she is the opposite of the solitary orphan, a woman who always inserts herself in social affairs. Local lore having it that Boldwood was once jilted, Liddy takes the opportunity to ask Bathsheba whether that has ever happened to her. Gabriel Oak is also in church, close enough to hear Bathsheba's response, and although the latter does not name her former suitor, she does admit to having been courted, and also to being too restless to consider marriage, though she rather liked the man concerned.

Liddy is by now showing herself to be of a type that von Franz defines as a woman with an undeveloped animus. At this stage, the animus is not distinguished from the shadow and is living in the realm of the personal unconscious rather than as a personification of the collective unconscious.

> When they have not worked on the animus, [women's] mental functions often remain fixed on gossip and thinking about their neighbors. They get interested in a divorce in the neighbourhood and want to know how it came about. They talk in a half-psychological way. ... But it never gets farther; it remains on the level of curiosity, and they never get to the bottom of anything ... instead it remains stuck in a kind of half-developed mental operation, neither disinterested nor objective, which, I think, is typical for an undeveloped animus.'
>
> (1993: 188–9)

Vinterberg perceives clearly that nineteenth-century farming of necessity occurred in public, given the number of manual workers required for many tasks, and that it also offered regular opportunities for fun and celebration. One such occasion is the annual dipping of the farm's sheep when, noticing Miss Everdene watching, Gabriel challenges her to join in the work. She accepts immediately and, to cheers from the farm hands both male and female, wades into the tank and helps move the animals through the water. She and Gabriel enjoy sharing the labour with each other in a light-hearted manner. In the moment, their playful activity with the sheep corresponds to an alchemical image of the couple's unconscious pair (anima and animus) being cleansed and united at the same time.

This pastoral scene is interrupted by the arrival of Mr Boldwood who asks to speak to the young farmer. He wants to show her his fine gardens and grounds before leading her into the great house where he asks for her hand in marriage. He has received an anonymous Valentine's card and believes that Miss Everdene must have sent it in good faith and would like to marry him. In fact, Liddy had teased Bathsheba into sending the card, meaning it flippantly. Understood psychologically, Liddy and Bathsheba have colluded in playing the role of the trickster archetype which serves to compensate for the rigid disposition of collective consciousness. Thus, the trickster's devious behaviour exposes the shadow side of the Self. When Mr Boldwood understands that the card was no *bilet doux* but merely sent as a jest, he feels painfully mocked. What, urged by her gossiping companion, Bathsheba had sent light-heartedly, too late she realises has cut him deeply. Hannah holds that 'projection is doing another person harm and then not doing everything one can do to take it back' (2018: 85). Conscious of her error, the young farmer takes personal responsibility and Mr Boldwood responds to her gesture by giving her time to consider his offer. Such awkward moments are familiar in human interactions. Wounded by rejection, Mr Boldwood's desire for marriage and his lack of relationship to his anima has made him vulnerable to seduction. The Bathsheba/Libby trickster plot has been empowered by their animus/shadow pairing. However, John Beebe regards the trickster as the only means through which one may work with the anima/animus archetypes (1981: 48).

During the evening following her interview with Boldwood, Bathsheba happens upon Gabriel working late sharpening knives. She asks him to teach her this skill, intending to hide her interest in finding out whether the farmhands have spoken about her meeting with Mr Boldwood. When Gabriel reports that they expect her to be married before the year's end, she asks him to deny it to the men, in effect doing her dirty shadow work and requiring him to take on a task that is her responsibility. Gabriel declines to tell stories about Boldwood just to please her. Instead, he delivers a poor opinion of her playing pranks on the wealthy farmer and leading him on in a manner unworthy of her. Aroused by this frankness, Miss Everdene's animus beard, already showing signs of stiffening again, promptly rises to anger: "I cannot allow a man to criticize my private conduct. You will please leave the farm at the end of the week." When Gabriel throws down his tools and says he will leave at once, the animus beard delivers its *coup de grace*, "Then go. I never want to see your face again." Once again, Bathsheba is clearly animus possessed.

Echoing Gabriel's disaster on his own farm, an overnight calamity strikes Miss Everdene's flock of sheep which have broken a fence and eaten young clover. An indistinct boundary crossing has occurred between Bathsheba's psyche and her sheep, threatening not only to poison the sheep but consciousness itself. She has just dismissed the only man able to release the gasses that will otherwise kill the animals. This meaningful coincidence demonstrates that Bathsheba and her sheep are connected by simultaneity *and* meaning. '[This] the synchronicity principle … becomes the absolute rule in all cases where an inner event occurs simultaneously with an outside one.' Bathsheba sends one of the younger men to summon Gabriel back, but when the lad returns he brings the message that she is to go in person and request him civilly in a proper manner. Miss Everdene's bloated animus immediately expostulates once again, this time in front of the men, "Where does he get his airs? I'll do no such thing." Her overblown reaction is a vivification of her animus that has cut her off from her own feeling life. Gabriel, however, has anticipated her reply and sent his rejoinder ahead of time, "Beggars can't be choosers!" She goes to him and speaks in an emollient manner. "Please don't desert me, Gabriel. I need your help!" The sheep are saved thanks to his skilled surgery, and peace is restored between owner and shepherd. But the question remains whether the words she chooses to draw him back to the farm are still too unconsciously motivated and ego driven.

> Our ego's desires, our being unwilling or unable to let go of our wilful demands, followed by issues of jealousy and envy, all help to pave the royal road to animus possession that rapidly occur when we fail to take responsibility for our plots.
>
> (Hannah, 2018: 48)

In summary, Hannah's words succinctly portray the harsh reality that the more power driven the ego personality is, the more the unconscious exerts influence on conscious decision-making.

Sometime later, Boldwood will resume his campaign to wed Miss Everdene. He asks Gabriel Oak whether she will do what he hopes and marry him, to which the shepherd replies, "If it is not inconvenient to her." Boldwood finds Gabriel's words cynical, but they are not far off the mark in expressing the plots of women and men. Hannah writes in depth about these plots in *The Animus*, for both Bathsheba and poor Boldwood are caught in their own plots, outright anima possessed by the psychological functions of the anima and animus.

> When I use the word *plot* in the sense of women's 'plots'… I mean that their animus is spinning a plot with a purpose or goal of which the woman herself is relatively unconscious … it is not wholly unconscious but is more a matter of compartmental psychology. Now men also occasionally get caught up in plots, but with men, plots tend to be wholly in the realm of the anima. It is not so much compartmental psychology; they are actually unaware of them and cannot even know them until they become conscious – to quite a high degree – of their anima.
>
> (2018: 171)

When the carnage of his sheep obliged Gabriel Oak to leave his farm and search for work, he had found his way to Everdene Farm thanks to a tip from a few words exchanged with a young woman who was watching soldiers recruit local men to serve in the army. She first suggested that Gabriel should consider signing up and pointed out an excessively self-aware recruiting sergeant as her fiancé. When Gabriel resumed his search for employment as a shepherd, she advised him to try Weatherbury where a farm badly needed help. Sometime later this girl's fiancé, Sergeant Francis Troy (Tom Sturridge), enters a church where he has an appointment to marry Fanny Robbin (Juno Temple). The groom waits, but his bride has mistakenly gone to the wrong church – a clear sign that something in her unconscious was activated. When the vicar has to officiate at another wedding, the sergeant leaves without Fanny having found him. Nor do we see any evidence to hint that the sergeant has tried to find her. The wedding is doomed. We will come to find out that this unknown woman is an image of both men's souls, their anima. However, in her role as anima a distinct difference in a man's destiny is made clear. One type leads to life and love, the other to death and loss.

Bathsheba likes to walk round her farm at night to check that all is well and one night she disturbs a uniformed soldier who claims to be lost and looking to get to Weatherbury. His uniform has caught her dress (a metaphor that succinctly foretells her future). Holding Bathsheba's lamp so that she can disentangle her clothing from his gear, the soldier compliments her on her beauty, whereupon she orders him to leave her land. The next morning, however, the interloper has insinuated himself among the Everdene people stacking straw. Liddy, once again playing the role of Bathsheba's blind shadow, recognises Sergeant Francis Troy and offers her mistress a gossip's thumbnail sketch of him: noble blood, full of promise, very sharp and trim, well educated, good things expected of him, but he jettisoned it all to become a soldier. Something about his presence irks Bathsheba once again and once again she reacts instinctively (a response that often affords great protection against plots) and orders him to leave her farm. Troy responds with the sexual assertiveness he had displayed the previous night, telling her outright that she is beautiful. Confused, flattered, and far from in control of a temptation so unlike any she has faced before, she lets him manoeuvre her into a clandestine nocturnal meeting in the woods. Their encounter reveals that she is caught in a projection, a certain uneasiness that existed from their first encounter, exposing the weak point in her unconscious life. Something in the shadow of the orphan is disturbed, allowing her animus to mislead her. Had she been confident in the feeling life, the animus would not have been able to interfere; but some-where deep inside, she wants passion in her life and gives in to the instinctual side of her animus desires.

Decked out once again in his scarlet regalia, Troy dazzles her that evening with a display of swordsmanship that could injure or kill her.[2] In a naked display of power, he hovers about her, a woman who admits she has never before been kissed, let alone subjugated to his conflation of sadistic martial threat with sexual desire – perhaps performing and animating the animus made flesh. His swordplay is brutal, so too his seizing a prolonged, deep kiss that leaves her transfixed. His seduction is a kiss of death laden with a beastly hunger closer to rape than love making which triggers the orphan's starved need for an intense connection. Tragi-cally, Bathsheba has confused intensity with the capacity for depth. Meanwhile the solo violin's soaring arpeggios voice the emotions that Sgt Troy is arousing in her suddenly awakened feelings. Notably the rhapsody continues after he walks out of the woods leaving Bathsheba behind, stunned by her emotions. The music's fever, like her own, will fade only when Gabriel Oak warns her to keep away from her suitor: her good shepherd knows that Frank Troy is untrustworthy, his name an outright negation of his nature.

The animus likes to project itself upon all kinds of heroes. Troy's dangerous display of swordsmanship strikes at Bathsheba's complacent belief that (strictly identified with ego consciousness), she is the master of her own fate. His sword, signifying his persona, has penetrated through her inner shield, her inward-facing masculine partner. Unprotected, Bathsheba is left unaware of how vulnerable she really is. When the persona rather than the ego connects to the contra-sexual partner, one is really in for it.

It falls, then, to Gabriel Oak who, while reiterating that he is no rival for her affections, acts as her living psychopomp to warn his employer in the strongest terms against her suitor. Gabriel can smell out the man's foul unconscious drives and believes that Miss Everdene should get rid of him. His instinct and intuition are forces driven by his feeling life, proceeding from a deep interior root and connection to his anima. The anima, being the inward-oriented attitude of a man's personality acts as a bridge to his unconscious life and a wellspring filled with intuition. Gabriel is in service to the feminine principle and therefore does not adhere to one-sided masculine authority or judgement. His words give her momentary pause but no more than that because her suitor is approaching across the fields. What she does instead is write to William Boldwood and decline his offer of marriage, thanking him for his kindness. Behind her courteous words to him lies an as yet wholly untested confidence that she will find a secure married future with Frank Troy, that being the route toward which she now turns, still blind to this man's calculating desires and self-adoration. Inevitably we once again emphasise Bathsheba's injured instincts when we see her projecting her animus on her seducer without being able to perceive him for what he is. And only when projections are withdrawn does a kind and loving relationship become possible. The blinder love is, the more it is instinctual and the more it is attended by destructive consequences, for it is a dynamism that needs form and direction (Jung: Vol. 13 §391). Once again, her instant decision-making falls subject to the animus.

When the newlyweds return to the farm, they are at the centre of a lively celebration at which Frank Troy introduces himself as the farmhands' new master. Outside in the yard and keeping his eyes on the weather, Gabriel is acutely aware that a storm threatens (a whole set of metaphors here). He asks the new Mrs Bathsheba Troy to release six men for no more than an hour to secure the harvest from ruin. Troy intervenes, countermands Gabriel's request, and like a god insists that there will be no storm on his wife's wedding night. No less than a climate change denier, he exhibits the dangers of egotistical inflation in believing he holds power over nature. His pride and poor judgement are symptoms of inflation, revealing a lack of connection to his instinctual life. In fact, his one-sided toxic masculinity is a compensation for feelings of inferiority and reveals his complete lack of eros and capacity for a real relationship.

In a passage that foretells Bathsheba's fate, Emma Jung asserted that a woman's completely successful projection of her animus on a man seldom lasts for long, especially if the woman is in a close relationship with the man in question. Indeed, one of the imperatives of individuation work is to withdraw anima and animus projections.

> Then the incongruity between the image and the image-bearer often becomes all too obvious. An archetype, such as the animus represents, will never really coincide with an individual man, the less so the more individual that man is. ... When this discrimination between the image and the person sets in, we [women] become aware, to our great confusion and disappointment, that the man who seemed to embody our image does not correspond to it in the least, but continually behaves quite differently from the way we think he should.
>
> (1934: 11)

Obliged without forewarning to face his self-centred conceit, his "false bride" who was won through power is crestfallen, and increasingly so when, drunk on brandy, Troy leads the men in a licentious song celebrating men's sexual appetite, whereupon, led by the new Mrs Troy, their womenfolk leave the party. The abandoned bride soon notices Gabriel singlehandedly battling the storm to save the hayricks, covers her finery, and goes outside to work alongside him. It recalls the time when she shared with him the labour of bathing the sheep. It is risky because the wind is fierce and the tarpaulin heavy, but she is unafraid until the shock of a nearby lightning strike causes her to lose her grip on the fabric. Gabriel grabs hold of her arms, helps her back to safety, and shares her relief in laughter, a scene which, in the tumult of wind and storm, speaks as it always has done, of the gods' unquenchable spirits, be they pagan or Christian.

It hardly needs saying that a wedding is a universally respected ceremony. Through it (no matter what the particular rituals observed by different communities may be), the new partners along with their families and supporters celebrate in public their declaration of shared love for one another and, by no means incidentally, their progress from one phase of societal life to the next. From a psychological perspective the wedding feast signifies a union of the opposites and can be regarded as an initiation. Through her marriage to Troy, Bathsheba has been forced to gather all the things in her that were formerly dissociated and therefore not properly related, an act of self-recollection as she comes to terms with herself. In this regard, marriage is a path to individuation and with conscious effort assists in the growth of the personality. Through a synthesis of this orphan's split-off parts, a new unity with the Self is made possible.

Set against this framework, it is plain from what we have already written about Troy's brutish display of power and Bathsheba's animus problem, that the marriage is heavily skewed toward the power complex and conventional patriarchal values. Power corrupts love. Troy already speaks of Bathsheba and Everdene Farm as his possessions. In the context of his lascivious greed, Bathsheba's fearless readiness to expose herself to the fury of the storm takes on an absolute, purifying quality. The shock of the storm and her husband's crass mindset deliver just the right intensity to wake her up! von Franz asserts that when operating correctly, 'the feeling function gives the information and measure' (1980b: 73). First comes authentic confession, "Gabriel, I've been a fool." By connecting to both the dark and light sides of her personality, Bathsheba is slowly developing a more balanced attitude toward the opposites. As a testament to the reality that she finds herself in, until this important integration work has been achieved, the animus is predisposed to marry the unrecognised shadow. Such is the subjectivity of love which is ego-oriented and full of projections. Only when one has a confrontation with the persona and shadow, does a genuine interest develop in the Other whereby harmony and real love are within reach. Lead by intense conflict, the path to individuation and the Self is experienced as torturous. More than an innocent girl's fascination with a soldier in a scarlet jacket (though that too), she now perceives belatedly that Troy aroused her jealousy (doubtless a coldly unconscious plot) by telling her he had loved and lost a woman more beautiful than she. Envy, the characteristic shadow material of the orphan, had kicked in.

Hannah observes that Jung said,

> … jealousy often comes from lack of love or the ability to love. This is undoubtedly true, but jealousy of one which is conscious – and suffers – is paid for (to some extent), because you cannot, for instance, possibly uphold a flattering image of yourself as a self-sacrificing angel if you are aware that you are torn apart by the ugly forces of jealousy and possessiveness within.
>
> (Hannah, 2018: 5)

In this pivotal moment of self-revelation, Bathsheba is consciously suffering and has had a genuine encounter with her shadow, transforming the situation and forcing an alteration in her attitude. It is a new experience for her for which reason she is only able to tolerate her feelings of vulnerability for a moment. Realising that she has left herself open to Gabriel's comment, she switches instantly to her usual defensive tactic: "I don't want an opinion on the subject … In fact, I forbid it." Gabriel's steady advice is succinct: "Go to bed." On this occasion for the first time, however, she thanks him with authentic feeling.

Come the morning Gabriel is completing the night's work by tidying the yard when he spots Mr Boldwood at the gate, invites the older man not to turn away and remarks on his looking far from well. By this time Bathsheba had long since apologised to Boldwood for her prank and more recently written to say that she cannot marry him. Now he humbly admits to Gabriel (talking to him like a confidant who cannot bear to have the woman he loves beyond measure misunderstood), that Bathsheba never jilted him but that nevertheless he is beset by terrible grief. Indeed, psychologically he does appear to be on edge and begins to speak and act in relation to her in the manner of a man who has lost his soul, revering Bathsheba as an omniscient figure with almost divine qualities. When a man falls completely for his anima projections, something substantial is lacking in his relationship to the world. A confrontation with his problem must occur, in which the opposites, conscious and unconscious may potentially reach a balance. This will not be the older man's last confessional exchange with Gabriel, but its sensitivity is marked by Boldwood's request that the shepherd should not say a word about this conversation to Bathsheba.

When discussing Gabriel Oak's precipitate proposal of marriage to Bathsheba, we mentioned that his yearning for relationship derived from both his intuition as an instinctive act and something archetypal that he acted on too quickly. Timing is everything and doing something too soon or too late can destroy the whole thing. However, the relationship between Bathsheba and Gabriel has deepened. Guided by his keen instincts that have restrained him from becoming inflated, his sense of timing reflects the harmonious relationship between his inner and outer life. Both his warning to Bathsheba against her reckless betrothal and his sensitivity to Mr Boldwood's anguish indicates that he is a modern-day Orpheus and has matured into a well-rounded individual and a responsible member of society. Through his own suffering and experiences, Gabriel has acquired the power of knowledge equal to wisdom, implying that pure knowledge is naturally fearless when accessed from the level of the objective psyche. It is Frank Troy who soon finds his new life as master of Everdene tedious and, confirming Bathsheba's new and painful perceptions, shows himself as the *puer aeternus*, the eternal boy that he is. Liddy had described him to Bathsheba as someone of whom good things were expected, but who abandoned it all to become a soldier. Indeed, in both respects he falls in line like a soldier, a member of the collective who has not developed his own mind. Yet he fits only one side of the archetypal *puer/senex* pair, lacking firstly the maturity to value hard work (something both Gabriel and Bathsheba have proven they do), and secondly the ambition and drive to develop his own individual life. He resembles the knight of cups who, all dressed in his assumed military glamour, fails to become King.

Living the high life of the *puer aeternus*, Troy seeks out his pleasures in Casterbridge, betting large sums which, as his wife advises him, are draining money needed to pay the farm's expenses. Possessed by the emotional intensity of power, the *puer* is an inflated hero, and consequently doomed to failure. von Franz (1980b: 50) states that true gamblers do not care about the money but they want to win. Troy's wasteful behaviour demonstrates his arrested development; and his inability to comprehend limits brings crisis in its wake when, having gambled extravagantly on the outcome of a bare-knuckle fight and lost all the cash in his pockets, he notices a destitute woman begging. Not any woman, this is Fanny Robbin, his lost and ravaged bride. She tells him that she is carrying his child. Overcome by instant sentimentality, Troy vows to bring money and find her a place to live the next day. As is his wont, he makes grand gestures that sweep aside not only practicalities but also a sorrowful reminder that their previous promise to marry had been broken. Indeed, behaving in his vainglorious way as though he expects to suborn to his will both his wife and his lover, he turns away from Fanny to order Bathsheba (who has observed the encounter) to get into their carriage, manhandling her when she demurs. Troy's actions reveal the reality of his lack of development; the more sentimental love is, the more brutal is its shadow following behind.

Bathsheba refuses to give her husband more cash, dismissing his deluded claim that he works for the farm. Troy's anger flares and, warning Bathsheba to be careful not to do something she will regret, he rides out next morning to the secret rendezvous he had promised Fanny. As ever he is immaculately dressed – and at Bathsheba's cost since their marriage. If he were able to recognise his own lies, Troy would have to accept that he has made Fanny another empty promise since he has nothing to give her. He waits at the appointed place on a bridge; but, like a neurotic repetition of their wedding day, she fails to arrive at the appointed time and he grows impatient and turns away without making any attempt to find her. The bridge is an emblem of the psychological terrain that neither of them is capable of crossing.

Fanny has not lived to face the final humiliation of failed love and has died in childbirth during the night. Her untimely death represents how useless love is when absent of insight and understanding. The injured feminine in both Fanny and Troy has failed to secure redemption. The undertakers' cart actually passes Troy waiting for her on the bridge, with the inscription on her coffin concealed by its canvas cover. The men take her to Everdene farm, Fanny's last known address and where she had worked as a servant for Bathsheba's uncle. His heir insists that the casket be brought into the house out of respect for the young woman. She and Liddy keep watch over the coffin, the mistress sorrowing over the death of Fanny and remarking, "I seem to cry a great deal these days. I never used to cry at all." Her tears are evidence of her evolving feeling life as she grieves the aborted life of feminine awakening with the unborn child. And when Liddy goes to her bed, Bathsheba the orphan is left alone beside Fanny's open casket on finding her husband's lover cradling her stillborn baby. In a posture of sacred repose, she is unknowingly grieving the life of the woman who led Gabriel to her. Without warning, Troy returns to the house and bursts in on this scene. He weeps when discovering that Fanny has died and turns savagely on Bathsheba to declare, "This woman, dead as she is, is more to me than you ever were, or are, or can be. You are nothing to me now." Anima possessed, the injured narcissist lives in a state of inhumanity and is incapable of realising love until it has been lost.

Next morning the undertakers return for the coffin. Troy, once again kitted out in scarlet despite having quit the army, leaves Everdene on foot behind the hearse. Is this his farewell to Fanny? Or is it his salute to army life, the only existence that gave him some sense of a cohesive self and identity? Is it a mute repetition of his insulting renunciation of his wife? Or could it mark his intention to end his life? In short, his behaviour can be explained by a need to silence the sterile grief of abandoning the woman he assumed had rejected him at the altar. The calamity of his state of mind has been solely of his own making and now he walks to the coast, strips off his finery, and swims out to sea, joining Fanny and his unborn child in the oceanic depths of the unconscious. By losing the only link to his anima, he loses the animating connection to his unconscious which he can only recover through dying. In his uroboric fantasy of pleasure and love, Troy now joins Gabriel's sheep fallen in the collective waters. He is equally incapable of differentiating consciousness from an ability to distinguish an appetite for life from a resignation to death.

The year turns, harvest comes around again and Bathsheba returns to the Corn Market to sell her grain. In that most public of places, a constable breaks the news that her husband has drowned, and he has brought Troy's uniform home as evidence. As the representative of collective rules and values, the officer's announcement portends that something has fallen into the unconscious.

Bathsheba immediately dons mourning garb, not the bereaved lady's ostentatious costume but a labourer's rigout. She now has to lift turnips from a wide field with only Gabriel and one other farmhand for help. At the end of the long day's work, she is too exhausted to get her boots off before falling onto her bed. As she had warned her husband, Everdene Farm cannot pay the debts that he had amassed.

Having discreetly noted how things fare at Everdene, Mr Boldwood approaches Gabriel Oak with a proposition. He invites Gabriel to manage not only Bathsheba's farm but also his, Boldwood's, own place. Further to persuade the younger man to accept a deal which will be profitable for them both, Boldwood has retrieved Old George, the shepherd's dog that Gabriel had to leave behind when quitting his farm. From the psychological perspective, keeping the dog symbolises Boldwood's loyal disposition. But instead of growing consciousness, he is developing a second anima plot with which to approach Bathsheba, and indeed makes her another offer of marriage. He undertakes to pay the debts that Troy left unsettled, to protect her for the rest of her life and to make it possible for her to run Everdene herself even as a pastime if she wishes. He offers her shelter, safety, and comfort as his wife without any regard for what he needs emotionally. From this perspective, retrieving Old George represents the dark side of eros and a kind of love madness for Bathsheba. Apropos, Hannah comments that power and financial plots are more natural to men than women, for these plots have more to do with Logos than Eros (2018: 249).

Mr Boldwood yearns for love and companionship. He has mastered the desires of the outer world but has no access to the feelings of aliveness that a relationship to the anima brings to a man's life. This becomes apparent when he probes Bathsheba's mind asking firstly whether she likes and secondly whether she respects him. She answers "Yes" to both questions, but he persists and asks which of those is true. Does she like or respect him? Her response is magnificent and to a large degree expresses the proficiency of a woman who now *relates* to her animus. It sufficiently expresses what she has learned through her experiences with all three men. No longer animus possessed she replies, "It is difficult for a woman to define her feelings in a language chiefly made by men to express theirs." At this juncture, Boldwood makes an offer which amplifies an error of judgement that he made when first proposing marriage to her: "If you worry about a lack of passion on your part, a lack of desire … if you worry about marrying me merely out of guilt, and pity and compromise, … well I don't mind." He means kindness by this, but his words accurately list the very feelings that Bathsheba is now consciously aware of. The rich man is in effect offering the woman he intends to wed a companionship devoid of passion or reciprocal love.

Bathsheba now speaks to Gabriel about Mr Boldwood's second proposal with a new frankness, telling him that she is committed to reaching a decision by Christmas, a terrible responsibility: "I hold that man's future in my hands." She realises that her persistent suitor is offering to suffocate her with money, patronage, and dogged kindness and fears that she may hold the key to his well-being should she reject him. As all projections do, his needy love leaves her burdened while he attempts, albeit unconsciously, to tie her down and make her feel responsible for his happiness. To Gabriel's inquiry about her feelings for Boldwood she admits that she does not love him, adding, "But love's a worn-out miserable thing for me now." Her love problem has now reached its crisis point.

Marie-Louise von Franz summarised in a succinct passage the psychological structure of the complete marital relationship. The complex pattern that evolves between the partners stands in vivid contrast with the locked-in possession that William Boldwood – despite his seemingly obliging and humble words – intends to impose on his wife.

> In every couple relationship there are actually four figures involved: the man and his anima, and the woman and her animus. … Only when the two partners can relate to all these figures can one speak of a complete relationship, and therefore love in modern terms becomes a vehicle of the process of individuation and the development of higher consciousness.
>
> (1993: 77–8)

The anima-ridden Boldwood now prepares to host a great Christmas party with the intention that this should be the occasion when Bathsheba must accept him. The centuries-old ceremony centres on the seasonal tree and its flaming lights not only to celebrate the birth of Christ but also the flowering of consciousness deeply implicated in his coming. However, Boldwood cannot conceal his deep anxiety: it will be no coincidence that psychologically, the climax of the tension between the opposing factors of consciousness and unconsciousness will occur while celebrating Christmas. As staff hired for the occasion finalise their preparations in the great house, he takes Gabriel to one side and quizzes him, his key questions centring, of course, on Miss Everdene (as he still calls her). But when the tormented man asks whether Bathsheba will keep the promise which Boldwood has persuaded himself she has implied, namely, "Will she do what's generally accepted as being right?" Gabriel replies as we have already mentioned, "If it is not inconvenient to her." Boldwood remarks on Gabriel's newfound irony; but he then pays the younger man a double-sided compliment. He first notes the affection and care with which Gabriel regards Miss Everdene. Then he thanks Gabriel for acting like a man (i.e. for his willingness to stand aside) now that he, William Boldwood, will become the successful rival.

At the Christmas party, Boldwood, Gabriel, and Bathsheba are each ill at ease; but when Gabriel announces that he intends to go home to his cottage, Boldwood insists that the pair must first dance together. It is a bizarre gesture on his part, as if he unconsciously recognises the natural psychic rhythm that resonates between them. In tune with his intuition, Boldwood's idea appears to be an unconscious compensation that adheres to the axiom that justice will be served. As they waltz, Bathsheba begs Gabriel to advise her what she should do and he responds, "Do what is right." Her wise shepherd explicitly states that she must take responsibility for her own mind and life; she must reach deep inside herself to find what she thinks and discover her own ethical position. In this respect it contrasts with a moral judgement focused on the affairs of the collective values that are judged either right or wrong. It is a critical moment in the development of her animus, discovering her own individual *Weltanschauung*; the moment of realisation of the absolute nature of the Self. Filled with tension, she makes her excuses, quits the dance floor, walks out of Boldwood's door and turns toward her home only to be brought to a halt by the sight of what looks like a ghost (and is indeed the ghost of her animus).

It is actually Frank Troy, pulled alive from the sea by fishermen, who has slowly made his way across the country to Everdene. Clad now in his sergeant's uniform, he comes to find his wife. The psychology underpinning this brief meeting with her echoes the form of his past dealings with her. There's a calculated and ironic flavour to his discovery that he had been declared dead and that he preferred it that way for a while. Asked by his wife why he has come back, he says, "The strangest thing. I missed you." Bathsheba, outraged by his strategic abuse of her loyalty, will not let this pass: "You said I was nothing to you." The fact that she cannot forget his vile words amuses this faithless, infantile man, who abandons all pretence at affection at once. He demands money and orders her to sell the farm to raise it. When she refuses to go back to Everdene with him, he seizes her yelling, "I'm your husband, and you'll obey me!"

Boldwood, in his own state of heightened tension, is well aware that Bathsheba has not come back to the dance floor. Fearing that something may be wrong, he picks up a shotgun and hastens outdoors in time to witness Troy's enraged assault on Bathsheba. Boldwood fires a single shot and kills the former sergeant outright before handing himself into the police. Thrown by the older suitor shooting dead the younger husband into archetypal relation, Boldwood and Troy are revealed unforgettably as forming the Senex/Puer pair. Troy's blind suffering has kept him from avoiding the worst outcome when living an unconscious life. Weddings and death "are regarded as turning points in human life and the one always points to the other" (von Franz, 1987: 52).

A scarcely less sorrowful coda closes William Boldwood's tale than Troy's existence. As manager of the two farms, Gabriel informs Bathsheba that the other man's life will probably be spared, the death of Troy likely to be adjudged a crime of passion. Bathsheba asks Gabriel to show her the marital suite that Boldwood had prepared. It abounds in extravagant gifts: sumptuous hat boxes; hangers burdened with fashionable dresses; and drawers laden with strings of pearls and jewels. Every item carries the name which the groom intended his bride to assume, the entire lavish display revealing his obsession with her and the preparations he had made to receive her into his life as his anima, a goddess-like figure held in lockdown. By asking Gabriel, her Shepherd, to show her the overwhelming pomp of Boldwood's marital suite she becomes conscious of the choice she might have made for both of them by opting for the jewels of the outer life.

In due time, the seasons turn, a fine harvest is gathered in by a full complement of hands, and Gabriel announces to Bathsheba that he intends now that the farm is thriving, to leave England and move to America. Unlike some of their earlier impassioned confrontations, their leave taking is characterised by mutual respect and kindness. In this monumental moment, Gabriel's own transformative process while working for Bathsheba is revealed. He has proven to be better than both of Bathsheba's suitors, a man encompassing the feminine principle with its intrinsic relational values. Gabriel's development signifies a reconciliation and union of the opposites, releasing him from every one-sidedness. No longer driven by the collective values implicit in his early proposal of marriage, or his unconscious hunch he has relinquished his own ego desires to serve the Self. The symbol of the lamb has converted from a gift to a sacrifice. Through his own individuation process he has discovered the self-knowledge to know how far he is willing to give himself up. We see and feel the couple's deep relatedness and mature mutual dependence that has developed over time. Theirs is now the Royal Quaternity that encompasses four figures: Gabriel's conscious with Bathsheba's conscious, Gabriel's unconscious/anima, and Bathsheba's unconscious/animus: the archetypal pair are a living dynamic imbued with the spark of the Self that carries the qualities capable of coming up against the 'herd instinct.'

As they kiss, the familiar, sweet music that celebrates the farm's beauty and prosperity gives way to a reprise of the lovers' theme once again led by a soaring fiddle. This, however, is no self-centred celebration of a sexual incandescence such as Troy's that had been his only gift to his bride. As the couple walk hand-in-hand back toward the farmstead, the two themes come together: the lovers and the loveliness of the land blend. We witness the whole making effect of Eros and Individuation linked together that reveals a truth: in every deep love experience the Self is involved.

Notes

1 Psychologically, to be tamed means to give up her power attitude. The shadow aspect of the ego must be transformed into a vessel of strength (Jung stated the ego needs to become as small and as strong as possible).
2 Here we see the effect of opposites linked with the colour red. On one side it augments vitality and reinforces warmth, while on the other it builds aggressiveness and the tendency toward quarrelsomeness, temper, murder, and carnage (1977: 142).

Chapter 5

Knight of Cups

The Pilgrim's Progress from This World to That which is to come: Delivered under the Similitude of a Dream Wherein is Discovered, The manner of his setting out, His Dangerous Journey; And safe Arrival at the Desired Country.

(John Bunyan, 1678)

John Gielgud reads these words, the title page of *The Pilgrim's Progress*, as a prose overture accompanying the title sequence of *Knight of Cups* – an emphatic link between the two works. Despite its sparse narrative elements, the explicit set-up of *Knight of Cups* holds the tension between two moral worlds. Bunyan's militant Protestant Pilgrim triumphantly reaches his goal, overcoming every obstacle in his way (though not without difficulties and sacrifice). Constant in the face of temptation he holds to his purpose to gain the other world. Unlike him, Malick's Knight (softly caged in the velvet luxuries of Los Angeles) abandons what should have been his heroic quest and retreats into a miasma of the soul.

Bunyan's twentieth-century editor, Roger Sharrock, argued that Bunyan's achievement lies in creating not allegory, but myth (1965: 24). This is significant given that in the seventeenth-century allegory was a dominant method of writing texts that framed familiar biblical stories in the guise of morality tales. Allegory depended on a structural schema that encouraged readers to connect characters or emblems with their moral or biblical significance, as if locked together by a set of equal signs. For his part, Sharrock maintains that in *The Pilgrim's Progress* neither its characters nor the countryside through which they travel function like such an account book of moral virtues. On the contrary, 'Their moral significance cannot be neatly pared away from the sensuous form in which they are presented' (1965: 24).

Sensuous form has particular relevance to us because approaching this most sensual of films via erotic mythology is a rich way to open out its themes. Although it offers viewers no less sacred an understanding of the soul's potential development than *The Pilgrim's Progress*, *Knight of Cups* does not impose an ideology by means of an allegory conforming to dogma. In fact, by means of its very title, *Knight of Cups* inserts a caesura between the film and a Christian morality tale in that it foregrounds the divinatory practice of the Tarot. As Nick Pinkerton writes,

DOI: 10.4324/9781003545538-6

'the operation of chance within a defined framework – which might also describe a Tarot reading – has long been a crucial aspect of Malick's process' (2016).

Puer Aeturnus and Senex

In Britain the Tarot Knight is better known as the Prince, a title emphasising the youth's apprenticeship to the monarch. Early in the film, Malick signals through his narrator (Brian Dennehy, who also plays the father figure) how the film's father-son relationship fits the archetypal pairing of *senex* and *puer*. The ageless tale which the father recounts to his young son seems to have been handed down the generations to warn about a recurrent problem in which fathers and sons are caught on both the personal and collective level of the unconscious. The story (derived from *The Hymn of the Pearl*) tells of a knight commanded by his father, the king, to under-take a long quest and find a pearl deep in the ocean. But the son, having started out ablaze with energy and determination, soon succumbs to the temptations of pleasure, and drinks from a cup that cossets him in easeful sleep. Time passes. His father, the king, sends messages reminding the knight of his commitment; but, forgetful of the pearl, the young man sleeps on.

Approaching the father-son relationship through the *senex-puer* archetype places the film in a psychological *and* historical framework that allows for a deeper under-standing of the tale. In *Knight of Cups,* the longing for redemption is located in the father-son pair as surrogates for Father Time and Eternal Youth with all the bewil-dering paradoxes of their connection. In effect, the pairing exemplifies the problem of the feminine (the anima) in a man's psychology. If he is capable of creating a connection with his unconscious, an unforgettable surprise and memorable experi-ence may ensue, bringing something archetypal into the conscious realm.

Robert Wang, in his sumptuously illuminated Jungian version of the Tarot pack, describes the Knight of Cups as a personality type who has a charming, emotional and romantic nature. Mary Greer adds to this the observation that the Knight follows his dreams. Usually popular, he likes being the centre of attention; but he tends to be superficial in his relations with other people and subjective in judgement. His negative characteristics often include a capricious behaviour in relationships, cou-pled with thoughtlessness over the feelings of others, moodiness and jealousy (Greer, 1984: 236; Wang, 1990: 78–9). This archetypal figure, a viable thumbnail sketch of our present-day knight Rick (Christian Bale), is familiar to Jungians as the eter-nal youth (*puer aeternus*). Jung introduced the term in 1912 and Marie–Louise von Franz expanded it, describing a man who is identified with the *puer* archetype as one who remains too long in adolescent psychology. This archaic identity occurs when a young man is unable to detach his ego complex from its archetypal roots. James Hill-man says that this single archetype tends to merge in one; the Hero, the Divine Child, the figures of Eros, the King's Son, the Son of the Great Mother, the Psychopomp, Mercurius-Hermes, Trickster, and the Messiah. 'In him we see a mercurial range of these "personalities": narcissistic, inspired, effeminate, phallic, inquisitive, inventive, pensive, passive, fiery and capricious' (2005: 50).

Rick possesses several of these qualities but lacks the sparkling wit of this personality type in its effervescent phase (Wang, 1988: 78). That absence hints at an undertow of sorrow darkening his outlook. We find him, like the leading male characters in *The Tree of Life* and *Ex Machina*, facing the mid-life crisis, having outlived the golden innocence of youth, his sense of invincibility further shaken by the suicide of a brother. Suppressed memories rush in and jolt him into resuming his long-delayed journey toward enhanced consciousness, 'All those years,' he reflects, 'living the life of someone I didn't know.'

Like all archetypal figures, the *puer* stands in opposition to contrary values, in its case represented by the *senex*. This archetype, according to Hillman, is represented by Saturn-Kronos.

> Saturn is at once archetypal image for wise old man, solitary sage, the *lapis* as rock of ages with all its positive moral and intellectual virtues, and for the Old King, that castrating castrated ogre... Saturn is image for both positive and negative *senex*.
>
> (2005: 42)

Jung understood Saturn as his personal daimon, defining Saturn as the ruler both of his horoscope *and* of the incoming Aion of Aquarius. The God Saturn is the founder of civilisations, social order and conformity; and the rings that enclose the planet reflect the idea of human limitations. Saturn in Aquarius implies reordering structures and developing innovation as it turns toward unknown terrain in order to gather and harvest wisdom off the mainstream path and beyond the norm. Keeping this in mind, we recognise that *Knight of Cups* has taken on a monumental task in conveying both the profound significance of the planet's mythology and the evolution of an individual life. Rick's confrontation with his father Joseph resonates not only with his personal journey but, as we shall come to see, a collective journey as well.

The *senex* compensates for the too idealistic attitude of consciousness which the *puer aeternus* cannot voluntarily assimilate. Rick's cantankerous father Joseph is his son's opposing type. Representing a traditional mind and collective disposition with a certain quality of inertia that resists change in dealing with living experiences, Rick's ageing parent, 'once the terror of the household, now hunched and muttering' (Gilmour, 2016), reveals almost no recognisable connections with the wise old king who dispatched his son on a sacred quest. Yet Brian Dennehy, playing both the loving story-telling father and his tyrannical *alter ego*, does connect them. When *senex* and *puer* are linked together and seen as a whole, they provide a sense of meaningfulness to the spirit of a man. Just as the film opens with Rick stuck in identity with the *puer* rather than the hero which the royal father desires his son should become, so Joseph, far from the steadfast wise old man invoked by the fable, cannot escape the *senex* who has lost contact with his own creative impulse. Jung warned that identity inhibits individuation. We are confronted with a split within the symbolic figure. The negative *senex* and *puer* problem 'are consequences rather than causes, they reflect a prior disorder in the archetypal ground of the ego' (Hillman, 2005: 47).

Hero figures take a variety of forms whose labour is to set things right. Rick's whole story is concerned with what happens to him as the main character whose guiding task requires him to overcome certain unusual difficulties. Archetypally, there is a constant shift between interpreting the hero as a symbol of the Self and a symbol of the ego. In his essence, the Hero character stays true to an inner author-ity. As the restorer of a healthy conscious situation, the hero is an archetypal figure that represents a model of an ego functioning in harmony with the Self. Such roles include the saviour of his people, the finder of hidden treasure and the survivor of the night sea journey in the belly of a whale (von Franz, 1996: 58). We have argued that Rick is the beautiful youth type: early in the film we are left wondering whether the hero implicit in the fable of the king lies beyond this Knight's grasp. It's a question which we shall return to.

The film centres around the relationship between a father and his three sons. This dynamic is frequently portrayed in fairy tales, the Grimm Brothers, for example, including 50–60 father-son couples in their stories. The narrative of *Knight of Cups* is organised around masculine characters among whom the female element is sel-dom seen, which illustrates the general problem that the film appears to address. This wholeness represented by four men indicates a dominant masculine attitude in the collective consciousness that does not sufficiently acknowledge a psychologi-cal aspect of the Self.

Rick is one of three brothers who has sought a way to adapt, albeit neurotic, to the powerful influence of their patriarch. One son found refuge in suicide: his death hangs heavily over the survivors. One of the latter, Barry (Wes Bentley), has escaped into chemical and alcohol addictions that alternate with volcanic rages, like Joseph's in rocking the bounds of sanity. Meanwhile their mother Ruth (Cherry Jones) has long found refuge from her husband's dominance by hiding in plain sight, to all intents and purposes absent from the family. The negative *senex* relationship to the *feminine* has been put succinctly by Hillman who declares that those born under Saturn do not like to walk with women and pass the time. They are never in favour with woman or wife (2005: 44). This insight helps us see that Joseph's personalistic psychology is dominated by a one-sided male standpoint lacking relatedness (Eros) to the feminine element. Seen in this light, Eros func-tions in opposition to the will to power. His obscure sight inhibits him from con-necting on a deeper level. His attitude manifests ultimately in a problem with his anima, the archetypal figure of the woman that was born in him and subsequently projected into his own mother. This first encounter with the feminine shapes a man's basic disposition toward women and gives his anima certain characteristics. Thus, in an undeveloped state, the mother and anima figure are merged in the man's unconscious. Not until he has his first emotional experience does the personal and archetypal layer of the unconscious get activated (which encompasses the whole mother anima archetype). Ruth's animus (the masculine contra-sexual partner in a woman) which has been shaped by her father and patriarchal culture has also contributed significantly to the anguished inner lives of her sons. The problems in her marriage to Joseph reflect the antagonistic internal partnership between their respective anima and animus.[1] Ruth's absence may be an indication that she has withdrawn her animus projection onto her husband or it could mean she simply could no longer tolerate the chronic tension created in the subterranean environment by their anima and animus conflict and left. Rick's mother has not offered him anything more than the torn fabric of a matrix on which to hang his own projections of the all-powerful mother – the mother goddess.

von Franz writes that when the anima shows its negative aspects – as she does especially when the man is not conscious of her – she manifests as irrational states, sentimental or frigid moods, hysterical outbreaks, or sexual fantasies remote from reality. Not least, she leads the man to find the wrong partner (1999: 247). Don Juanism is for von Franz one typical psychological disturbance of the *puer*. He seeks in every woman the image of the perfect woman who will give him everything, constantly looking for the mother goddess.

The *puer* manifests itself in this way in Rick. Like Barry, he has drunk deeply of addiction, captured by a daemonic longing for the feminine due to his mother complex while fleeing from his father's authority. Unconsciously under the influence of both parental imagoes, Rick is reluctant to take on commitments in the outer world and has escaped into a world of fantasy shaped by immersion in aesthetic beauty. Richard Brody observes that,

> Malick doesn't depict Rick as a man of woe but as an introvert thrust into an extrovert's playground, as someone who has trouble throwing himself wholeheartedly into the throng because he has the habit of standing back from the event even while within it… and, all the while, he's filled with images, not ones that he's actively composing but ones that compose themselves in his mind.
>
> (2016)

All in all, Rick's anima is removed and distant, sickly disconnected from the source of creative life and his own sense of meaning and purpose.

Aesthetics of Emerging Consciousness

As Brody implies, the audience finds its attentions occupied by Rick's memories, fantasies, and reflections. The rhetoric of *Knight of Cups* resembles that which Malick had developed through *The Tree of Life* and *To the Wonder*. As in those two films, spectators cannot readily construct a classic narrative arc thanks in part to the fragmentary but vivid expression of Rick's erratic experiences and his unsteady reflection on them. The film's themes have, therefore, to be sensed through a stream of emerging consciousness which Malick devises ways of mobilising both in the psyche of audience members and those of his characters. *Knight of Cups* entices us to experience Rick's delights, bewilderment, and self-discovery mainly through the sensuous pleasure of our own eyes, ears, and imagination.[2] In actuality, Malick engages the audience's senses like those of wild animals that have complete possession of their natural instincts for orientation. That is where the mystery lies, in the imagery and sounds that modulate our access to the psyche of a man (along with his brothers) who has something wrong with his instinctual life and is therefore stuck in mid-life unable to change without undergoing crisis. Kong Rithdee recognises that our visual experience of *Knight of Cups* is predominantly 'non-linear, impressionistic, and has the clarity of a beautiful, foggy morning ... the gliding camera like a wandering soul' (2016).

Although we never see Rick at his desk, the way in which he relives memories of former lovers (which now, after they have parted, take hold of him like iridescent fantasies), suggests that he might have found a grounding in his professional screenwriting – more of which later.

Prologue and Portent

At sun-up in Death Valley's cosmic landscape, Rick meanders apparently with no sharper focus than a tourist dabbling in its crystalline salt flats. Landlocked far below sea level in a desert that could hardly be further removed from an ocean-embedded pearl, he has fallen away from the route leading to self-discovery and resembles a lost soul. Yet he is searching for something.

Without warning, Malick (like Kubrick in *2001: A Space Odyssey* leaping the aeon between humanity's ancestors and space flight) cuts hard to the *aurora borealis,* an emerald serpent seen holding close the midnight curvature of the turning Earth. A wonder, this numinous vision displays our planet as a Pearl, the Grail in glory. When we take the leap of imagination to engage with the revelation, the epiphany, cannot be mistaken. Gielgud intones Bunyan's description of Christian preparing to set out on his long walk, "a man clothed with rags ... with his face from his own house, a book in his hand, and a great burden upon his back" (1768: 39). A moment later, Rick (in counterpoint with Pilgrim's realisation that he has too long-delayed his own journey) confesses his own long absence from himself: "All those years, living the life of someone I didn't even know." That someone is his shadow self who interferes with a viable relationship to his anima. He has always projected his anima on the women in his life; but Rick lacks a guide equivalent to Pilgrim's Bible. This emphasises the grave importance of the anima in a man's psychology. The anima assumes the role of the *psychopompos,* or soul leader, who draws him onward to the next stage in the transformation of his personality changing his attitude and psyche.

That said, the seventeenth-century Pilgrim and our twenty-first-century seeker resemble each other in that (comparing the journey toward God of the one with the quest to advance individuation of the other) the path toward their goal for neither man runs straight or true. Having started out in mid-life, both will lose their way more than once in disastrous detours and reversals. As Jung often said, authentic transformation cannot happen without emotion, and at the start of *Knight of Cups*, it remains to be seen whether Rick will truly open himself to his feeling life.

The opening sequences feature three distinct locations: Death Valley; the Earth seen from space; and Rick's point of view driving through a Los Angeles tunnel, the single shot when he recalls the emptiness of his life. How are they related in diegetic time? The seemingly obvious clue is Rick's inner voice confessing his years of self-alienation, juxtaposed against Bunyan's painful epiphany. But while this juxtaposition underlines the main theme of *Knight of Cups*, it does not connect the early sequences in conventional narrative time. Instead, the structure hints that the method that Malick previously used in *The Tree of Life* (2011) recurs here further developed. Bernard Aspe noted how in *The Tree of Life* language comes after the story, and the whispering voices-over are structurally retrospective. They do not so much express what a character is thinking as let us understand what he or she ought to have thought but does not realise until much later. For Aspe, the device demonstrates the prerequisite imperative to becoming a psychological being, namely reflection (2011: 20–1). In *Knight of Cups,* Malick goes a step further by eroding the plotline near to vanishing point. As a consequence, like Rick, film goers have little choice but to puzzle and reflect deeply on what can be drawn from what they see and hear. For example, as the film unrolls, it becomes no easier to fix the opening sequence in the chronology of Rick's life. Occasionally, we cut to bone dry landscapes, distinctive rock formations, and sun-cracked roads; but whether these are Rick's fragmented memories or portents of future revelations in Death Valley remains for a long while indefinable. As Brody writes, '*Knight of Cups* is close to a first-person act of remembering, and the ecstatic power of its images and sounds is a virtual manifesto, and confession, of the cinematic mind at work' (2016).

Wandering in a desert by daylight, Rick could not possibly have seen the aurora wrapping the earth's curvature. The audience, however, does get a few seconds to register the glory of these ethereal illuminations. For some it may be glimpsed, barely registered, and then forgotten. For others, the visionary perspective (viewed as if from outer space) may become a moment of revelation if its majesty draws our imaginations to sensing that it has an unexplained significance. For some people (e.g. those viewers who are identifying with Rick whose role of searcher the film invites us to share), this lone shot, isolated from the familiar cause-and-effect organisation of narrative exposition, may take on qualities of a synchronicity that seems to insist we reflect on it.

Jung's concept that synchronicity is an acausal connection through meaning (Jung, 1952) was developed by Victor Mansfield (Professor of Physics and Astronomy) who wrote that it 'simultaneously incarnates transformative meaning in the subject and in his or her world' (2002: 132). The image of a luminous aurora has no causal links with the film's storyline, yet for viewers its fleeting 'material' presence is there on screen. Among those in the audience as disoriented from their sense of direction as Rick and equally unable to redirect their lives, some few may discover that seeing the aurora meets a personal psychological need and anticipates meaningful insight on which they can reflect. These individuals may then discover that contemplation of the emotions and sense of wonderment which the image excites in them has a transforming effect on their lives.

Mansfield observes that synchronicity experiences always involve an interior intuition of meaning, and that is always unique to the person whose individuation is advanced by that meaning (2002: 133). Roderick Main complements Mansfield's observations by discussing the ways in which Jung's concept of synchronicity addressed the transformation from the disenchanted modern world that succeeded the enchanted pre-modern era and contributed to the partial re-enchantment of the post-modern world (2011: 156). For the present writers as scholars of film, there is no question but that the cinema is both a powerful agent of personal re-enchantment and too of communal enchantment. We accept Mansfield's argument that the meaning of each individual's synchronicity experience is unique, which entails that people in an audience who are stimulated by a particular experience in the same scene will not feel its transforming psychological power in the same way. Notwithstanding that, they may share with others watching the same film strong currents of emotion that it arouses, but their personal psychology guides them to an understanding (whether transformative or not) quite distinct from others.' Those viewers who register that the aurora is the Pearl have an advantage they share with Pilgrim in recognising it as the goal toward which their quest, if successful, must tend. However, at the start of *Knight of Cups* Rick has only his confusion and the sense of his empty existence that urge him to stumble erratically toward some lasting transformation.

A montage sequence of Rick's memories commences with childhood. With those memories inflected by fantasy (the way of the anima), when the childless Rick projects himself as a loving father carrying his infant safely from the sea back to the beach, it seems that he might be imagining himself as both infant and parent – the anima pointing the way into the future and into the future development of his personality. There follow scenes of energetic children playing happily, these soon overtaken when Rick, now a young man, careers along LA boulevards in an open-top car sporting with two flirtatious women. Soon recollections flood in of his pursuit of sensual fulfilment to satiation and beyond. As he loses himself in increasingly orgiastic parties, the masks behind which he hides grow ever more demonic, frenzy keeping self-reflection at bay until the sequence shudders to a visual crescendo in nightmarish, black and white stop-motion footage of a nude woman. A still close up of her face, printed on card, is attached, a duplicate face, to the back of her head. Broad crosses, brutal marks of erasure, are painted on her back where either breasts or wings for this angel-cum-demon once were, a ghastly mastectomy. She is the ravaged feminine whom we shall see time and again in this film.

> Like the "supraordinate personality," the anima is bipolar and can therefore appear positive one moment and negative the next. … Whenever she emerges with some degree of clarity, she always has a peculiar relationship to *time*: as a rule she is more or less immortal, because outside time.
>
> (Jung and Kerényi, 1978: 173; see also Pinkerton, 2016)

Finally, black paint whips across and obliterates both her Janus faces. Rick's troubled anima is presenting herself to him in the starkest images.

In these scenes, Rick finds himself the involuntary witness to lost time as repressed memories surface. Through life experiences, dreams and fantasy, the unconscious releases energy to consciousness to compensate for an individual's biases and may not reflect the chronology of memories but invites reflection. So *Knight of Cups*, imbued with Rick's fantasy life, does not construct a narrative in linear form. For example, Rick wanders by day through a Hollywood studio lot and by night across flat roofs high above the street while, a voice in his head, his father murmurs to him. 'My son, you're just like I am. Can't figure your life out. Can't put the pieces together, just like me. A pilgrim on this earth, a stranger … Where did life go wrong?' Perhaps the old man once said this, perhaps he never did, but the inner voice of the father-son relationship has clearly communicated and exemplifies a state of emotional stagnation, an identification with his father that has thwarted individuation. It's another instance of the whispering voices functioning as structural retrospection (Aspe, 2011: 20–1).

An earthquake sucks Rick out of sleep. Scrambling around his apartment he looks around him 'with an expression of dazed bafflement' (Pinkerton, 2016). The Saturnian boundaries have ruptured as the gateway to the unconscious opens. Taken as an image for his inner life, the quake's aftershocks never cease, for this is the archetypal moment when the damming up of Rick's life energy is shaken to the extent that his encounter with the unconscious begins. He will eventually recognise that everything in it has got clogged. For this is his experience of synchronicity, a shock encounter with the divine. It sparks a simultaneous meaningful link which evolves into his recognition "I am part of a Whole." Such synchronicities can present a kairos or opportune moment, an important time for the healing of an unborn state. A consciousness that is not yet born carries the distinctive characteristic of someone who is under the spell of a complex in the emotional life. In the meantime, memories of Rick's former life and loves continue to irrupt, exposing him to the unwanted resumption of a quest he had forgotten.

The Moon

Rick takes up with a young Hollywood starlet (Imogen Poot). With her pink wig, kohl-painted eyes, and delight in startling Rick by teetering on tall stiletto heels near dangerous roof-top edges, she can be puckishly provocative (Pride, 2016). She is an anima figure and excites him sexually beyond measure: 'Desire's so deep, I throw my life away,' he whispers. However, beyond this reckless flirtatiousness, she challenges Rick's fear of intimacy by offering it to him, albeit superficially: "You think I could make you crazy. Crack you out of your shell. Make you suffer," she says, breaking down his ego strength as she drills into his unconscious one word at a time: "I. THINK. YOU'RE. WEAK." Before he leaves her, she tells him, "You don't want love. You want a love experience." Thus, in effect she counsels him, albeit unconsciously, not to return to being dead.

Two opposing cultural value-sets threaten to submerge Rick. When still a couple, he and the starlet had roamed an aquarium gazing at whales gliding beside them, while an unseen clergyman voices the spirit's claims on him: "When you see a beautiful woman or man, the soul remembers the beauty it used to know and love … and that makes the soul want to fly, but it cannot yet because it's still too weak." The scene both encourages and reflects on the necessity for our hero to move toward the spirit of the depths (the symbolic value of the whale) and increased consciousness. Shortly after, we look back in time as two agents suborn Rick on the studio lot, coaxing him into dealing dishonestly to secure a project in which they all have a financial interest. One of these deal makers slips cash into Rick's unresisting hand who recalls that the Hollywood moneymaking machine had long offered him a secure existence mired in deception. He had preferred that to the emotionally vulnerable world of love, but thereby smothered the claims of his soul. Now, as he looks back, the starlet surfaces in Rick's memory as his first lover who was more than a superficial liaison. Recalling their time together, desire for her fills him once again with longing and regret.

The Moon, the sign under which the starlet appears, is an archetype linked intimately with the feminine and the unconscious. In its dark aspect it can symbolise deception and deep-rooted fears that seem to well up from nowhere (Wang, 1988: 52). However, from a psychological point of view, the feminine archetype is both positive and negative. The positive side of the archetype brings life to all things. On the negative side it is bound by fear and only *seemingly* comes from nowhere, in actuality it comes from the dread of being swallowed up by the feminine dark aspect of the unconscious. But such fears are not characteristic of Rick's quirkily insightful lover. On the contrary, she embodies the moon's positive capacity to reflect light, inflected through her intuition of both what she wants and what would enrich Rick's soul. Erich Neumann notes,

> The sudden thought and the intuition are expressions of the spiritual force of the unconscious, of the *lumen naturae* of the archetypally feminine night world, whose darkness suddenly becomes bright, as if by inspiration.
>
> (1994: 79)

Instead, it is to Rick that the moon's shadow aspect attaches as it had done to his eldest suicidal brother. In Rick's case it shows in his willingness to deceive people with whom he is contracted as a writer, and his concomitant fear of his feelings. "Desire's so deep, I throw my life away" he murmurs shortly before walking out on the starlet – at which moment Malick cuts to a shot of a car crash unfolding below her apartment block. Edward Edinger notes that an ordeal of frustrated instinctual desires is a characteristic feature of the developmental process (1985: 20). He adds, concerning the necessary frustration of desirousness or concupiscence,

> First the substance must be located; that is, the unconscious, unacknowledged desire … must be recognized and affirmed. The instinctual desire that says "I want" and "I am entitled to this" must be fully recognised by the ego.
>
> (1985: 42)

The Hanged Man

Recollections of the young starlet touch Rick emotionally and somewhat hesitantly he visits an astrologer's studio on Sunset Boulevard where no fewer than four clairvoyants attend to help direct his bewildered soul. It's an ironic nod toward Hollywood excess, a vice which Bunyan would have understood, but the choreographed performance of the four passes Rick by. Instead a single Tarot card, The Hanged Man, grabs his attention. The imagery of the card shows a figure hanging upside down with his hands free to achieve release if he wishes. Jung's own brief interpretation of the card was that it signified 'powerlessness, sacrifice, test, proof' (Greer, 2008). The goal of the voluntary sacrifice of conscious control is the transformation resulting from willing receptivity to a direct experience of the Self. Right on cue Rick's brother shows up on the street outside the astrologer's shop. Barry is Rick's shadow and, as the latter says, always pretends that everything's okay when it isn't.

The two men drift into a quarter of LA where addicts and the destitute squat on sidewalks beside their few remaining possessions. Barry, wired and unpredictable, leads his brother to a vacant loft above a sweatshop. It is his dosshouse, empty but for a couch, suitcase, and a TV set which he tries but fails to smash. Forcing Rick to share his suffering, he deliberately reopens the unbearable family wound, their eldest brother's suicide and father's responsibility for it. As Rick's shadow, Barry plays an important role by preventing a dissociation of Rick's personality. So, while the latter conceals his emotions (as usual), his mind rages at Joseph who, "Like a snake, swallowed him ... grasping ... vicious!"[3] No sooner do these words infest Rick's head than fantasies flood in: his father dodders round an abandoned office fumbling at a grubby desk. The old man tries to wash his hands; but they, like Macbeth's, incarnadine the basin with the blood of the son he has murdered – his eldest prince.

This fantasised office metamorphoses into a vast clubroom where, knowing that Joseph's professional life is in ruins, powerful businessmen ostentatiously ignore him. To displace his humiliation, Joseph orders his sons to justify him, "Redeem My Life!" Thus cued, a harpist noodles inauspiciously across her strings, and the scene cuts to Joseph's surviving sons pacing in funeral order behind their demented father. Muttering enraged self-justifications, he stumbles along rotting alleys and stairwells until unexpectedly murmuring "I turned you upside down, my son." With these sentimental words Joseph remembers starting Rick's new-born life; but they map equally truly onto the damage done by a father imposing an intemperate will on his offspring. This will not be the only moment in Rick's memory where his father *senex* touches on opposing archetypal truths.

The Hermit

In a hotel apartment, Rick, far from living isolated in contemplation, frolics with a twinned pair of naked blondes whose business is seduction. Whatever the pleasures of that afternoon, they have not lodged in his memory deeper than as a delightful escapade. Nevertheless, the recollection is augmented by his own inner voice

offering tribute to sex: "Life … a goddess!" The music heard at the film's beginning resumes, invoking a stately procession in the Steppes of Asia.

The Hermit depicted by Wang stands 'at the edge of a desert which symbolises
a transition between conscious and unconscious, between darkness and the light of
self-awareness' and lights the way through the dark night of the soul (1988: 34). The
Hermit driven solely by intellect and ambition and who lacks emotional engagement with the life-giving soul (the anima) will experience only a dry and barren
existence. Rick (by now a walking dead man) drifts into just such a metaphori-
cal desert, feeling alone among hundreds of guests at a grotesquely ostentatious
Hollywood party. He feels his separateness, an early indication of the loneliness
that must encompass him as he returns to his quest for the Pearl. The host (Anto-
nio Banderas) displays his pretentious home with its vast rooms which include
a banqueting hall where nobody sits at the table. The guests parade their vacant,
extravagantly fashionable personas and trade in flattery to impress anyone who will
listen. Egregious, self-celebrating celebrities insist on their piffling claims to fame.
The host brags that he falls in love 20 times a day and says, propounding a bogus
respect for women's "secret mystery," that he never stops loving a woman although
the way he loves them changes (he does not add that his self-adoration remains
constant). Another self-deceiving fraud ambushes people and boasts absurdly that,
having once been to Sarajevo, he feels so useless he prays that God should take
both his arms. These people, gripped by the denial of mystery, a leprosy of the
spirit, have no soul and when we are completely disconnected from our unconscious, we project our own soul (our anima or animus) onto our partner and are
naturally disappointed once reality sets in.

As drinking games, poolside shenanigans, and bored flirtation absorb the crowd,
none of these people catches Rick's attention for long. Yet he cannot summon the
resolve to quit this parade of Hollywood's finest. As he wanders, fragmentary echoes of his father's voice irrupt into his consciousness. "The Pearl … somewhere
in the sea … A chaos … hungry … longing for something other without knowing
what it is." Meanwhile the party wears on into the night when another disembodied
voice intrudes, and Rick's inner hermit enters his conscious: "Dear friend, I wonder where I was in all that time, a sleepwalker." This voice confronts Rick with
his ego's faulty attitude, "In love with the world; in love with love." Immediately,
however, the cynical voice of his crass host, negates the spiritual: "The world's a
swamp. You have to fly over it high up where everything's just a speck." Rick hears
these words straight from the playboy's mouth – his boasting of a self-centred need
to rise above the stinking dung of humanity. The self-same words may help Rick
become conscious of his own callow and exploitative attitude to life by inviting
him to take a wider, objective perspective.

Judgement

The Jungian Tarot Judgement signifies the evaluation made at the end of a
tension-filled process. In this sense, judgement is about discernment which has

been hard earned through self-reflection and consciousness with the important distinction that it does not amount to a final verdict; people experience the end of many cycles in the course of a lifetime. Jesus pressed this thought home in preaching to his disciples, 'Think not that I come to send peace on earth: I came not to send peace, but a sword' (Matthew 10:34). By the sword he separated his devotees from those who loved the members of their household more. So too, the Judgement card represents the archetype of rebirth, an interim report on the soul's progress as it labours to resolve unconscious materials (Wang, 1988: 57).

The chapter opens in the present as Rick's ex-wife Nancy (Cate Blanchett) tells him, "You changed." Her words cue a passage of intricate cutting back and forth between past and present as she leads Rick step by step into painful reflections on their break-up. The voice track switches between fragments of live dialogue and their internal, whispered recollections of the joys and sorrows that each experienced in the relationship. Her need to understand the nature of their marriage and why it ended nudges the silent Rick (whose reluctance to engage in introspection is plain) into reopening the shared wound that he first inflicted and then sealed below his consciousness. Yet, as his numb face reveals, it now causes him suffering. The to-and-fro debate alternating the couple's voiced and unspoken thoughts and emotions nudges the audience toward feeling their painful reflections on their marriage as well as his own self-judgement.

"The world absorbed you," Nancy says as they walk through the studio back lot, the emblem of the realm to which he is now indifferently wed. By contrast to her purposeful professional life (as a medic tending homeless patients suffering dreadful skin diseases), he is a drifter. Their marriage too suffered from his inability to be real. She recalls, "You never really wanted to be totally inside our marriage, nor outside it either." As her words sink in, Rick remembers walking back and forth in their house unable to decide whether to stay or leave. We cannot move forward in our decisions and commitments without the ability *consciously* to suffer. To move from 'being in love' to 'being loving' is the result of attaining the development of mature dependency, the hallmark of a healthy marriage.[4]

Fog drifts over one of Los Angeles's canyons and thence out to sea as this chapter moves toward its sorrowful closure. Each of them reflects silently on their love for the other, Rick, more honest with himself than before, admits to himself, "I was afraid when I was young. Afraid of life. I'm sorry you had to pay as well." He seems to have made peace with himself and is now able to face his wife. The fog lifts, they walk and embrace on the beach while Edvard Grieg's 'Solveig's Song' bonds the characters and audience in a shared sense of loss and affection. Rick says (to himself rather than to Nancy), "My hope. You gave me peace, mercy, love, joy. Be with me, always." Not quite breaking free from his inability to speak of feelings, we imagine his inner dialogue is an homage to *both* his anima and former wife. Sitting under the flight path, they watch planes flying into and out of LAX, and Nancy says to herself, "You're still the love of my life. Should I tell you that?" Could it have led to reconciliation had they spoken? What we can surmise is that both the anima and animus in the marriage quaternity have been liberated from the shadows. A plane leaves the runway and climbs toward an unknown destination, but they have missed the flight.

Too late to save the marriage, they have withdrawn their projections and, reconciled in their mutual grieving, have reached peace.

The Tower

The inescapable twists and turns of the path that every pilgrim follows force the hopeful traveller like Bunyan's Christian to undergo painful reversals. This is Rick's fate on the next stage of his soul's uncertain journey. Everything he had lately gained in judgement he appears now to lose. His imperfect insight into the dangers of being sunk in the material world is threatened once more by its seductions; and he also drifts away from the nascent capacity to talk (if only secretly to himself) about his soul's needs. Occasionally, however, a voice offers him words of spiritual guidance unsettling his disposition which, without that intrusion, would have reinforced his attachment to the material world.

Wandering beneath glittering towers of glass and steel, Rick is ambushed by yet another powerful Hollywood agent. Like his rivals this unctuous fellow deploys flattery, assuring Rick that he has an incomparable opportunity to reward himself for his long and hard work. The temptation is, of course, crude: 'I wanna make you rich.' Rick has only to give him the nod to meet whichever industry moguls he wants. In this setting, the high towers that dwarf people walking beneath them have a cultural and economic function, symbolising vast and fashionable (albeit empty) power for these are the morally teetering edifices that hold Hollywood's agents, lawyers, executives, and placeholders.

Military towers have an older function as tall, secure posts from which soldiers can survey surrounding territory either to defend ground they possess or to launch an attack and seize land they want. The relevant Jungian Tarot card incorporates a deeply ambivalent image of an armour-plated Martial Father wielding in one hand a flaming sword with which, as avenger, he destroys the tower. In one aspect, the ruined tower can be read as an archetypal image for the destruction of a decayed, patriarchal formation of life. Conversely, it also proffers the idea of rebirth since the father is also a protector and carries in his other hand a rose (Wang, 1988: 48–9), an expression of his tenderness and connection with his feeling life. The personal connection with Rick cannot be missed when we cut to Joseph as the agent leaves Rick with his father.

At first the old man's conflicted behaviour impacts deeply on Rick. Shambling across the roof of an unimposing office tower, Joseph again rages at Rick and Barry, charging them with ingratitude for his sacrifices as a parent and blaming them for his failure in business, once again projecting his own shadow onto them. Of his sons only Rick has developed the single most essential element of *real* masculinity, which is endurance. He can now stretch to recollections of his father's tenderness flickering on the brink of consciousness when he hears the old man say, "It comes to me now how tenderly you touched my face when you were four years old." For a moment Joseph drops the sword and proffers the rose of his love, whispering a reminder that the pearl beckons everyone as both guide and god, and encouraging Rick to resume the pilgrim's journey. The son appears to be experiencing a real shift toward integration, capable of carrying the tension between his father's rage and his love. Rick's new hard-won capacity reflects his relationship to his own unconscious (the internal other) and his less personalistic defence mechanism in relationship to the external other (whether his wife or father).

Meanwhile, Rick continues to struggle with his anima projections through his compulsion to look at beautiful women. von Franz reminds us how 'A man's anima whispers to him: what is beautiful is also good. He cannot separate his feeling from aestheticism' (1996: 130). At a glamour shoot, under the gaze and lights of a camera crew, the loveliness of a model enchants him. Slow, quasi-oriental music fades in as he muses, "I had a dream. I met a woman from another world. I was taken up above the earth. I shook with fear, wonder." He approaches Helen (Freida Pinto) and spends time with her; but she, intuiting both his enchantment and his fear of relationship, shows the wisdom linked with her name by urging friendship. She acknowledges frankly that her beauty has wreaked havoc in men's lives before, and indeed Rick cannot ground Helen's numinous image in her professional life. As usual, drawn to a sexy woman whose beauty leads his mind toward the erotic, he fails to see her in a real relational way. As he continues to identify with beauty as his highest value, he remains vulnerable to seduction materially or sexually. He had paid little heed to his wife's dedication as a medical practitioner and the same pattern repeats with Helen when Malick portrays her photo shoot as hard labour imposed by a ruthless media industry. If not actually brutal, the treatment of the models is undeniably brutish. Rick's vision of Helen as a supernatural beauty is absurdly at odds with the ribald, negative animus behaviour of the shoot's female director. Setting up a butch scene for the cameraman, she hurls orders at the models like a regimental sergeant major: "Fucking make it hard. You're a dirty fucking bitch. You're a 1975 housewife who takes steroids and fucks girls." Yet while the scene registers a horrid contrast between the subtlety of a soul's inspiration and the coarseness of a manufactured illusion, Rick does not get it.

Rick and Helen become close and he wants a sexual relationship; but she demonstrates her intuitive understanding, asking rhetorically whether he wants her to weave a spell and make him dream. Dreams are nice, she says, but you can't live in them. Their time together closes as the sweet melancholy of Solveig's Song resumes, and she returns to her apartment alone. Their parting resembles Rick's from his wife except that Helen is on to Rick's fantasies and knows that an affair cannot resolve them: "There's somewhere else you need to get to." Thus, both grounded and relational, she urges him with authentic affection to seek out his own future path. Helen, named for the ancient world's most beautiful woman, acts as guide helping Rick differentiate between the erotic and the feeling life of Eros.

Fortuitously Rick now meets a woman in her middle years, a visitor to his neighbourhood. Besides being friendly and wise, she is a transient stranger, which makes it easier for him to open up to her. He brings Barry to meet her too and together they find it possible to talk about the enduring terrors imprinted in childhood when they would hide behind a rocking chair before their father got home. The woman's conversation is informal, common sense, and (appropriately coming from a mother) intended to re-insert the men in the current of life. "I hope you have children," she says, demonstrating her instinctive judgement, because parents have to worry about their kids instead of themselves. This critical encounter reflects Rick's progress in his individuation journey in redeeming 'the mother imago' by lifting her up from her unilluminated position into the light and renewing contact with her.

Rick goes home to his flat to find armed burglars turning it over. They are incredulous that he seems to possess nothing worth stealing except a television set. In the moment, the robbery does not seem to disrupt his stoicism even when he hands over cash and his jacket. Afterwards, however, he starts driving restlessly by night along endless lonely boulevards, the car's speed exaggerated as it whooshes across the city. His thoughts switch back to the long years of ruining and not living his life while, conversely, his excessive speed registers his struggle with self-regulation.

He comes to a halt in a car park, A new and intimate female voice asks, "What mood am I in? Tell me. What do I think of you? No one cares about reality anymore."

The High Priestess

Karen's (Teresa Palmer's) words cue the next chapter which opens in a steel-blue strip joint. A stripper supplies a seductive metaphor for the archetype that has the power to bare a man's unconscious to his own view. The mutual seduction between the pair has as much to do with mind as body.

Karen:	'You live in a little fantasy world, don't you?'
Rick:	'Don't you?'
Karen:	'Yes. Because it's so much more fun.'
Rick:	'Do you enjoy yours?'

Karen agrees: 'Changes every day. I can be whatever I want to be. Don't forget that. You can be whatever you want to be.'

Karen's invitation to Rick to join her "in a little fantasy world" draws him into the very realm of dreams that Helen had advised could not be lived in. But Karen is the first temptress whom Rick meets in the present rather than principally in rueful memory. As he gets drawn to her, memories of, and regretful reflections on his earlier loves impinge on his consciousness so that he has no choice but pay attention both to those memories and what Karen is to him now. The rhythm of alternation between regression and progression stirs new awareness in him of not just of her role, but also of his part in their relationship.

In Jungian terms, the High Priestess unambiguously represents both the anima and the feminine. For a woman she is a Self – figure. The imagery associated with Karen reveals characteristic polarities of the anima: she can be loving and supportive; conversely, she can be deceptive and cruel (Wang, 1988: 21). Apropos, while flirting in the strip club with Rick, Karen notices "a little shadow" in him; but in the early stages of their dalliance it is the imagination's freedom that captures them both. Next morning Karen meets Rick in a diner and exuberantly he carries her across the street, deposits her in a shopping trolley, and wheels her away. He has paid for the object, so carries her off. He is living a fantasy that Karen inspires but fails to intuit that she is leading him on another kind of shopping trip as they head off for Las Vegas.

To help him enter the new life she has in mind for him, she tells him that drugs have opened up what she calls her Window of Truth, murmuring "Real life's so hard to find." A repeated low-angle shot of palms lining Venice Beach recalls Rick's dizzy notion that these trees promise everyone they can achieve what they want in LA, while Karen is telling him his mind is a theatre so he should get high as she does to enter this world of fantasy. Now revealing herself as a *puella aeterna* she mirrors Rick's escapism back to him, and the wandering Knight drinks once more from the alluring cup of unconscious temptation. "Then I fell back asleep," he remembers, "Sing for me. Dream another dream."

As Rick and Karen approach Las Vegas in his convertible, the radio picks up a priest quoting Psalm 104, celebrating the creator and his work "who laid the foundations of the Earth that it should not be removed forever." These words fade as they enter the ghastly city of fake architecture, its mock antiquity desecrated in the service of excess, less dreamland than nightmare. Soon Karen, flaunting an expensive fur coat and boots, boasts that Rick's money proves his love, while Rick's inner ear is filled by a voice inciting him to indulge greed: "And the world held up a mirror. Here. Take the things you want. They can be yours."

At this moment, Gielgud returns with Bunyan's words when Christian, trapped in Doubting-Castle, finds a belated moment of clarity.

> What a fool am I, thus to lie in a stinking dungeon, when I may as well walk at liberty. I have a key in my bosom called promise, that will (I am persuaded) open any lock in Doubting-Castle.
>
> (Bunyan, 1768: 156)

Christian's dungeon recalls Karen titillating Rick by closing him in a cage. Now those images act like forewarnings as she leads Rick past displays of wealth for which people enchain themselves. The pair drift on into a druggy, nightmarish world of endless partying where Karen disappears into the crowd, her function in immersing Rick in an increasingly poisonous fantasy world now displaced onto sinister masked revellers. As anima woman, utterly transformed now into a succession of nightmarish figures, she aims to take total possession of him. As we have mentioned, Esther Harding says that such women

> conquer men not for love of the man, but for a craving to gain power over him. They cannot love, they can only desire. They are cold-blooded, without human

feeling or compassion. Instinct in its daemonic form, entirely non-human, lives through them.

(1990: 118)

As Rick is sucked through a peripatetic theatre of drugged perversion (does he recall Karen telling him his mind is a theatre?), the anima reveals herself in grisly emblems. A woman floats upside down in a jar, like a pickled corpse. A man dressed as a skeleton wrestles with another figure and then mocks with a grotesque rictus the death of a murderer in an electric chair. Sombre chords juxtapose dancers' hectic movements while, suspended far overhead, another female endlessly repeats a ghastly routine. Buckling like a human chrysalis caught in mid-air, she sheds a tightly wrapped shroud again and again, but never finds life as a butterfly.

At last Rick's mind struggles to break free from its dazed satiation. "Go!" it instructs him, but he asks "Where?" and then "How do I reach you?" While tawdry light and firework displays close the Las Vegas sequence, Rick's mind leaps away from this meaningless scene and offers him the gift he asked for. He is gazing across wide salt flats in Death Valley focussing on a lone rock. It is a way marker, distinctive as any signpost Bunyan might have wanted to point out the road ahead; but for Rick it hints at the psyche's mysterious landscape without as yet mapping it.

Anima

It is worth reminding ourselves that when Rick almost literally first stumbles over Karen, he appears to be frozen in his emotions, a state of mind that mirrors his professional lack of vitality. As a writer of feature films, he must deal in fantasy; but nobody mentions his past scripts except to praise their success as money-spinners. His work has nothing worthy of remark be it in storylines, characterisation, aesthetics, the power to touch emotions, or offer spiritual, cultural, or psychological revelation. Nothing. Rick's powers of fantasising for the screen have hitherto been tepid compared with the barbarous scenes into which Karen and her fellow demons have led him. Could it be, as we hinted earlier, that the memories he is recovering, along with self-knowledge and augmented curiosity are awakening the dormant writer in him?

We have already noted that the role of the anima, like that of the animus, features significantly in the hard work of individuation. Both are representations of the internal psychic reality embodied in the opposite sex and thus are transformational figures. It follows that the anima, the soul image which the male experiences is an element in his own psyche and has to remain merciful if it is to redeem his inner femininity and soulfulness. As Jung pointed out, it is formed in part by the male's personal as well as archetypal experience of the feminine. Rick's anima, which has most recently found expression in Karen's character, is a product of genuine experience of the nature of the feminine. In the process of his gradual self-discovery, and as the most potent manifestation yet of his anima, she is the vehicle par excellence of the transformative character. For the anima is the mover, the instigator of change whose fascination drives, lures, and encourages the male to all the adventures of the soul and spirit, of action and creation in the inner and outer world (Neumann, 1963: 33).

The stripper's transformation from seductively inviting representation of the feminine to her repulsive embrace of excess, horror, and death has to do with anima's links to the release of contents (not only personal but archetypal) in the unconscious. We have already encountered several instances of women who reveal the workings of Rick's unconscious. The stereotype (as opposed to the archetype) resides in the typical roles required by Hollywood and presented to global audiences as ideals for womanhood. Instances abound in the young women who frequent Rick's milieu of exquisite physical perfection – the actors, would-be actors, models, and others – whose images Hollywood's bland fantasies stultify. To help the further evolution of consciousness, a man has to go into complete introversion, meet his own anima, and engage with his soul. In this milieu, Karen is rightly tagged as anima and high priestess. The road of excess leads to the palace of wisdom.

Death

When the Tarot card for death evolved so as to express Jungian themes, its original, literal meaning developed additional connotations. Readings of this card now reinforce those discovered elsewhere in the Jungian Tarot. A skeleton bearing a scythe in one hand and an hour-glass in the other continues to occupy the foreground, but a female figure stands behind death, her arms reaching out to embrace the traveller. Her presence implies a return to the Great Mother in that she who once bore the child stands ready to receive it again when life comes to an end. The card can also be read as signifying an unending cycle in which death precedes rebirth, and this sits well with the Jungian idea that a major phase of life must draw to an end in order that another may begin (see Wang, 1988: 42–3). death and rebirth in this sense can follow an overwhelming intervention of the anima such as Rick has just experienced. Those observations notwithstanding, it would be a mistake to presume that this card has become wholly detached from its original, literal meaning.

A coyote slinks out of a well-groomed garden and Rick follows it on foot down a suburban road. A measure of stealth befits a man who has a married woman Elizabeth (Natalie Portman) as his secret lover. Both are overwhelmed by the madness of new love, as when they rush fully clothed into the ocean with a full-throated church organ roaring on their ecstasy. Rick murmurs, "So this is what we are, a fire." They spend long hours wrapped blissfully in each other, locking out of their minds everything else (including her marriage). However, most affairs are caught in the lovers' inability to make a decision about their future while they remain merged in the honeymoon phase of their relationship. Indeed, their time passes in delight until Rick asks Elizabeth to marry and is shocked that she cannot look him in the eye. He pleads with her not to wreck her life locked into a failed relationship; but he is mistaken, and infidelity is not the main cause of Elizabeth's diffidence.

She has conceived and, not knowing whether Rick or her husband is the father, has secretly terminated the pregnancy. The torment of a double grief takes hold of the lovers, their relationship sundered agonisingly beneath the burden of a death which haunts them both. The Judgement Card looms once again in the shadows of connection and separation and the unborn life reflects the depth of their unconscious entanglement.

A brief scene follows poignantly recalling one in *The Tree of Life* where the heavily pregnant Mrs O'Brien clad in white linen leads the souls of infants yet unborn along the river of life. One of them will come into the world as Jack, her firstborn. Now, in *Knight of Cups* Malick allows fleeting glimpses into an uncanny, mist-filled house. A little girl in a ghostly white dress plays with a tangled puppet, preparing a miniature show for another figure in white linen, possibly the spirit who would have become her mother had the pregnancy run full term. A sorrowful adagio is heard and from outside this scene, watching intently, Rick whispers, "Forgive me!" As a ghostly notation of rejected motherhood, Elizabeth's fate is not too different from Ruth's, the woman who might have become her mother-in-law.

Alone again in Death Valley, Rick (lost in scrub, aloes, and grief) perceives that people have love inside them that they cannot express. The desolate landscape becomes the recipient of his sorrow but, though his tears fall, he cannot yet find what he is looking for. At home Joseph kneels and prays for God's mercy and in his heart addresses his elder son, "I know you have a soul." He seeks help from a priest (Armin Mueller-Stahl) who, albeit in compassionate tones, delivers the harsh Catholic teaching that God shows his love by sending humans suffering; and that suffering binds them to something higher than themselves, higher than their own will: "We are not only to endure patiently the troubles he sends, we are to regard them as gifts." Putting this in terms addressing psychological development rather than personal morality, Jung concedes, 'As always, every step forward along the path of Individuation is achieved only at the cost of suffering' (1954: 411). Joseph's suffering has by no means ended: Barry, incandescent with rage, returns to the family home and attacks his father.

Despite the implacable tensions in the family, Ruth has maintained the unused dining table as the centre where the family should gather and share time together over their food. Barry's anger explodes in this room where, shattering a flower vase and smashing furniture, he wrecks her last symbolic place in the family, leaving Joseph clutching broken gladioli while Rick tries to clear the debris. Out on the street beyond the house, the camera tracks a shabbily dressed woman. Her face never in frame, she shambles along, one hand clenched behind her back. Ruth, cast out by her menfolk, with nowhere to go and her humanity denied, seeks refuge from the hell they have made. The camera tracks in on the unbolted door of a garden shed.

Recovery from this trauma is not easy for the men. Down in the all-but-dry concrete channel of the Los Angeles River, Barry doubles up in anguish while Rick tries to comfort him. And soon Rick reverts to wandering across the city, asking himself how to begin repairing the rupture with his father. Once again, he meanders in Death Valley, gazing at the magnificence of the barren landscape while in his head calling on his father to give him courage and strength. Joseph, equally distracted, wanders around suburban streets. Eventually Rick returns to the house, but Barry does not accompany him. Rick and his father embrace when the old man acknowledges that Rick has surpassed him, finally able to welcome that as 'the way it's supposed to be.' The father's (senex) state of unreflecting awareness now surrenders to the son's (puer/knight) ability to reflect by means of gains in consciousness. Both men have achieved an increased ability to discriminate (revealing why the judgement card is critical in the process of individuation). They have brought the Puer/Senex Archetype into closer relationship and healed the split on both a personal and archetypal level.

As interpreted by von Franz, the prince or knight is a reconciling personality far superior to those people who fight with each other, being beyond such conflict and representing a superior being in himself, namely that true personality which differs from the persona with which he had formerly been identical (1999: 321). The climax of this scene thus resides in the sacral formula "I and the father are one." Rick is not a hero who transforms the world, but a hero/prince who transforms himself by atonement. The healing of the split between himself and Joseph brings a return to a loving relationship, their embrace counterpointing the sight of Barry mooching alone and directionless around street corners. Finally, the latter drifts out of frame, the injuries that rack him unresolved and the burden Joseph imposed on his other sons more than either could bear. Barry's moving off the scene indicates that Rick no longer stands in opposition to his shadow. When this occurs, his anima is no longer contaminated by the shadow which now lives in the archetypal realm where she belongs and becomes his guide and psychopomp.

We asked earlier whether the archetypal heroism implicit in the fable of the king lies beyond the grasp of both Joseph and Rick. When the dual aspect of an archetype has been polarised and split, a problem of one-sidedness occurs in the unconscious realm of the ego structure and there a fundamental negativity may occur. The archetypal core of the complex loses its inherent tension and necessary ambivalence. This unconscious energy creates a great vulnerability in the personality organisation and diminishes the amount of psychic energy available to creative conscious living. At some developmental time in the male's life he is not going to be able to bear the weight any longer. In our story, the father has demanded that his sons should take life onward where their parent was unable to go, unaware that the greatest burden a child can carry is to live the unlived life of a parent. But the myth is clear. Joseph, unable to change in the face of his family crisis, presents a traditional collective disposition. As a figure having a certain inertia unwilling to change in the face of crisis, it prefers to sacrifice the future, the child, seeking to acquire only enough energy to persist in its intransigence.

If Rick is now emerging as the urge within the collective unconscious toward building a new dominant of collective consciousness, he must (as the maker of a new king) become a symbol both for his father's future possibility and for what his father has loved most in the world. We must keep in mind that Joseph has not died as the king but has quietly abdicated from the extroverted world. The psychological equivalent of this is the integration of the Self through the conscious assimilation of split-off contents in the unconscious. Self-Recollection, which Rick has been undergoing since he first accepted that he did not know himself, is indeed a gathering together of the Self.

Freedom

Thousands of people are enjoying a clear day on Santa Monica beach, swimming, playing games, and relaxing while from a footbridge Rick overlooks the scene and the lanes of packed traffic that move slowly along the Pacific Highway. But these sights are not his prime focus: a blond woman seen here for the first time is cavorting next to him on the overhead walkway. This is Isabel (Isabel Lucas).

This final chapter is not linked with a specific Tarot card; nor does it deliver our twenty-first-century Pilgrim to the gates of heaven at its denouement as Bunyan did with his seventeenth-century Christian. Yet, since reconciling with his father, Rick has found the first of two human guides, the old king, whose remembered voice again advises him, "Find the light you know in the east. As a child … The moon, the stars, they serve you, they guide you on your way. The light in the eyes of others. The pearl."

Rick's other guide, his anima, now lives where she belongs. Not entwined with the shadow in the realm of his personal unconscious but in the archetypal domain. As we have stated, if a man is capable of integrating the anima, something archetypal is gained in the realm of his humanity. And this is his new partner. Everything about his life with Isabel suggests illumination, peace, and beauty. He is no longer the *puer aeternus* stuck in boyhood; nor does Joseph remain locked to the *senex* archetype. Rick is free to explore the world and himself more completely as Isabel calls him to renew his life: "Turn! Look! Come out!" Together they fashion an authentic relationship in which each of them leaves space for the other to thrive while finding their pearl, the light in the other's eyes to guide them on their way. The audience senses the freedom in their loving bond through paired emblems that link the wild and the domestic. For example, in their yard a trained bougainvillea cleaves to an inner wall, displaying vivid pink beauty. Yet while their spacious house shelters them it also opens lines of sight and entices them out to naturally weird boulders shaping the land around them. As a couple Rick and Isabel inhabit the world vigorously. Whether clambering over rocks in the Californian desert, wondering at the spreading vista of a wind farm, or playing relaxed games of tennis, these shared pleasures draw Rick away from his familiar world-weariness. In exploring nature, the couple find spirit in it, a discovery which embraces the sense that they are part of the whole.

As Brody notes, the main incidents in Rick's life have been his relationships with women (2016). More than physical attractiveness alone, Isabel's mystical being is, to mention just one characteristic, expressed gorgeously through her subtle movements when she swims alone at night in their illuminated pool. Fundamentally, however, it is Rick who has changed as a consequence of learning more about himself. Joseph's final exhortation to "Find ... the light in the eyes of others. The pearl," has released his son to see Isabel more completely and in her own right rather than (citing John Berger in altered context) clothing her in his own desires and needs as he had his past lovers. Now, in knowing Isabel, Rick experiences genuine synchronicity 'always an arresting and numinous experience, and there-fore ... *sacred* knowledge' (Mansfield, 2002: 135).

Knight of Cups draws to a close as the newly confident Rick says to himself, begin! Once more we see him drive into Death Valley, this time climbing across boulders to a hilltop below which the wide spread of salt flats lies open. Cumu-latively his visits to Death Valley amount to elements of a single journey.[5] The intermittent rhythm with which these fragments punctuate Rick's inner journey of the soul hints at a key concept of Jung's, namely the circumambulation of the Self. It is this slow but intense penetration of the unconscious maze that brings Rick that moment of synchronicity, simultaneous meaningful linkage that connects in his psyche the beauty of his lover's eyes, the joy of living, and the realisation that he is part of a whole, a shock that is felt as participation with the divine.

Whether Rick travels to Death Valley before, during, or after the pressure of his memories of women gains his conscious attention, the audience can only speculate. However, we can see now that had he not gained insights from the feminine, he would have been lost forever like his brothers. As, not without pain as well as joy, we share Rick's gathering conscious and unconscious impressions, we may begin to recognise his achievement as a model for today's pilgrim. While Bunyan's honest fellow was directed infallibly by his Bible, the many voyagers today who do not accept the old route maps of the orthodox faiths must find their own individual ways to approach understanding of the Self. Perhaps the broad-est path for the many people, male and female, caught in the toils of antiquated patriarchal orders, is found in the psycho-social shifts in Western culture that are leading us toward the revitalization of the feminine principle, with its promise of a new vibrant zeitgeist.

Rick's painstaking search guides him on his Bunyanesque path by means of a variety of way markers, some human, others objects, and (as in Las Vegas) oth-ers again being phantoms. Some assist this present-day pilgrim as he searches for his goal and others flatter to deceive. His long journey enriches his life and fur-thers his individuation; but it is confined to the Earth, reaching no higher than a skyscraper's top nor lower than the parched depths of Death Valley's seabed. As the film's writer and director, Malick takes us higher and nourishes the collective psyche with a reminder of the Earth's place in the planetary system. At its most dra-matic, his camera vouchsafes a glimpse of the emerald serpent and makes instantly, brilliantly clear what Rick slowly discovers in the terrible beauty of Death Valley. When the worlds of the personal and transpersonal in *Knight of Cups* are regis-tered as an entity, the film invites us to reflect on the profound significance of our co-existence with our planetary environment.

Notes

1 von Franz summarised Jung's account of marriage and argued that there were four people in every relationship, conscious to conscious and unconscious to unconscious (1993: 77–8).
2 Malick's exquisite relationship to his own anima expresses itself through his lyrical, reflective style as a director.
3 Joseph, the insatiable python, sets at nought the emerald serpent that cherishes the Earth.
4 W. R. D. Fairbairn's object relations model of development considers real relationships to be more important than fantasised relationships for emotional development. He considered development as progressing along a continuum, the last stage typified by an interpersonal life that reflects the inner life, characterised by reciprocity, the recognition of differences, and the acceptance of healthy dependence (1952: ix, 145).
5 His clothes are the same each time we see him there.

Chapter 6

Song to Song

Kiss to Kiss

Throughout much of his life Jung courageously explored the mystery of love and regarded human relationship as the key experience toward its realisation. In *Memories, Dreams, Reflections* he comments on the daunting task of trying to find the language which would adequately express its paradoxical nature. The opposite blend of positive and negative, trust and fear, attraction and repulsion, hope and doubt, demand reconciliation for those on the path of love and individuation. Jung did not think of real love in its connotation of desire, but as something beyond the individual, something far superior that included the meaning of wholeness. He writes that "Love alone is useless if it does not also have understanding. And for the proper use of understanding a wider consciousness is needed, and a higher standpoint to enlarge one's horizon" (Jung, 1983: 391). In *Song to Song*, we explore the mutual individuation of two main characters and the undeniable value of love experiences in its ultimate achievement.

Tommaso Priviero has written carefully researched commentaries on Jung's inauguration of what became a detailed exploration of Dante's experiences of the human soul. Priviero notes that in December 1913, Jung had copied in his *Black Books* two entries from the *Purgatorio*. In translation, the first celebrates Dante's submission to Love (Priviero, 2018: 44).

> I am one who, when Love
> Breathes on me, notices, and in the manner
> That he dictates within, I utter words.
>
> (Dante, *Purgatorio*: XXIV, 52–54)

The second extract is concerned with the nature of the soul and the intellect.

> And then, in the same manner as a flame
> Which follows the fire whatever shape it takes,
> The new form follows the spirit exactly.
>
> (Dante, *Purgatorio*: XXV, 97–99)

When Priviero investigates Dante's (and prior to him Virgil's) epics, they might appear at first sight to leave Jung's assertion unsupported that he had never been

DOI: 10.4324/9781003545538-7

able to explain what love is. Jung had, however, recognised from childhood and reported in *Memories, Dreams, Reflections* that he had two personalities, one associated with ego consciousness and the second connected to the realm of the depths.

Jung looked at the *Commedia* in a meditative and pragmatic manner, starting from the conviction of a profound analogy between the experience described through the *Commedia* and his own visionary self-explorations at the time of *Liber Novus*. The original difficulties he grapples with before the startling psychic material that he comes across, led him to describe his experiences as a descent to Hell, or a katabasis (Jung, *Liber Novus*: 237).

Priviero elaborates (2020: 69) on Jung's recognition that "Dante's role begins to play a crucial part" which evolves into an illustrious model for a medieval visit to Hell, an aspect which Jung puts on centre stage in *Liber Secundus* where he makes the majestic claim,

> An opus is needed, that one can squander decades on, and do it out of necessity. I must catch up with the Middle Ages – within myself. We have only just finished with the Middle Ages – of others. I must begin early in that period when the hermits died out. […] My I, you are a barbarian. I want to live with you, therefore I will carry you through an utterly medieval Hell, until you are capable of making living with you bearable. You should be the vessel and womb of life, therefore I shall purify you. The touchstone is being alone with oneself. This is the way.
>
> (Jung, *Liber Secundus*: 330)

Priviero makes the further point that the *Commedia* is not solely an account of the katabasis, but becomes above all a reference to the anabasis, the return from Hell. It is therefore the victorious counterpart to the time of the descent (2020: 70). Jung himself claimed in *Psychological Types* (1971: §376–7) that the birth of modern individualism would have originated with a medieval element, since the worship of the woman meant worship of the soul as in Dante's love for Beatrice, her image evolving into 'a figure that has detached itself from the object and become the personification [which Jung] termed the *anima*'.

Thus, with the aid of Jung's insight and Marie-Louise von Franz's summary of Jung's conception of the four levels of love, we hope to shed light on the human quest to know love. Elaborating further with the help of the cinematic imagery in *Song to Song*, we give language to what is at the core of all human love, namely the archetypes of the Self and the *coniunctio* with its greater emphasis on feeling. As the culmination of the archetype of love, the conscious and the unconscious along with the masculine and feminine unite.

Von Franz provides the following psychological summary of Jung's four levels (2006: 42):

1 Archaic identity or *participation mystique.*
2 Mutual projections.
3 Human relationship.
4 Eternal union through fate.

Faye (Rooney Mara), a young woman still in her twenties, opens *Song to Song* by introducing herself, thinking not of the present but her past. "I went through a period when sex had to be violent. I was desperate to feel something." Nothing felt real to her. "Every kiss felt like half of what it should be." At that time in her life, she had rejected her feelings and consequently a part of her life. She thought she needed to know the right people, to get close to them, and show them what she wanted. An obviously attractive woman, when Faye reveals what she needs to the people whom she gets to know, she has a good chance that those needs will be satisfied insofar as she has succeeded in manipulating them. She has told herself, in short, that she needs experience: and any experience is better than none. Reflecting the first level of love; archaic identity is a natural state in which one is immersed in the belief that things are just as we experience them. We don't recognise what we have been "swimming in" until we are out of the unconscious waters of *participation mystique.* The film commences where Faye begins to work out her projections onto her love relationships. In the stages of love mentioned above, her honest reflections provide a platform for the viewer's own projections and the complexities involved in the unending hardships of love relationships. The opening of the film is really an image of the *uroboros*, beginning in her reflections on her past and ending with her eventual realisation of her love experiences.

There is more in this vein but all in all it amounts to an uncertain framework on which to organise her life so that it serves her dreams to sing her song. Unfortunately, she appears not to know in what direction she wants those dreams to pull her. She has since her teenage years had a lover and thinks coolly of their relationship in transactional terms: "I thought he could help me. I paid my dues." Faye's confession reflects a passionate love which serves only the demands of the ego whose aims are self-centred rather than being a genuine love for another person. Real love can only be experienced by ending the unconscious *participation mystique* originating in family relationships. Faye seems to mean what she says when she first speaks of this relationship, but the terms she uses take on changing meanings according to what at any given juncture the audience understand about her lover's altering behaviour toward her. There is a question which we eventually notice that Faye has left unasked and which relates to what she wants to achieve that is more precisely focused than "I wanted to live, sing my song."

The film soon switches away from Faye's hesitant observations about her youth. It cuts abruptly to footage of boorish fellows surging back and forwards in slow-motion across a dusty square in front of a stage from which a rant incites the crowd ... "We don't answer to no one ... We make our own rules ... warrior style!" It is a moot point whether these goons are drunk, high, raving, or fighting each other. To the last man for sure they share an aggressive masculinity which remains a constant despite the superficial distinctions between their uncouth swarming and the scene to which we soon shift at a pool party being extravagantly hosted by Cook, a wealthy music producer-cum-playboy (Michael Fassbender). Here the bored elite circulate and make a pretence of admiring their host and the vanities that he is showing off at this, his annual party. It is a scene that plainly invokes Logos (the masculine principle celebrating the ruling dynamism of control and power) as holding the upper hand over Eros, the feminine principle of relatedness. We shall discover in due course that Eros needs to be freed from the *dividing* clutches of Logos psychology and must learn how the power of unconscious motives carries a profound limit on the actions of free choice. The Eros principle *combines* the opposites and creates a genuine attitude toward love as a real psycho-spiritual reality that embraces the feminine principle. Logos joined with Eros is needed to reach wholeness.

David Jenkins identifies Fassbender's character Cook as a recurrent figure in Malick's filmography.

> Like Sam Shepard's farmer in 1978's *Days of Heaven*, Christian Bale's John Rolfe in 2005's *The New World*, and half the characters in 2015's *Knight of Cups*, Cook is a Mephisthophelean archetype, holding out the promise of material satisfaction and worldly wealth, jamming up the desire of living "kiss to kiss, song to song" (as Mara's character puts it). He is the snake spoiling the Garden of Eden. To drive the point home, Malick shows him buying drugs off a man inked up like a reptile, and slithering across the bedroom floor on his belly following a sexual bacchanal with two unnamed women.
>
> (2017)

One of Cook's guests at his extravagant party, BV (Ryan Gosling), is a songwriter and musician whom we have glimpsed earlier walking among festival goers while musing on the need to sing and help people by lifting their hearts. In that respect, he might represent a helper who seems to have the capacity to free Eros from the control of a one-sided masculine attitude that does not know how to relate to feelings and emotions. Now meandering among Cook's guests, BV is like a distant musical cousin to another singer, Patti Smith, whom we shall later hear performing in the Austin music festival. Cook wants to persuade BV to release a record on his label and is enticing him with various blandishments. No question but money is likely to be the main temptation. Another, seemingly frivolous attraction, centres on what Cook boasts of as his "Doctor," a ceramic jug making its annual appearance charged with a mysterious and inebriating liquor. Constantly urging onward a musician whom he intends should make money for him, Cook asks if BV likes the people at the party and then, playing the ever-ready entrepreneur, tells him to introduce himself to them. When BV demurs, saying he doesn't know the folk in question, Cook whispers to one of the beauties loitering by his swimming pool telling her to strip off and dive in, she does so immediately. In effect it seems an entirely pointless instruction: it may make the boss man feel empowered but has no impact on any of the guests.

That said, there is another undeclared temptation on offer to BV, namely Faye herself. It has become noticeable that we are dealing with love in its initial form of desire or concupiscence, the primary agent in the process of transformation. Desire comprises a spectrum that ranges from physical sexual exploits on one end of the scale to spiritual contents on the other. Concupiscence implies joy, appetite, lust, pleasure, and a blend of instinctual and fleshly desire. Although neither Faye nor Cook has mentioned their relationship, we learn in due course that from the age of 16 or 17 she worked for him as his receptionist. At some point in time they had become lovers, which they still are. Their relationship portrays a 'perversion of Eros,' desire that includes only one side of the spectrum and mainly satisfies the need for pleasure. That noted, at Cook's party, BV and Faye (who may be following her boss's instructions) quickly become acquainted when she drifts up unassumingly beside him and offers to share with him La Shun Pace's searing gospel track on her headphones.

In the opening moments of *Song to Song*, the audience has become familiar with Faye's dark hair. Now, however, when she and BV meet alongside Cook's long pool, Faye is wearing a blond wig. Her alternately dark and bright-haired wigs have unmissable archetypal associations. This gives us an image of female completeness. However, their stark contrast indicates an inner disunity, a split in her personality that must undergo a process of discrimination and integration. Integrating these opposites will protect her from the dangers of a one-sided idealisation of the feminine. Faye's alternation between dark and light-haired wig is a personification of the Eros principle. The struggle between light and darkness runs through the narrative of the film. The dark hair implies depth in thought and reflects the unconscious; blond hair indicates brightness of thought and consciousness. The couple's meeting is so casual, it might be a chance encounter, but it leaves unanswered (given the assiduity with which the promoter is pursuing the musician) a troubling question whether Faye's lover-cum-employer is using her as the bait with whom to hook BV. Jenkins notes that

> *Song to Song* exemplifies [Malick's] unique and ultra-sensual mode of montage-based storytelling, where human characters are constantly submerged in an endless, glowing stream of consciousness. Here, the eyes are not the only window to the soul – the twitch of the hand, a twist of the neck, the accelerated breathing pattern can also offer vital signs of life. The eyes are less important than what those eyes are looking at, and who's looking back.
>
> (2017)

We would add to Jenkins' own observational eye that the sightless and unmet aspects of Malick's characters are frequently in need of healing. Malick's inner insights keep us alert to the erratically emerging relationship between Eros and Logos.

The unpredictable construction of these early scenes therefore bears mention because (not atypically of several films written and directed by Malick), unexpected aspects of their aesthetic organisation draw attention to themselves. In these early scenes, to return to one example previously mentioned, the presence and organised chaos of the rioting males are difficult to locate in the narrative structure.

Faye and BV soon find themselves enjoying each other's company. Before long he's asking whether she has a boyfriend, adding, to cover possible embarrassment on her part, that she can tell him whatever she wants, even a complete lie. Faye is shrewd (or we should probably say *experienced*) enough not to respond to this jejune offer, not least because she has just been seen lying in Cook's arms. Soon BV drives the young woman out beyond the city limits to a place she has not been before. Nothing could be more different from the bald slopes of grey granite that, with their attendant massive boulders might just as plausibly be found in the Matopos hills of Zimbabwe as within reach of Austin, Texas. Excited by the rawness of the scene and the contrast between the rough landscape and the immaculate cityscape they have left behind, BV and Faye (no blond wig now) tear around like children splashing through puddles, a scene that will return to each of their minds more than once. Their play is wild with the authentic exhilaration that these natural scenes licence in contrast with the meticulous formality of every element in Cook's design, whether of his garden or the immaculate house.

Soon, driving back toward the city's outskirts, the couple find themselves coming within earshot of a crowd whose wild chanting fills the air. The great singer Patti Smith exhorts the crowd to applaud themselves: "You are the future, and the future is now!" We interpret this as a synchronistic moment that underlines the meaning of what not only the couple have come across unexpectedly, but also the crowd who have just experienced it, not only in terms of present time, but some unknown potential that it may hold.

As scenes briskly follow one another, the barest outlines of connections between characters begin to emerge. At home, Cook fucks Faye, but although she accepts his advances, she is not greatly aroused by his dominating nature. Is by any chance BV's warmer personality now tending to exert the greater attraction on her? As von Franz succinctly writes, "the worst obstacle in the way of human relationship is the power complex, the wish to conquer or possess the other person" (2006: 43). In other words, what we are witnessing could be the nascent beginnings of a transformational "enantiodromia" (the reversal of an extreme into its psychological opposite) in her life.

Faye's father (Brady Coleman) visits her in the city and buys her lunch. Faye is by no means emotionally as close to him as he would like to feel; nor does she warm to his suggestion that her parents should make a visit to the city together. Her indifference hurts him, and he is reduced to probing for information about how she organises her life. Her reluctance to share information confirms the man's sense that his daughter carries significant angst about their relationship. Family relations are awkward: on the one hand, she readily admits to having a boyfriend who is a big earner in the music business; but on the other, she will not name him nor will she respond to her father's inquiry whether she trusts the man. We recognise that her intimate relationships are mired in projections. From a psychological point of view, "projections spring from family patterns, transference of mother and father, brother and sister images, creating dark and unrealistic erotic attractions filled with infantile demands and prejudices." Jung couldn't emphasise enough that "one should, as far as possible, withdraw all projections in life. They make life poor and steal libido" (von Franz, 2006: 71). It is left to the audience to do what the father cannot and interpret these mixed signals: the big earner is of course Cook and not conceivably BV. The signs are that Faye's emotions are being tugged this way and that between one established lover and another revealing that she is caught in a powerful love problem. Faye's emotional entanglements indicate the unconscious factor represented by the stark contrast in wigs that we have already mentioned and which she must fully experience to resolve. As the chief source of consciousness, Faye's *emotions* indicate that an unconscious factor has been split and needed to be experienced with both men. Cook represents the authoritarian father figure who will give her financial security while BV stands in for the mother who can offer love and connection. Meanwhile, Faye is too embarrassed to acknowledge that she gains little income from her work: showing vacant apartments to would-be lessors and walking dogs, she exposes her lack of self-worth and idealistic puella psychology. The dark puella falls into the shadow. However, when integrated psychic space is created for the animus to develop, a spiritualised femininity will grow.

Faye and BV take increasing delight in each other's company and divide their time between her work showing apartments and her persistent attraction to dreams of a fantasy existence. "I thought we could just roll and tumble," she murmurs to him, "living from song to song, kiss to kiss." To complement her wild imaginings, BV paints her face, and they play lovers' games, switching clothes to amuse themselves. Does this scene represent a perpetual state of childish delusion about themselves? Disconcertingly, out of the blue and among her declarations of love, she drops in a few words of warning advising him not to trust her. When BV asks why not, Faye hesitates before covering her tracks crudely by announcing that she just wants him to be careful. Hesitation is becoming a telling feature of these new and intimate conversations: it seems that her desires are running in alternating streams. Warning BV reveals her genuine feelings of affection for him as well as her capacity to be self-reflective and honest with herself. However, she has not acquired all the experiences she needs to achieve the self-knowledge necessary to trust herself. Faye's are not the only relationships coming under strain.

One afternoon Cook and BV are lounging around the rich man's house and garden. Because of the Puer type of man's fundamental need to be free, they are typically not well grounded. As a type of personality, they fly high and shy away from anything that requires some perceived permanent level of responsibility. Although he is talented and creative, BV's resistance to being 'tied down' has blocked him from having stable relationships and financial success. One sided, he suffers from a power complex and must find a way to reclaim his power if he is to mature. In contrast, Cook in the role of senex has gained mastery over the material world but can only make a profit from buying or stealing another man's creativity. The contrast between the two men displays the truth that when one does not have a healthy relationship to money, one lacks a healthy relationship with the world. Once again Cook works over the younger man's plain resistance, seeking to persuade him to make a record for release on his company's label. Opting for power play (Cook's habitual way of proceeding) he tempts BV to make more money than he has ever done by promising that whatever BV wants, he can make it happen. Does he want costly sunglasses or jackets like Cook's own expensive clothing? And as BV jokingly switches jackets with him, Cook asks (not exactly in jest), "Do you want to be me?" Cook's primal instincts successfully seduce BV's unconscious drives as he "tries on" the persona of the other man when they exchange jackets. Like a shark, Cook goes for blood, smelling BV's talent as somewhere more money and power can be made. Then, flaunting his wealth, he throws in what he intends to be a killer punch, announcing his intention to dispose of his exquisite, contemporary house. "It's *all* for sale. I don't like it. It's all the same." The impresario's indifference to affecting an attachment to the beauty of the pile he possesses shocks BV. With these dismissive words, Cook reveals his power shadow that has complete disregard for anything 'other'. It helps us understand that the shadow cannot think in paradoxes, thereby making him incapable of being psychological. His flippant attitude toward women, men, or material things exposes his only aim, which is to be on top. The need for relationship is completely irrelevant.

Indeed, everything is by no means as serene in this paradise as its perfect architecture and immaculate garden suggest. Coincidentally, Faye finds herself advising Cook that he has too much pride, a sentiment to which her lover responds sardonically that he had always thought pride was a good thing.

As if emphasising the tensions concealed by visitors to Cook's opulent mansion, a furious woman suddenly picks up her handbag and strides out of the building without warning. Witnessing this, Faye comments that in her own experience people who spend time in Cook's company often change (indeed she admits that she has done so too) and the spectator may conclude that Cook has aroused the unknown woman's anger. Faye's observation is a testament to the psychological reality that where passion and attraction are involved, both parties are affected. In fact, however, that would be to jump to the wrong conclusion because Cook is actually brooding on aspects of BV's character that we have not yet encountered: "He leaves us alone this way because he wants to be free. All his life he's tried to get free. He doesn't know how." Cook's financial interest lies in securing BV's monetary commitment to him, so it should make it worth Faye's time to check that he has been representing the musician's personality accurately. Later that same evening, BV having left Faye and Cook alone, the latter is seducing Faye and making demeaning comments about her and BV. "You aren't who you think you are. He doesn't love you [whereas] I like you this way." Faye responds to Cook sexually, but by no means joyfully. The violent lovemaking that she spoke formerly of needing still seems to have its hold over her so, while roaming in Cook's garden after having had sex with him, she decides to continue with that relationship as it is: "I wanted to be free the way he was. I went on seeing him. I let myself be smashed." Rooted in desire or concupiscence, emotional relationships may become contaminated by coercion and constraint. Expectations swathed in projections become a burden for the partners, making both feel unfree. What dark denizens in her psyche is she projecting onto Cook that she is willing to suffer for? She has a fantasy that by making brutal contact she will find freedom. "Erotic, relational energies can urge conscious realization, if one can face the reality that is projected into a "You," and discern its primal source ... Love could be mercurial agent of the *coniunctio*" (Owens, 2015: 23). Owens's realization here draws directly on Jung's reflections on the emotional struggle of all humans to free themselves from existing fetters. However, to achieve such an open state of experience (both interior and exterior), requires psychological development. Through the acquisition of self-knowledge, the inner truth creates a condition of innermost freedom.

When she is with BV, Faye allows her thoughts to return to the attraction of extramural sexual adventures. She has as yet no intention of confining herself to one or the other lover. Soon she draws BV's attention to a photograph in their room of a stylish Edwardian man, describing the sitter's sexual recklessness in terms which in due course come to fit with what we can recognise as a plausible account of Cook's life: "He did everything. He exhausted every poison. He knew every form of love, suffering, madness so that he could reach the unknown. He experimented!" Her words resound with an echo of Jung's in his acknowledge-ment of the importance of Freud's singular vision in bringing sexuality within the scope of psychological discussion. "Human relationships involve instinc-tual sexuality; this is an undeniable fact haunting us from within. But there was another haunting instinct: the longing for creative intercourse with the nocturnal light of the soul. Jung had experienced it. This primordial instinct was evidenced in the ancient story of the *hierosgamos* or *coniunctio,* the "holy wedding." While Freud stressed only the sexual aspect of love, Jung saw its mystical implications" (Owens, 2015: 23–4). Faye's instinctual drive for love *with* freedom reflects an impulse to attain a higher level of consciousness. "This urge to a higher and more comprehensive consciousness ... if it is to fulfil its purpose, needs all parts of the whole, including those that are projected, into a "You"" (Jung, 1945/1985: §471). Or, as Owens parses Jung's words, there was another haunting instinct, namely the longing for creative intercourse with the nocturnal light of the soul (2015: 23–4). We shall return to Jung's celebration of the true marriage of the soul as he strived to unite its conflicting powers in a manner finally discovered by some of the characters in *Song to Song*.

Faye's thoughts move on to celebrate her own sexual freedom when, for exam-ple, she makes a point of scorning people who try to scare her off by attaching to her reputation labels like Wickedness. It is apparent that Faye is quite comfortable relating to the dark side of her nature and rejects those that do not. She boasts to BV that "You liked it that I did what I liked: I pulled you down in the car;" and at this moment the shot cuts to Faye pleasuring BV as he drives.

Presently Patti Smith resumes:

Life! Are we ready to suffer? Don't be afraid. I saw my husband. I saw this boy across the room. And I just loved him the moment I first saw him. And we had a life. And it was beautiful, and it was difficult. And I thought I would be with him for the rest of my life. But he died.

When we project an unconscious part of ourselves onto a love object, we can experience "love at first sight." This notion reflects the first level of love. Sometimes it is a complete projection of one's own soul onto another but at other times it is a union of the Self. Fortunately for Patti, the first glance was a mutual spiritual experience that involved the Self. Although bereaved, the widow's summation of her marriage has a distinctive vitality and fullness: her exuberant joy enriches her acceptance of the difficulties that come with every marriage. Significantly, she embraces too her honouring of the grief she suffered when death took her husband from her.

Song to Song will return to Patti Smith's twin themes of joy and suffering later in the film. For now, we know she has experienced the paradoxical blend of love in a real relationship that Jung speaks about in *The Psychology of the Transference* (1945/1985: §471–3) which includes hate, happiness and sadness, hope and hopelessness, etcetera. Patti embodies the important alchemical symbol of the widow who was originally represented by the Egyptian goddess Isis, the great teacher who was not only vicious and murderous but also a healer. Marie-Louise von Franz writes,

> The name 'widow' refers to a specific stage of her life… psychologically it refers to the stage when the masculine spiritual principle of consciousness has died, and the feminine principle of nature and the unconscious takes over and rules over a mysterious process of spiritual transformation and resurrection.
>
> (2006: 104)

Patti Smith has more to say with undiminished passion and has identified the audience which needs to hear her eloquence. Before she shares her wisdom again, however, much is to change in the lives of Cook who takes himself to a Mexican seaside town in his private jet together with BV and Faye for companions. The way that the participants imagine this short holiday might turn out proves very different from the actuality.

As Faye prepares to board the plane, she remembers that at this period in her life she remained profoundly restless. "I wanted to escape from every tie. Every hold. To have a life at any price. Not to settle. To go up higher. Free." Does her self-centred tone of voice imply that she would consider herself cheated were she to receive any less? Or is her desire an expression of her longing to be released from the chains of the dark side of her unconscious and the unredeemed animus that prevents her from *singing her song.* From a depth-psychological understanding, escaping from every tie means freeing the animus from the grips of the shadow which will result in a connection to the creative life of the *light* animus. The shadow is less glamorous and does not correlate to the ideals of perfection. And like the animus, it is important to remember that the shadow is an archetype that can seize us! The animus should serve the woman, not dominate her. But first, conscious separation work from the shadow must ensue. At this point it appears that Faye has been called to the individuation journey where it includes the processes of differentiation and separation that help one recognise what belongs to them and what does not.

Certainly, the party arrive in their Mexican destination in good spirits and high expectations with Bob Dylan's "Rollin' and a Tumblin'" providing the backing track. BV slyly presents Faye with cut flowers, as if behind Cook's back. Vendors comb the beach selling a wide variety of trinkets, baubles, and toys. And as if Cook were determined to entertain his guests (still seeking to charm BV into joining his company of artists) he makes degrading monkey noises and leaps around like a wild creature, before mimicking the seagulls that flock overhead. For her part, Faye reads a good luck charm sold to her by a man on the beach who selects tokens picked by doves: "The bird said we'd love each other forever. Love never fails." For our part, we can interpret the message from the doves as another synchronistic moment. In Greek Mythology the dove was singled out to represent romance and was associated with Aphrodite. Eros is in the air!

Moving away from the beach come the evening, the male visitors enjoy horsing around in a shebeen with the locals, relishing games of rough and tumble, guitar music, and drinking games. Occasionally BV joins in with a local band and hoists Cook on his shoulder.

Recovering next day from a drunken night, the booze keeps the two men bound together for an hour or two as though they were lifelong comrades. BV pounds a keyboard while musing that: "It didn't seem like anything could break us apart. I thought we'd build each other up and make music together." For his part Cook again urges (albeit like a child ignorant of the ugly racket made by his attempts at song) that they should make a record together. Superficially cheerful though this arrangement may appear, the holidaymakers add up to an awkward trio given that Faye is concealing her interest in both men and vice versa. BV chooses this moment to ask Cook how long he has known Faye and learns that she was a receptionist for him from the age of 16 or 17, confirming our understanding that Cook is a projection of her animus and father complex. BV wanders into the church to absorb this knowledge, while Cook and Faye encounter each other in a corridor. Perceiving that the group's dynamics have altered, Cook advocates that he and Faye should decide what's right and wrong in their sexual conduct. However, his approach to this idea proves inept and something is stirring in Faye's unconscious so she dodges his attempt to play a power game.

An elderly local woman has been shopping for food near where the visitors are staying and begs them for money. BV quietly hands her cash, for which the crone offers simple words of gratitude. This minute incident mysteriously alters the relations between his generosity and the American mogul's braggadocio in ways that will be seen to have changed Cook's mindset from the moment the three visitors meander into the church cloisters.

On disc Johnnie Taylor sings "God Is Standing By." Rather than being led by her unconscious projections and ego's desires, Faye's increased consciousness will lead her to the inner birth of the Self where God is present to fulfil the longings of her soul. As von Franz writes (2006: 45), "At this level love becomes an experience of the self, inner wholeness and God, which cannot be understood intellectually but only through love." And now, Malick's wondering exploration of love connects *Song to Song* with the Christian bridal song, *Song of Solomon*.

5.1   I come to my garden, my sister, my bride,
I gather my myrrh with my spice,
I eat my honeycomb with my honey,
I drink my wine with my milk.
Eat, O friends, and drink: drink deeply, O lovers!

5.2   I slept, but my heart was awake.
Hark! my beloved is knocking.
"Open to me, my sister, my love,
My dove, my perfect one;
For my head is wet with dew,
My locks with the drops of the night."

5.3   I had put off my garment,
How could I put it on?
I had bathed my feet,
How could I soil them?

5.4   My beloved put his hand to the latch,
And my heart was thrilled within me.

5.5   I arose to open to my beloved,
And my hands dripped with myrrh,
My fingers with liquid myrrh,
Upon the handles of the bolt.

5.6   I opened to my beloved,
But my beloved had turned and gone.
My soul failed me when he spoke.
I sought him, but found him not;
I called him, but he gave no answer.

6.1   Whither has your beloved gone,
O fairest among women?
Whither has your beloved turned,
That we may seek him with you?

6.2   My beloved has gone down to his garden,
To the beds of spices,
To pasture his flock in the gardens,
And to gather lilies.

6.3   I am my beloved's and my beloved is mine;
         He pastures his flock among the lilies.

6.4   You are beautiful as Tirzah, my love,
         Comely as Jerusalem,
         Terrible as an army with banners.

6.5   Turn away thine eyes from me,
         For they have overcome me ...

This traditional *coniunctio* image develops poetically through *The Song of Solomon*. It too reflects deeply felt love that is heart-achingly painful in the way that Patti Smith had earlier described: love being as strong as death and existing outside of time. For her part, Faye realises suddenly that this has been the first time in her life that she has felt everything to have sprung from the past hour. She leaps into BV's arms, a moment of ecstasy as if she were hearing Patti Smith encouraging her again, "Don't be afraid. I saw my husband. And I just loved him the moment I first saw him."

Although Faye will indeed hear Patti talk to her about love on another occasion, the words of neither woman are heard at this moment. Rather, it is Cook who gazes at the new lovers, experiencing that rarest phenomenon in his adult existence, namely a revelation. In his state of deflation, Cook becomes acutely aware of what he has never experienced. By way of contrast, Faye's desire to feel free *just like Cook* is arising from the yearning of her soul. Her present love experience equates to the inner lawfulness of individuation where one becomes totally and essentially oneself. It is the quest to unify the play of opposites within and heal the split in her heart.

Cook, meanwhile is watching BV carry Faye up an Aztec mound murmuring to himself, "They have a beauty in their life, a joy. It makes me ugly." Dreadfully, however, it is this, the dark truth of his complete lack of self-knowledge which he shall find inescapable. His sorrowful observation reveals an ego that only pretends to know everything. Clearly, depression lives underneath the surface of his personality and reflects his lack of relationship to his anima (inner ideal) and loss of soul. Pushed down from his heights, as Cook witnesses the reality of real love, he has a fleeting moment when his ego is not arrogant; but in compensation his shadow will become dangerously inflated. Love provides insight, something power is completely incapable of.

To survive the narcissistic injury, he must create an action that can compensate for the severe ego blow. Well aware of Cook's brittle humour, Faye sits subdued on the return flight home while the pilot inverts the aircraft so that, to the delight of his two male passengers, they enjoy one more (wholly illusory) freedom before landing, 'flying' in the aircraft's aisle upside down to its roof. The pilot's aggressive manoeuvre clearly mirrors Cook's secret revelation of himself that has turned his inner world upside down.

On landing back in Austin, life changes almost immediately, driven by Cook's characteristically bold behaviour. More or less on a whim, he picks up a good-looking blonde, Rhonda (Natalie Portman), an out-of-work kindergarten school-teacher who earns just enough to survive as a waitress in a diner. Cook's fast-talking wit, his Ferrari, his easy backstage access to outdoor music events and scenarios where he chats familiarly to celebrated musicians such as Iggy Pop, all persuade Rhonda that he might be the right kind of person to keep company with. She is probably no better off financially than her mother Miranda (Holly Hunter) who earns her wage by working as a cleaner of large apartments. However, the older woman has had to learn to accept the limits of what the world brings her. After her husband left her to bring up their children single handed, she had wanted the kids to have much more but soon discovered that her reduced family could not afford better than a tacky rental property with plaster peeling off the walls.

Cook, on the other hand, does not deal with relationships without displaying his power drive by flaunting his money. In this instance, having proposed success-fully to Rhonda, he buys her mother a property currently under construction in a new housing estate. Furthermore, he promises Rhonda that she can get out of the marriage without doing more than asking him to release her. Cook and Rhonda do marry, but with nobody else in attendance other than a woman who might be a clerk recording the details required for the legal declarations or (more plausibly) a publicist hired by Cook to keep his name in the public domain. Even Miranda is not present. Thus, one side effect of Cook's "will to rule" psychology results in isolation for everyone around, including himself. Like all malignant narcissists, he lacks understanding that the largest obstacle to experiencing a loving relationship is suffered through the power complex. Jung's dictum, where there is power there is no love, resonates here. Rooted in the infantile wish to conquer and possess, he desires ownership at any price, making individuation impossible. Logos without Eros does not have a clue how to relate.

Faye and BV return to Austin from their Mexican holiday initially enjoying an emotional high, sharing time together, chasing each other around in parks by day, and clubbing by night. However, as Faye develops emotionally, her capacity to carry feelings of guilt is also growing, an important indication that her psycho-logical split (formerly symbolised by the dark and light wigs) is beginning to heal. Struggling with guilt will eventually bring increased consciousness and is one of the most important religious questions one should grapple with. She tells herself she has to come clean with BV about her relationship with Cook, but she does not know how to broach the topic. Eventually BV asks if she has lied to him. She replies that BV is someone who always wants to know the truth, but she prefers not to speak about such sensitive matters because sometimes telling the truth hurts the person hearing it more than concealment. From a depth perspective, good judge-ment comes from a *fluid* relationship between the mind (logos) and the heart (Eros) and too the conscious and the unconscious. This level of integration provides the capacity to discern what should be kept a secret and contained within from what should be shared with another. One must struggle with the question, does this information belong to just me or you? Does my partner have the capacity to deal with such a truth? However, if the question and the answer derive from mutual shadow projections rather than genuine curiosity (regarding the life of the unconscious), only misunderstanding and strife will erupt. For the time being, Faye has intuitively made the right decision. This is a rare moment between them when she approaches frankness, yet nervously veers away from it.

Meanwhile, rooted in human insecurity, BV and Cook have a number of increasingly acrimonious meetings. Superficially, they are falling out because Cook insists that BV looks down on him, takes too much, and furthermore does not pay him as the boss what the latter claims he is owed. In so far as Cook sees it, writing songs is a trivial matter. How many people in Austin does BV think are writing songs? Openly sneering and devaluing, Cook asks BV whether he really thinks his songs are that good. BV's riposte refers the other man to their original deal, saying it should be the 50–50 split they had agreed. It adds to BV's bitterness that he knows full well that Cook has put into his own name (which is to say that he has in effect stolen) the copyright of all the songs that BV had written under their alleged 50–50 deal. Cook falls to his knees in the street in a mocking gesture intended to persuade BV to bow to his will. Overwhelmed by emotions aroused by the businessman's blatant disregard of him as his supposed mutual partner, BV becomes spitting mad, literally.

Cook promptly goes behind BV's back and talks to Faye without revealing his latest dealings with BV. Cook proposes to give Faye a record contract. "How's that make you feel? That's what you want, right?" As before, his demeaning sneer has its twin roots in both envy and the sense of having secured a victory. From a psychoanalytic understanding, envy is wanting what another has so one is instinctively compelled to destroy the other (i.e. to putdown the other in order to feel better about oneself). Envy is always aggressive, and there is no surprise in that, but what do astonish us are Faye's reactions when she leaves her meeting with Cook. At this moment, her responses amount to a wholesale reversal of what in Mexico she had embraced as her first life-affirming experience of love. Seduced by Cook's manipulations, she falls into a regression, a time when she felt some (albeit negative) form of psychic stability and murmurs to herself, "I love pain. It feels like life … Sometimes I admire what a hypocrite I am … Strange what you get used to." In fact, she is relishing sliding back into her fascination with the dark emotions that she had embraced when specifying suffering as necessary for her to access feelings of aliveness while engaging in sex. Is BV too tame, too gentle a lover compared with Cook, to excite Faye? Alternatively, does she prefer playing games that depend for the excitement they generate on the deception of one or more lovers? That seems plausible too. Psychologically, she is vacillating between opposing poles of love, gentleness, and brutality. Something in her unconscious is activated, perhaps hiding from developing awareness of the tension of these opposites. Alternatively, perhaps she is in a regression that is moving toward a more conscious state of suffering that leads to rebirth.

BV has long postponed visiting his father who has, or so BV's mother habitually claims, exhausted her through endless battles given over to breaking up the family.

The wars between his parents have discouraged BV from returning. His younger brother (Tom Sturridge) also finds it hard to live in his parents' home, but BV has seized the advantage by moving out first. Now, as a half measure, BV travels to visit the rest of the family and in particular talk to his mother (Linda Emond), trying to lift her spirits and get her to see herself as a healthy, vigorous person. His mother, however, complains that she is sinking all the time, addressing her elder son like the obsessive hypochondriac she has become. Disconcertingly, it has become obvious to BV that his mother is incapable of recognising her power and therefore is in complete identity with being a victim. His realization brings Jung's words to life in 'The Psychology of the Transference' that "the unconscious can be integrated only if the ego holds its ground" (1945/1985: §503). With such a weak ego, his mother is doomed to live out a tragic life played out by the neurosis of her bodily symptoms. BV also speaks to his brother, admitting his reluctance to see their dad, though in his heart he realises that eventually he must do so. The cumulative domestic tensions are so intense that they bring clarity to Cook's previously obscure assertion that throughout BV's life he has tried to get free but doesn't know how. Only now that the internal stresses within BV's family reveal themselves as an oppressive burden does Cook's comment show up as expressing some awareness of BV's need to break free from his family dynamic. But for now, the latter has to learn to endure his suffering. Escaping from the bounds of *participation mystique* will free up his libidinal energy that has been in lock down.

> This task entails the most painstaking self-examination and self-education, which can, however, be passed on to others by one who has acquired the discipline himself … they show up acutely when a human relationship brings them to the fore and when they are noticed by the other person as well as by oneself. Only then may he discover that committed relationships are not just a prison
>
> (Jung, 1945/1985: §503)

As in fairy tales, the hero must go home and have a confrontation with reality. Reconnecting to the old reality is an important aspect of Eros that holds the opposites together.

Faye joins BV at his mother's place and tells BV that she has met Cook in town, and he wants to sign her to his record company. BV tells her that it's a big opportunity and she should seize it. He adds that she knows how he feels about Cook, but that his personal antipathy shouldn't affect their professional relationship. Occasionally BV wipes an eye with the back of his hand. This is such a moment, and it looks as though his unacknowledged feelings are surfacing. He and Faye hold each other close but it is now she who weeps, not BV. When the latter asks why, she explains that she is happy. Perhaps he is no less than she is feeling a connection to the other's unconscious *inner* partner. In this significant moment, we are bearing witness to a genuine heartfelt meeting between her animus and his anima. That being said, perhaps in the practical world it is BV who has calculated the clever manoeuvre with which Cook seduced Faye and has out-played him. At all events, each of the three companions in the trio can now be identified by the other two. As we shall see, the archetype of the trickster is playing its part toward a resolution.

Back in Austin, a not entirely welcome encounter occurs for Faye that seems plausible enough among the crowds moving through a music festival. Faye happens to have met a previous fellow musician and girlfriend of BV who has flown into Austin to give a concert. The meeting upsets Faye because Likke Li is a singer who has once again asked BV to go off with her. Likke and BV discuss this in an oblique manner (in effect sensing out where they are in their lives). Their exchange is frank, affectionate, and painful: both of them feel burdened with unresolved closure from their previous time together. The yearning comes out in their questions and observations, simultaneously telling and intimate. Both of them know full well that they are touching on powerful matters: 'The road not taken' as Felsenthal wrote in her review (2017).

BV: What's it feel like to be a girl?
Likke: Like I have special powers.
BV: What don't I know?
Likke: How to feel. How to be sick to your bones. How to yearn.

(She throws dust in his face)

BV: You're casting spells.
Likke: Does it hurt?
BV: Mm-Hm
Likke: Yeah?
BV: I don't even think you know you're doing it.
Likke: I mean …
BV: Just going around chucking spells on people.

As dusk draws in, Likke swings around BV on an empty, open-air dance floor while on the speaker system Del Shannon grieves for the loss of his former love in "Runaway." BV asks if she is happy and Likke concedes that she has sometimes thought about their sharing happiness. Now, once again, while taking leave of him on the airfield where her little plane stands waiting for her in misty rain, she confirms that she would have followed him around again if he had asked her. But BV is aware of her dark anima seductions, revealed in their dialogue when he tells her that she is just going around chucking spells on people. Likke plainly sees no advantage in waiting for a man who will not commit to her. She knows what she wants and has decided she would have settled on BV if he were to have chosen her. Likke and BV sing together a shared farewell duet and happen with telling irony to harmonise in the very garden where Patti Smith will mentor Faye and advise the latter not to allow BV to escape her. But now Likke shrugs fatalistically and leaves Austin.

By way of contrast, however, having switched away from her apparently life-changing reorientation in Mexico, Faye has still not succeeded in committing her life to BV. In the interim, she goes to one of Cook's apartments muttering "Foolish me!" and "Devil!" It becomes a rare moment that combines self-recognition with the understanding that Faye is 'acting out' stupidly. She goes to bed with Cook and promptly shares her innermost thought to him, tearfully telling him that she loves BV and no longer wants to sleep with her boss. The mogul exhibits no hesitation and tells her that she should get out. Consciously sharing her secret and thereby revealing her integration work, Faye makes her gesture of renunciation final with a fully booted exit across the bed that they have just shared. It is an unsettling performance by a woman who has been possessed by her animus and now fucks her false lover for what she intends should be the last time.

Although the affection has not suddenly come to an end between Faye and BV, and they continue for a while to use lovers' language with each other, it seems that for her the breaking off of one relationship must entail the ending of the other and she notices that things have changed. In the background, like a reminder of needless loss, Likke Li accompanies herself on the piano in the melancholy song "I Know Places." Meantime, although BV attempts to amuse Faye, he has also become suspicious of her. The dialogue between the two of them grows increasingly uncomfortable as BV cross-questions her. Why is Cook after Faye if he's not attracted to her? Did they ever sleep together? Although BV insists that they don't need to keep secrets from one another, his questioning actually grows increasingly insistent. And every time she gives him the answers that he requires, BV presses her for even more information. At one point in this cross-questioning, BV obliges Faye to discuss with him what sounds as though it might have been an occasion when one of her schoolteachers had sexually interfered with her. Too familiar with his father's rages and his mother's depression, he aggressively confronts Faye in an instinctual effort to get their unconscious entanglement unstuck. Both BV and Faye are miserable.

Eventually each confesses to the other. Faye admits she was wrong to have slept with Cook and asks if BV will forgive her. The words she utters on the soundtrack are not spoken audibly. On the contrary, she states that she is still not unhappy about it. And then, adding to the impression of her confused emotions, she finishes with the thoughts, "I don't seem to bring people happiness anymore. I wasted your love." BV offers his own *mea culpa*, reporting that he tried to be kind to Faye, but it only made him colder. Will he learn from such mistakes the poisonous repetitious compulsions of those with which his parents had for years afflicted each other? Not so fast it seems …

The audience for *Song to Song* has already tasted Cook's reckless appetites through Faye's readiness to test the limits of excess. Now Cook's new wife Rhonda (who is already adapting to ingratiate herself with him), offers unwisely to surrender whatever part of herself he wants. Rhonda's impoverished background has made her hyper focused on outer worldly appearances. Because of this, she can be regarded as Cook's persona, the mask or role he plays in the outside world, rather than his anima. Cook is so identified with his persona that his wife (not him!) is experiencing the disturbance in his personality and is beginning to take on the emotional consequences. He asks her to let him "untie her hands" and in return he wants to sense her desire to do the same to him.

Rhonda meanwhile attends a pompous campus community church service. It's an event where the words of the minister are intended to sanctify the devout soul with nothing less than gratification that the congregation has supported fulsomely her urging the handsome circulation of their cash. When Rhonda returns to Cook at his beach house, it is to experience another kind of religious fervour much more to her husband's taste than hers. He urges the "Doctor" on Rhonda, the sticky liquor which we previously saw him offer to guests at his pool party. When he administers the infusion to his newly wed wife, it is no surprise to discover that Cook is suborning her in roughly similar behaviours of unconscious dependency in which he had previously held Faye. The latter, however, had evidently not been revolted by his description of the tincture as "dipped in God" with the addition of the boastful *non sequitur*, "They've never been where we've been." Soon, horribly inebriated, Cook mutters spools of pseudo-mystical speech: "You won't die ... Here I reign, King ..." However, his repetition of such increasingly crazed outbursts encroaches persistently on Rhonda's sanity. She cannot fail to see that Cook keeps wild company and that it draws him, as he intends, into episodes of madness, bouts of deep excess that terrify Rhonda. She is the only woman present when two Afro-Caribbean men join the party. One of them, as Jenkins (2017) writes, is "inked up like a reptile." This man augments the weirdness with performances of grotesque self-injury while Cook's visions stagger out of his brain through broken, overloaded images and fragmentary speeches. "I was once like you. Didn't know what I know now. Think what I once was. What I am now." His mania is thrusting him far beyond such raving as Rhonda can bear. He expresses it now through ghastly black-and-white scenarios of carnage and limitless slaughter. And as Cook has surely meant all along, he eventually cows his wife into admitting that she fears him. He is the trickster who (rather than having stepped) has slithered way beyond self-control. Plainly his blatant desire is to tie whomever he is in relationship with to his foetid unconscious.

Jung sets Cook's psychological inflation into context by furnishing it with a sharp edge in the following analysis which concludes his book on *Psychology and Alchemy*.

> An inflated consciousness is always egocentric and conscious of nothing but its own existence. It is incapable of learning from the past, incapable of understanding contemporary events, and incapable of drawing right conclusions about the future. It is hypnotized by itself and therefore cannot be argued with.
>
> (1968: §563)

These words inflict Cook's inflated consciousness with exactly the kind of blindness to which Jung refers here.

Faye, who at times has people's dogs in her care while their owners are on holiday, has a chance meeting with a Parisian visiting Austin. The visitor is Zoey (Bérénice Marlohe) who also likes animals, and the women find that friendship at first comes to them readily thanks to the animal that the dog's owners have left in Faye's charge. They discover that they share deeper sensibilities when they compare observations on the way that an unusual painting arouses similar responses in each of them, and they soon become lovers. We can interpret this sexual act as symbolic for Faye's longing to connect to the feminine. Nevertheless, as it happens, this is just one of several short-lived affairs linking characters who are already in contact with each other's shadows and whose affairs are also destined to come to an abrupt end. Titillating attractions are the shadow of Eros.

Specifically, and not at all by accident, BV, while scanning the guests at yet another party held to amuse the privileged well-to-do, and also held in yet another spacious garden along the riverside, reflects that he is getting used to drifting and waiting. On this occasion, BV is drifting and waiting for Faye; but she happens to be flirting with Zoey when BV catches sight of them circulating round the same party together. At this very gathering, BV meets another woman, Amanda (Cate Blanchett). She has just returned to live at the family home in Austin from the east where she has recently completed her education. Amanda, a woman who seems to keep a close eye on the way people whom she meets behave, disconcertingly announces to BV's face that he appears to be keeping a secret from her. She has taken note of his spying on Faye's behaviour with Zoey. Meanwhile Zoey has been doing some espionage herself. Calling on insights gained as an international travel-ler and a stranger in an unfamiliar community, she is able to describe the precise characteristics that she discerns in Cook and the coterie including Faye and other people around them: "They play with sex. They make it cheap. Maybe you need this world. The falsehood, the show. Maybe what stirs your blood is having wild people around you. You might have to be a sinner."

Zoey proves a shrewd observer of Faye and her circle. She is not only responsive to the mutual attraction between herself and Faye but also wary of the emotional wreckage that the latter puts in jeopardy. Zoey tries to sum up her own bewilder-ment at the other woman's behaviour: "I feel we are so connected, and I can't really understand. It's like …" Her introspective words are drowned out by the gurgling of pond water pumped through a fast-flowing drain, the implication being that Faye is not paying attention to her sophisticated visitor. Zoey in fact appears in only one last brief scene when, about to fly out from Austin, she bids a sorrowing yet affectionate farewell to her faithless lover, fondly admitting that she no longer believes anything that Faye is saying. She adds that now even the sound of Faye's voice upsets her. Zoey has a sophisticated understanding of human relationships and, true to her own name (the Greek term for 'life'), she chooses the life of being consciously related. In contrast, left to her own devices, Faye lacks this clarity of mind, as we have had ample opportunity to witness.

Faye must learn through raw experience. Indeed, belatedly, as a would-be con-cert musician, she now pays some attention to her own predicament, about to be marooned on stage, so to speak, in a private nightmare. "What if I don't become an artist? Don't have one life, don't have the other? Running around, trying to be somebody. Snatching at life." Whereas Zoey has made use of her objective eye in identifying and evaluating bogus human contacts, Faye (as we heard her declare at the start of *Song to Song*) appears substantially to have left it to her relationships to provide her emotional fulfilment. Unhappily, her relationship problems have been based on her own unconscious projections. Cook has for years used her as a malleable partner whom he can expose to his power games, Faye being too weak to resist his egotistical demands. Cook makes of her what he will and (although her own earlier faltering conversation with her father reveals that she is aware that Cook exploits her), the solution she seeks out is to take BV as a second lover with a different personality, brighter on the surface but driven by the need to feel free, and as yet equally incapable of sustaining a long-term relationship.

As it happened, Faye had already spent time with BV before Zoey left Austin. Faye's reunion with him, by her own not entirely dependable account, had an overwhelming impact on her. It might even, she thinks, be a turning point in her life. "I forget everything but seeing you again," she exclaims. Her own verbal excess lifts BV to a typically larger-than-life response. With once again Bob Dylan's "Rollin' and Tumblin'" pounding through their room, he makes a joke of toppling off his chair and then heaving her into the air while bearing her weight on his feet. Faye dances exultantly to the track, admitting to never having thought that she had a soul: "The word embarrassed me... Always been afraid to be myself. I thought there was no one there." Her fear of being soulless reflects a felt awareness of her lack of relationship to her inner life and animus. She boxes the air exuberantly as flashbacks of herself and BV kissing in the cloisters of the Mexican church course once more through her memories. Yet even at such moments, her humours oscillate erratically. At some such moments Faye is beside herself with delight; yet there are other times when she has moved between dwelling places and, in the wait for him to move closer to Austin, goes through misery: "I forget what I am ... whose I am. You're so far off, I'll die if you don't come soon." She adds self-reflexively, "I don't like to see the birds in the sky because I miss you, because you saw them with me." And sometimes, Faye's mood grows yet darker as when, reflecting on herself, she cries out to BV, "Come! Save me from my bad heart." Her words resonate with Jung's torment, when he writes in the *Red Book: A Reader's Edition*, "My soul, where are you?" (p. 127). However, by this time BV, whose heart is not one whit purer than Faye's, has moved in to share Amanda's room in her family's grand palace that commands a splendid stretch along the river side.

Blinded by inner motivations, in the early stages of love we are all "impure." Becoming introspective and reflective matures the personality to the point that we may arrive at a psychological understanding of our soul and develop a relationship with our inner companion, the anima or animus. By getting into a proper relationship with ourselves we quite naturally move into a proper relationship with our outer partner and finally experience the reality of a real relationship. Reaching the third level of love is an achievement of a lifetime!

At this phase of what is a complicated plot, Patti Smith sings "Birdland" into a tricky visual montage of, first, Faye with BV; then BV and Amanda going to the latter's bed; and later, Faye alone in a vivid green dress. Steeped as it is in the colour of the living principle, her dress gives us an inkling that transformation may be in Faye's future, for the surreal characteristic of the song's visible images stands out against the quality of the linguistic imagery: rational, irrational, probing and prowling the unconscious. Here birds, the flight of which Faye has just recalled sorrowfully, appear over the singer's head in endless black streams, racketing and harrowing sources of terror. Later, Rhonda also observes birds streaming over her head, flying in long columns. However, she believes that she is witnessing the revelation of a mystery that wants people to uncover its nature but, wretchedly, unlike Patti, she appears to be deluded.

Cook and Faye are seen fucking in a room overlooking his pool. Or alternatively, is it possible that they have been doing nothing of the kind, granted that she has lately been seen walking out on him with finality. It seems possible, given the psychological changes which will soon afflict Cook, that he is now fantasising his mistress of many years once again pleasuring him as she has done often before. In that case, Cook's hold on reality may already be displaying a subjective energy of barely resistible force.

A tearful and awkwardly dislocated Faye is hovering alone outside a pair of little houses which her sisters and their small children inhabit harmoniously. Set against that family background, her childlessness cannot be missed. In voice-over which contrasts sharply with the tenor of her reflections, she reports having revolted against goodness, believing that it had deceived her. She believes too that she did not need what made life sweet for her siblings, and that she could do better than others. As usual there are several delusions in the voice-over that may be her animus until the scene cuts sharply, even brutally to where, weeping, she prowls round her father on (of all locations) the forecourt of a filling station. Distressed by the realisation that she has not made him as proud of her as of her sisters, she accepts that she is not whom she had believed herself to be, not even a good person. Her father tenderly waves aside her apologies, trying to soothe her when she remembers how many sacrifices he had made for her so that she should have a chance to do the things that he couldn't. As she proceeds, we hear her filling out her life's narrative while removing her projections. Her interior dialogue reflects a painful understanding of opposing points of view as she vacillates from the inflation of her animus opinions to a deflation from her struggling ego. Honest self-reflection will help her to integrate these opposites and develop the capacity to differentiate herself from others and experience a man as her equal. A healing effect for the animus will resurrect her feminine self and feeling life. As she searches for the greater pattern of her life she observes, "I'm not who I thought I was," Then she questions, "Am I a good person? Even want to be? Or just seem like one so people will like me?"

Next, we drop into an ongoing lunchtime conversation between BV, his mother (Linda Emond), and Amanda. BV has jestingly asked his mother to talk about her family. This is both an instant wrong turn and a trickster's coarse joke to upset this nervy woman. When BV briefly leaves the table, his mother faces Amanda with the unwelcome insight that she, Amanda, is unhappy; and when BV returns, Amanda leaves the table and BV's mother reiterates that Amanda is the wrong person for BV. Later, the lunch party having been brought to an awkward and abrupt end, BV tells Amanda that he wants to change but does not know how to make that happen. Amanda responds that in the circumstances one has to sacrifice something. It seems as though either Faye or Amanda must make way for the other woman. BV has by and large passed thus far as a cheerful and light-hearted fellow who means well by the people he befriends or falls in love with. It is a shock when, however, he delivers an explicit summary of the ruthless values by which he lives, telling Amanda "When you give somebody your word, it doesn't mean anything, you just take it back." He follows this triumph of diplomacy with the remark that he should try his best not to say things he doesn't mean: the mercurial trickster in BV inadvertently strips his duplicity bare here. Shocked, Amanda tugs at her necklace and breaks it, scattering the beads across the floor of the riverside café at the very moment when BV saunters out of her sight and life. A montage of imperfectly juxtaposed shots presents random angles along the river.

Rhonda has noticed that the world builds a fence around people and ponders how they can get through it. Presently, however, she observes the birds streaming overhead, flying in long columns through rich blue skies and, excited by this vision, remarks to herself that "There is something else, something that wants us to find it." In this moment (which exultant choral church music extends through the following scene), she senses confirmation that there must be something in the beyond that calls us – something birdlike which has feathers and flies to heaven as an embodiment of a spiritual being. Could this be leading her to the mysterious presence she intuits? Unhappily, the following indications disabuse her grievously. She climbs a tall, spiral stairway and enters a garishly decorated apartment where she finds her newlywed husband, Cook. Here, as always consumed by insatiable desire, he not only has sex with Rhonda and a prostitute but (with his customary rapacity) stakes his claim to more from both: "I want the part that I don't know – that you don't know yourself." Arrested in the second half of life, Cook is entranced by only the sexual character of Eros. Instead of serving his anima, he dominates her and projects her onto all the women he surrounds himself with. This can only end up in depression as he entirely misses the value of love in one's life.

After Cook is satisfied, the two women share an interlude during which they dress themselves again. Rhonda asks the prostitute how long she has been doing this work and the other woman tells her tale of painful loss. She had dreamed of becoming a teacher, but when her fiancé died, she had to fall back on this work as a means to an end. She adds, verging on tears, "It was so much better when he was around – but God has a plan and I guess this is part of his plan." She hopes that God will hear her prayers so that she can move forward and do something worthwhile with her life, something her dad will be proud of. This is by no means the first time we have heard a dismayed woman expressing humiliation at her failure to live up to her father's hopes for her success, Faye being the other. The father is the first embodiment of the animus and determines a woman's spiritual temperament, shaping her individual mind and sense of independence. The prostitute's advice reveals herself to be a faithful and sensible person willing to offer Rhonda generous guidance based on feminine wisdom and her professional experience:

> Make the money. Don't let the money make you. Create the illusion, but don't let yourself believe the illusion. Don't let yourself get caught up. I sell a fantasy, not my body. I sell an illusion. I sell, you know, a daydream to these guys. And I try to keep the cookie jar closed.

Rhonda has to ask the other woman what the metaphor means and learns the simple and safe pattern of human behaviour. The prostitute carries a certain objectivity that knows how to keep the relationship between herself and her client purely transactional. She keeps the subjectivity of the love experience out of the equation. The prostitute's 'House of Wisdom' is where the *coniunctio* takes place. As an archetype, the most famous historical whore was Jesus's bride, Mary Magdalene.

This is not the only encounter between Cook and Rhonda (as a couple) with a pair of young rental girls. Rhonda, however, is increasingly alienated by her husband's coarseness, observing one night, "You burn me." She asks him, "Who are you?" Cook states the opposite of what he means, telling her: "I can't take this world straight." Then he switches to another corruption of the soul that he favours, questioning the young women as if stripping them naked while in fact they are dressing after paid sex. Always the dealer in power, Cook now wants the present two hirelings to talk about what scares them, an inquiry he had previously forced on Rhonda. The two girls admit to no fears, except when one of them, introspecting reluctantly into what truly *does* upset her, admits that she does not know her family. In essence, it is a legitimate fear because if you do not know your family or ancestors, it is difficult to know yourself. No one other than herself has ever been willing to take care of her. These two youngsters, probably in their early twenties, are physically attractive but their lives seem at best to be slipping away into emptiness, a vacuity which threatens to dissolve into meaninglessness.

Primed by now to see Cook's behaviour as typical of his increasingly brutal conduct and inferior Eros, we witness him flailing at the two young prostitutes. He fails to frighten them, but he surely does intensify Rhonda's terror. She is hanging out of the apartment's window, maddened by a raucous ululation in her head as she despairingly tries to escape the psychological cruelty which Cook methodically projects upon her. Desperately needing maternal consolation, Rhonda flees to her mother's home, bewailing her husband's deliberate descent into the madness with which he torments her so that she confesses the fragility of her ego state: "Mom, I'm afraid of myself. The hatred in me."

Responding to her daughter's despairing request for help, Miranda runs a bath for her. It seems like a ritual cleansing intended to meet the young woman's desperate need to wash herself free from the polluting waters of Cook's unconscious. Hypnotised by his oppressive authority, she feels that she contaminates everything she touches. "I used to think I could never be wicked. Wicked people were a long way off from me." How remote does Cook's casually delivered promise now seem that Rhonda can quit their marriage should she simply ask him to let her go?

How do Rhonda's responses to the aggression of her husband bear on her sense that there is something else in the world that tries to find us? Is there something that the chorale mixed in the film's backing track hints at? On the surface there is an incompatibility with the divine. Rather, auto-aggression seems to be indicated as the route to something else – the route to escape. Rhonda has joined yet another weirdly quasi-devout church congregation to have her dog (improbably enough) christened 'Bang!'. Is her dog's name a projection of her own instinctual life and her wish to live and kill Cook? Her recently recognised shadow seems to indicate that her unconscious is turning into a deadly force. Certainly, the sense of psychological incompatibility spills over as between quadrupeds and bipeds.

Walking disconsolately along a busy urban street, Miranda almost wanders off the kerb into a briskly moving car. This too feels like an omen, the near miss of a traffic accident being swiftly followed by Miranda's glimpse of Rhonda's abandoned vehicle (driver's door hanging wide open) which leaves the mother distraught, howling in grief and sensing the future in the present. The messages from the unconscious warn, in their fractured intrusions, of an ending.

Miranda might well have had to face the actuality she dreads except that Cook happens to be the one who stumbles across the drowned and dead Rhonda. Lifting her corpse, he carries the body to the artificial grass platform that fronts his property. Symbolically, Cook's movement connotes that his natural habitat resides in the unconscious waters along with his wife and makes clear that one-sidedness drowns consciousness. Consistent with Rhonda's troublesome passivity, she (rather than aim her anger outward at Cook) has resigned herself to her fate. There is no baptism here for rebirth, just inner violence and death. Their tragic marriage is an emblem for the un-individuated relationship. Fate forces us to grow but without a loving experience one is doomed.

Unaccompanied, BV at last visits his father. Having postponed the trip often and again, BV now weeps unrestrainedly recognising the ageing man's wretched condition, apparently beyond speech, beyond any redemption his oldest son might offer him, and hovering close to the end of life. It seems as though the unresolved frenzy of the old man's rages has ravaged his body and soul. Yet there is unexpected sweetness to be shared here too which touches BV when one of the neighbours stops by with carrots and apples for the ponies that BV's father owns. The neighbour appears to be older than BV's father, but, in terms of warmth, not to mention his thoughtful behaviour, he is a gentle, almost idealised figure of a rural Texan. The contrast between the two old men seems to reach tellingly deep into their innermost beings.

We mentioned some time ago that we would return to Patti Smith's twin themes of joy and suffering later in *Song to Song*. In a bizarre way the curious disjunction between the two old men helps Patti Smith identify the audience within the film which she realises needs to hear her wisdom. Leaving aside the fleetingly encountered old men, the audience that Patti makes her particular target comprises by this stage in her narrative just a single character. This is Faye herself because she hovers in a condition of moral unknowing which Patti intuits would benefit from being exposed to a fuller understanding of the importance of doubt. Total clarity would hardly be desirable since the opposites of hope and doubt belong together. Jung commented that absolute clarity was actually a sign of poverty. When Faye follows Patti's advice it will lead her further down the path of liberation and inner development.

BV and his brother have been invited to yet another party. So too have Patti Smith and Faye. Smith sings a few lines of a song marking the passing of a good man, a broad hint that BV's father may not be long for this world. Meanwhile, unable to resist his taste for sallow witticisms, BV re-introduces himself to Faye, pretends that he does not know her and inquires if she has a boyfriend. Once again BV heads deep onto emotionally risky terrain, jesting with dark humour. The two former lovers sit at a keyboard, and chat. BV asks Faye about Zoey and Faye shuts out his typically invasive inquiry, insisting that she doesn't have to talk about a former lover. Her directness reveals an increase in self-agency and developing animus. However, responding to Faye's riposte, BV admits frankly that Amanda was his girlfriend. In what for him is also an unusually direct access to honesty, he admits that he went out with her, but then never called her again. Faye inquires whether he had loved Amanda and hears him admit that he hadn't realised it at the time. Instantly the tensions between the couple ease, with Faye offering her passionate benediction to BV, "You found me: You held out your hand ... I wish I could take back every wound ... every doubt."

Faye remembers some revelations that she had tried to repress after Zoey had pointedly reprimanded her for taking sex, which she names the gift of life, as a plaything. The French woman had rebuked her for cheapening sex by playing with it. Zoey does not fully understand why she should be drawn to a woman who behaves toward her so vilely; nevertheless, her intuitions tell her that Faye appears to need this world of falsehood and bravado. "Maybe what stirs your blood is having wild people around you." And it is this impulse (which Zoey sees Faye has no intention of suppressing) that persuades the Parisienne to bring their relationship to an end. We understand Zoey's attraction to Faye as her shadow companion, the dark side of her personality that she has no need to live out at this time of her life. Although naturally attracted by the spark of this type of relationship, she makes a conscious decision not to get involved with someone that has such a flippant attitude toward the unconscious. It is also a recurring thematic cue to Patti Smith who for the second time shares her thoughts on screen about her marriage. As Julia Felsenthal writes, Smith has a powerful moral point to make urgently and most affectionately to Faye:

> Serene and wise, she takes the listless Faye under her wing, and shares her own memories of falling for her husband Fred, who died of a heart attack in 1994. It's worth remembering that Smith dropped out of the New York art scene at the peak of her success, chose a different kind of life in Detroit, started a family.
>
> (Felsenthal, 2017)

Smith tells Faye, "I was married in 1980 and I've been a widow since 1994 but I still wear my ring 'cause he's still my husband. You know, we didn't get divorced, so. This is my wedding ring and this [one] I bought for myself after he died. It's what they gave runners who didn't win a marathon but did finish the race. I never thought I would live long, you know? I'd be an artist and die young of tuberculosis or something like Charlotte Bronte."

Patti asks Faye, turning to the question that the latter probably dreads, what she has done that was bad. The younger woman tells her that she just got involved with this man whom she thought could help her. Patti points out affectionately that Faye made a mistake, nothing worse. "You're gonna do fine," she tells her. With this, Patti spots BV hovering nearby, and her attention switches to him as she urges, "Is that your fella? Fight for him. Really love him. Don't let him get away."

Patti continues to sing and, as before, her music – its lyrics and songs – are not obvious partners. The language can be fierce, wild, celebrating natural forces and in service to more than it knows. It is extravagant yet of necessity is delivered in the service of nature. Her songs bring a *feeling* of harmony, expressing an uninhibited steady flow of life energy, Eros that promises fulfil-ment and lifelong love.

Certain powers now ripen in Faye allowing a new vibrant future to emerge. From here, Faye reads the text aloud. Together the two women render a prayer that scintillates in its purity. A song of boots and prayer with Faye speaking the lyrics and promising BV the future.

> For mercy has a human heart
> And pity a human face
> And love, the human form, divine
> And peace, the human dress.
> Then every man of every clime
> That prays in his distress
> Prays to the human form …

We flash back to the elderly Mexican beggar seeking help with the cost of her shop-ping and offering thanks when BV puts cash in her hand. Her words under scribe a simple and potent blessing.

> Love, mercy, pity, peace.
> And all must love the human form.

The grey granite of the hills beyond Austin glows pink, stained gorgeously for a while by the evening light.

BV	is tickling Faye's feet with his tongue; and soon the couple commit to each other; to moving west; to supporting his damaged family and to the simple life.
BV:	"I gotta go back and start over. Like a kid. Mom's gone crazy. My brother's up to no good. I didn't have the right heart in me."
Faye:	I won't stop loving you. I don't think I can.
BV:	You're the only one that I love. And even after all that we've been through.

From what initially appeared as escapism and a compulsive need to 'be free', Faye and BV have found and retained true liberation, learning to share their open hearts. Through their hard-won work, they have withdrawn their projections which ultimately leads to their reunification and mutual redemption. Their love story is an archetypal one, one which von Franz (2021) explains in the Fairy Tale Rapunzel,

> a counter movement has been put in motion from the deepest suffering to joy. The couple remain united together and go into the realm of the prince, which we interpret as a kingdom "beyond all images." Symbolically contained within the union of the couple is the union of opposites, through which also the opposition conscious-unconscious is transcended.
>
> (Volume 3, p. 272)

Faye (Passenger in BV's car): "Mercy was a word. I never thought I'd need it. Or not as much as other people do. You asked me if I wanted to come out, too. I've never been out west before. But I'll come and find you."

We cut to BV, now kitted out in a labourer's clothing and headgear. He is wandering about over a building site in a desultory manner. The Foreman on the construction site delivers a pointed rebuke to BV as one of his team of men.

You're not making it. You're gonna have to pick your speed up. If you don't, we will have somebody to replace you. I'm just tired of it.

These sharp words, straight and to the point, say everything that BV needs to hear about his underlying attitude to work. Indeed, as we soon perceive, the rebuke has turned him honest … We notice how the team's working relationships have changed when the Foreman urges them onward cheerfully: "Let's get up here and bake a ham." The crew laugh, taking pleasure from work going well.

Faye (VO): "You wanna go back to the simple life? I want the same. Let nothing come between us. Ever." BV walks around the site and then, perhaps in their memories, she and BV walk together across the grey granite slope. She says: "Let nothing come between us. This. Only this."

Priviero (2018: 51) notes that "Throughout Jung's self-exploration, the movement toward the unity of the opposites resounds as a persistent inspiration. But it is possibly in no place more sharply described than in a passage from Jung's encounter with Philemon and his wife Baucis."

Jung (to whom our final words on Malick's extraordinary film must be devoted) wrote of his own experiences in following Dante Alighieri by venturing into Hell and then returning triumphant from it,

> …a certain solitude and isolation are inescapable conditions of life for the well-being of oneself and of the other, otherwise one cannot sufficiently be oneself. A certain slowness of life, which is like a standstill, will be unavoidable. The

uncertainty of such a life will most probably be its greatest burden, but still I must unite the two conflicting powers of my soul and keep them together in a true marriage until the end of my life, since the magician is called Philemon and his wife Baucis.

(The Red Book: 314)

Thus, in a single sweep, Jung simultaneously captures his understanding of the *coniunctio*, referring to the transcendent union of the opposites (conscious/ unconscious) and, in addition, by allegorically celebrating their long marriage by invoking his and Emma Jung's spiritual ancestors.

The celebration that concludes *Song to Song* speaks in its own way to the securing of love between a couple who, in the face of many difficulties, succeed in overcoming them.

Chapter 7

The Analyst and the Shaman

Part 1

Killing the Clinician: A Sacred Journey

Joanna

This book is an homage to the relationship John and I have developed over the past 20 years. We first met in the summer of 2002 at a Jungian conference in England. I was nearing the end of writing my PhD dissertation for Pacifica Graduate Institute on film and the individuation process. I felt compelled to attend the conference so I could meet my external reader, Don Frederickson, a professor at Cornell University. On the long flight from California to London, I was reading one of John Izod's books as part of the research for my dissertation. Upon my arrival, I checked into a small English inn located close to the conference at the University of Essex. I freshened up for dinner. Within the quiet dining room, three men were engaged in lively conversation. I spontaneously stood up and humorously cautioned them that I could hear everything they were talking about. I then walked over to their table and boldly proclaimed, "One of you *must* be Don Frederickson!" My intuition was spot on; the other two men were John Izod and the Jungian physicist Victor Mansfield. To say it was a powerful synchronistic encounter would be an understatement. John and I became fast friends. As we got to know each other, we recognised how much we had in common. We were both single, full-time parents who shared not only a deep love for our children but also for the art form of film and Jungian psychology. Another fortunate coincidence came to light when John mentioned he was visiting his niece in California the following month. His visit to California sealed our friendship.

Sometime during our long-distance communications, I had a dream that John and I would write a book on films about grief and loss. We took this communication from the unconscious seriously and decided to write our first paper on the film *Million Dollar Baby*.[1] Our first book was published in 2015,[2] which included all the papers we had published since our earliest collaboration in 2005. At that time in my development, my psychological interpretations were mainly influenced by my

DOI: 10.4324/9781003545538-8

clinical training as a marriage and family therapist, my psychoanalytic supervision and analysis, and depth psychological studies at Pacifica Graduate Institute. I was a walking psychological blend of Freudian and Jungian psychology.

When we first met, it had barely been 17 months since I had been hospitalised for a serious burn accident. My accident presented another crossover with the third man sitting at the dinner table. Vic had written the book *Synchronicity, Science, and Soul-Making,* inspired by a serious accident he had suffered.[3] I find it interesting that I would meet John, my future writing partner, after my initiatory experience.

The following provides a brief summary of my ordeal and descent into the underworld: Walking along a trail at the volcanic site at Mammoth Hot Springs, the earth collapsed underneath my feet. Suddenly, I was immersed to my chest in a circular mud hole filled with scalding water. Diagnosed with second- and third-degree burns, the emergency doctors at the local hospital stabilised my traumatised body. I was airlifted to a burn unit at a hospital in southern California and immediately transported into a bath of warm waters. For three weeks, I was completely embroiled in another world as I vacillated between states of torment and dark ecstasy while the nurses scrubbed the skin on my legs and arms in the daily debriding bath ritual. Unintentionally, I had entered a sacred vessel, a living *krater,* where spiritual renewal and rebirth occur. Baptised in the fiery maternal womb, it was as if my body became the krater itself, a vessel in which the pair of opposites, water, and fire, were joined together in an immediate experience with the Chthonian Great Mother archetype and the secret of individuation.

Mircea Eliade[4] described a descent such as mine as an *involuntary initiatory ordeal,* a symbolic ritual that involves dismemberment and carries the archetypal pattern of death, regeneration, and transformation. The process of initiation[5] may appear as a sudden change in vocation, a mysterious illness, or, as in my case, an unusual event. The story of my descent is permanently marked by the serpent-skinned scars on my arms and legs and seared into my soul. The sinuous movement of the scarring, which I call my "natural tattoos," suggests a symbolic image of the dynamic transformational process I underwent. Tattoo markings, especially on the hands and arms, were regarded as distinctive signs of initiates in ancient mystery cults. From a psychological perspective, Jung clearly conveyed that the urge to individuate was accomplished through a series of initiatory experiences throughout one's lifetime.

John and I wrote feverishly while he was teaching in Scotland and I was running a private therapy practice in southern California. We both found love and got married. I moved to Ventura with my new husband, and, for 12 years, I commuted weekly from our home in Ventura to my office in Laguna Hills. At the halfway mark of my two-hour commute, I would pause at the Los Angeles Jung Institute in order to attend their presentations. My psyche responded to the seminar experiences by giving me the following dream in August of 2013: *I am standing under the doorway at the entrance of the lecture room holding a blue egg.* After pondering the meaning of the dream, I understood it as a message from my soul directing me to explore the Jungian Analyst program at the Institute. Although I never had any ambition to become a Jungian analyst, I thought it was critical to follow the symbolic meaning of the blue egg. I attended the Open House at the Jung Institute the following October.

At the Open House presentation, the director of the Institute asked the attendants to write down what they hoped for by entering the program. I wrote about my longing to be part of a depth psychological community. My response was in alignment with the Institute's objectives. However, I also learned the Institute required 100 hours of a Jungian analysis before applying to the program in the spring. My clinician/ego identity was deflated and angry. After all, I had been a licensed therapist for 21 years and had undergone an eight-year-long psychoanalysis! My Freudian analysis had focused on the descent, the personal unconscious, complexes, and shadow. As we know, Jung also articulated the necessity of descent, but in addition, he included its opposite: ascent. Jung was interested in a prospective, future-oriented approach to therapy that emphasised the healing value of one's dream life. Unlike Freud, dreams were not merely a façade behind which their meanings were hidden. Jung emphasised that dreams are a part of nature that add to our psychological and emotional growth. In that Jung writes:

> A dream can be an experience of the greatest importance for somebody. If he grasps its meaning, it will become an experience for him that he will value more than all the kingdoms on earth. These are experiences we cannot rationalize.[6]

It took me months to cool down enough to begin my search for the right Jungian analyst. In retrospect, it was correct to slow down my application process. Giving birth to the contents of the blue egg would entail a slow incubation process. In May 2014, I entered a Jungian analysis with Dr Charles Zeltzer. Within a year's time of dream analysis, I followed a waking fantasy and a dream and applied to the C. G. Jung and Marie-Louise von Franz Research Centre in Depth Psychology in Switzerland. I entered the program in the spring of 2016 and, as a result, my relationship to the unconscious contents in the blue egg; my animus, and the Self, have on a fundamental level, changed my psychological orientation and the way I live and work. For those on the path of individuation, understanding the symbolic language of the unconscious is a depth psychological task that leads to a human community grounded in Eros (the principle of relatedness). The longing I originally wrote about at the L.A. Institute Open House has been fulfilled through my analysis and analytic training at the Research Centre.

Like the psychological shock I experienced during the Open House at the L.A. Institute, I've had two notable experiences during my training at the Research Centre. The first was at a dream colloquium during the first block course I attended. I asked one of the board members about her "clinical" methodology. She simply responded, "I am not a clinician." The board member was direct and explained that she allowed the dream life of the analytic patient to inform the treatment. I felt confused and completely disoriented. Secondly, after participating in the program for over a year, a client told me her insurance company sent her a letter stating that my license had lapsed. I assumed it had to be some error; I had always taken my responsibilities seriously. I discovered that the Board of Behavioural Science, the "ruling body" of my marriage and family therapist license, had made a clerical error. They had never changed their records, despite my notifying them of my new office address. Consequently, I had never received a statement to pay any renewal fees that were due every two years. Five years had lapsed before this reality reached any level of conscious awareness. The licensing board took a harsh, super-ego position and demanded I re-take the exam. They refused to take any responsibility for their own mishap and said it was ultimately my responsibility. This is true; I had not noticed the missing bill. Yet I firmly refused and told them I would find another way to keep my therapy door open.

From distant Scotland, John Izod guided me on a shamanic journey to retrieve my exiled soul. I was traumatised; my livelihood and commitment to my clients were under serious attack. Contained and understood by my Jungian analyst, I made a conscious choice to walk away from the rule-bound collective organisation (Jung deemed the super-ego to be a substitute for the Self). I promptly applied for a license through the Medical Board of California as a research psychoanalyst. I was forced to take conscious responsibility for the ethical stance of my soul. Time had caught up with me. My inner development was no longer in tune with my conscious attitude. I had not been working as a traditional "marriage and family therapist" for quite some time. As I waited for my new license to arrive, I travelled to Switzerland for the fall block course. I was prepared to take my first set of oral exams, one of three (I had to take six in total), which was the neurosis exam. After practicing for 25 years, the competent "clinician" in me participated in a lively conversation about therapy. As was customary during the examination process, I left the room so the four board members could discuss my oral exam. I was invited back into the examination room and asked to re-take the exam. The board members told me they did not hear me speak from a depth psychological orientation in regards to the notion of healing; specifically, that *the neurosis heals us, we do not heal the neurosis.* As Marie-Louise von Franz stated:

> The healing factor is generally hidden in the very factor that is making one neurotic. A neurosis is always a package with an unpleasant outer shell, and when you open the package you find the elixir that cures the neurosis. The neurosis itself contains the healing thing. You need not look elsewhere, for neurosis, according to Jung, represents a failed attempt of nature to cure a psychic imbalance.[7]

The board members' devotion to the objective psyche refuses to take shortcuts, and, in service to the student's individuation path, acts as ethically as possible. As the president, Eva, compassionately said to me, "Joanna, we are all students." Jung's words resonate to my core:

> One cannot individuate as long as one is playing a role to oneself; the convictions one has about oneself are the most subtle form of persona and the most subtle obstacle against any true individuation. One can admit practically anything, yet

somewhere one retains the idea that one is nevertheless so-and-so, and this is always a sort of final argument which counts apparently as a plus; yet it functions as an influence against true individuation. It is a most painful procedure to tear off those veils, but each step forward in psychological development means just that, the tearing off of a new veil.[8]

I walked around old town Zürich in a daze, slowly absorbing the blow to my ego that was being forced to submit to the process of my inner growth. At that moment, I suffered a kind of death; the clinician in me was killed. Mircea Eliade emphasised that the most important part in an initiatory ordeal (the exams) is the ceremony of death and resurrection where the novice must be killed. The morning of the exam, I had awakened with a disturbing dream of a dear friend who had committed suicide. We know that when someone dies in a dream, it presages how a specific personification that is represented by the dead person has come to an end. It is also typical during times of initiation that the dead show up in our dream life. Shortly after I returned home to California, I received my new license. The following spring, I sat for the neurosis exam and passed. At breakfast, Gotti, the former president of the Research Centre, said to me, "Joanna, you could have taught the neurosis class." His words blessed my difficult passage.

Ten years have now passed since I entered a Jungian analysis, and eight years since I began my studies at the Research Centre. Completing my thesis and analytic program has given my initiation a religious significance whereby I accept my burn ordeal as indispensable to my mystical transformation. Eliade urges that we do not forget that "initiatory death is always followed by resurrection; that is, in terms of psychopathological experience, the crisis is resolved and the sickness cured. The shaman's integration of a new personality is in large part dependent on his *being* cured." I find it a fascinating synchronicity that becoming a Jungian analyst has coincided with the completion of John's and my second book. Over the years, John's and my writing lives have been nothing short of a labour of love. Our fruitful relationship embraces the alchemical symbol of the *mysterium coniunctio,* an embodiment of our mutual individuation journeys and relationship to the Self. In the archetypal realm of healing and creative life, there are four of us: John and his anima and me and my animus, all in a union of love. The analyst and the shaman, on the same healing path toward wholeness and completion that occurs in the depths. Marie-Louise von Franz explains that the shaman is a "specialist of the soul" and is more like a psychologist.[9] She explained that his or her function is to deal with cases of possession – what an analyst would call "complexes" – ensuring the "dead" (the complex) finds its appropriate place to rest. The hard work of individuation is not only for our ancestors but also for our descendants. John, whose psyche is rooted in his childhood homeland in Africa, an Emeritus Professor of Media Studies and a trained Shaman; and I, deeply rooted in my Greek ancestry, a Doctor of Psychology and initiated to the depths through a torturous event (common to medicine men and shamans), unite together as Shaman and Analyst. The unconscious is longing to be understood. It is our sincere hope that our work will serve to illuminate others.

Part 2

Elfin King: Awakening a Shaman

John

Guided to embrace the cherry tree by my shaman, Two birds,
With eyes wide shut, I hugged the gean,[10] my mother,
Gazing at curtains of our blood as they flowed upwards,
rising past our eyes, hers and mine, … a mystery.
In turn, and after my mother, both Philemon and Jung became
my shamanic, intimate ghosts.

Learning how to become a shaman usually begins with descent to the lower world and the search for a power animal. Those steps start from a point in the ordinary world with which the individual is already familiar. Known as the *axis mundi*, it is the location in the actual or imagined world which a person who ventures into the non-ordinary world can seek and return to, confident that it provides a sure reference point from which to orient one's bearings.

As it happened, however, the classic descent to the lower world was not a feature of what turned out to be the start of my personal journey. I took no steps as such but started on a series of early morning flights of imagination while my children were still asleep. In fact, I was attempting to do two things before starting the day's work. One objective was to make sense of Robert Wang's Practical Guide to the Jungian Tarot. I hoped that it might stimulate meditation by encouraging the study of the Major Arcana of the Tarot.

My progress was slow. I found it challenging to interpret the images, altogether trickier than understanding Jung's writings. Morning after morning I found myself gawping at one particular conundrum, unable to make sense of a specific image, the Magician, and the symbolic attributes that illustrate his card. These included such antique images as not only the sun, moon, and lighted candles but also an alembic. The last of these was a long-superseded device formerly used for distilling. It consisted of a gourd-shaped object in which liquid was heated and the beak of which conveyed the resultant vaporous products to a receptacle in which they were condensed. Alembics were used by scholars and mystics, and in a different context remained familiar to scholars who, seeking understanding of spiritual truths, studied alchemy long after the seventeenth century.

What drew my eye among the imagery mentioned was not the alembic but a stationary house fly. Why was it there? What did it signify? My frustration lasted for days until one morning I perceived something that I had overlooked. Since the card was imprinted with the image of a fly, I realised that I could get the insect to fly in my own imagination. So I began every morning to ask it to carry me on what turned out to be an exhilarating journey of the mind reaching across continents to visit a friend in America while she was still asleep. Years later, and only then, did I discover that the house fly was in fact my first "power animal." I had no idea what such a creature might be until being taught by a shaman.

It is relevant to write briefly about my life after leaving school: I was born in England, but my parents emigrated to Southern Rhodesia after the Second World War when I was eight years old. My father continued his career making information and training films in Salisbury (subsequently Harare, Zimbabwe's capital). Unlike my parents, and in common with my sisters, once settled in school, I became an individual who learned to recognise that, from the age of eight I was at the start of a life with two personas, simultaneously a colonial expatriate and a white African. In Rhodesia in that era, the adolescence of a white schoolboy was dominated by two phenomena: firstly, the head teachers' imported enthusiasm for rugby and secondly, obligatory training after the age of 14 for military service.

Teaching was for the most part dominated by rote learning until those of us who entered the sixth form were fortunate to be taught by William Rayner, a migrant from Britain who came to Africa to teach English literature having graduated with an Oxford degree. Over the following years Bill became the warmest of friends both through the application of his intelligence in reading of Central African politics as understood by white migrants of his (as opposed to earlier generations). Significantly, it was Bill who introduced me to the work of C. G. Jung through *Memories, Dreams, Reflections*.

I left Rhodesia in my early 20s, at the end of a formal five-year commitment as a clerk articled to a Chartered Accountant's firm. I then returned to Britain to take the decisive step of enrolling for an undergraduate degree in the humanities at the Leeds University. Then, having completed a doctorate in literature, I found employment as a lecturer in English Studies at the New University of Ulster. A few years later I moved to Scotland to teach, research, and write not only literature but also film studies at the University of Stirling.

Shamanism

The word "shaman" has roots in Siberian culture, but variants of related ancient practices occur in communities and cultures worldwide. Some decades after leaving Zimbabwe I was reminded (by then over 60 years old) that I was more aware of shamanic practices than I had remembered. Actually, people who have moved away from their former lives in Central or Southern Africa commonly share the sense that the continent has marked them indelibly. For example, I knew a family doctor who did not press local people for money if they could not afford to pay his fees. Not infrequently such clients brought him small gifts of food. However, one old man claimed that he could rid the doctor's garden of poisonous snakes which he did, demonstrating his shamanic powers in a most effective way.

In practice I gained my formal knowledge of shamanic practice through the inspirational teaching of two women. The first of these was Twobirds, Wings of the Mountain Storm based near Inverness in Scotland. She began her instruction with an exploration of the concept of 'the non-ordinary world.' The phrase refers to an imagined world identified in contrast with the so-called *axis* mundi, the latter being somewhere that people already recognise as an actual place in the ordinary world. As a practicing shaman, I have used my wife's drum and enjoy the exuberance of joining in session accompanied by colleagues. By good fortune, the drum has not only a good ringing tone but also boasts a dramatic image (painted on the drum). This is nothing less extraordinary than the rendering of an uroboros, the mythical creature condemned to devouring its own tail in perpetuity.

The distinguishing characteristics of a power animal are likely to include features identifying it as belonging to the non-ordinary world. Thus, the behaviour of an imaginary domestic animal such as a dog is likely to differ strikingly from that of the actual creature, having characteristics which reveal it to be extraordinary (as implied by the very term "power animal"). The first creature to identify itself to me as a power animal in the lower world was a black panther. Early in our acquaintance, it revealed a characteristic typical of power animals by showing that it wanted to get to know me. In contrast, some power animals show themselves briefly to a newcomer in the lower world but then, having taken a look, may back away warily. Such a creature may not feel itself prepared to bond comfortably with the human who is considering it as a future partner. In contrast, the fantasy creature that shows signs of wanting to become a person's power animal may encourage the human to notice its interest so that a contact of this kind can develop into a rewarding personal attachment. Nevertheless, it is wise not to take the early expressions of its trust for granted because they may not endure should the human and the power animal discover that they are not compatible.

The black panther can be casually referred to as 'mine,' but certainly not on the pretence of claiming ownership, which would be absurd: as a power animal, it is linked to the collective unconscious and on a personal level as a projection of my personality. Of course, like anyone else, I could read about panthers and discover how they live in their natural environment. However, it is not the animal's physical existence, but its imagined qualities that interest me. As a companion escorting me protectively while we descend to the lower world, the panther impresses with its intense focus. It can and usually does run at the speed of an arrow, focussing its undivided attention on whatever at that moment absorbs it. Our shared access to the lower world is usually via a grand descent along a spiral pathway. Richly lined with walls of glittering black coal, this broad path makes for a fine walk and feels like a shared parade when the panther joins me in all his majestic pride on the walk down into the lower world. On other occasions it prefers to hold back and meets me as I reach my destination. However, in just one instance, the panther did not behave as I anticipated, and on that occasion, it was being told what to do by another shaman, Claudia Gonzalves.

In the foregoing, I have referred to elements of the training offered by Twobirds. She teaches classes which typically attract up to 20 people, a commitment which occupies much of her time, for which reason she does not offer one-to-one instruction. Claudia, on the other hand, does. When I realised that I needed intense support to help me through a gathering emotional crisis, I asked her to lead me on a journey and show me how to deal with the fear to which I had succumbed after watching my mother decline with Alzheimer's disease and die at the age 92. My fear, which had become relentless by the time I sought help from Claudia, was that I might eventually fall victim to the same condition.

My journey with Claudia started with her drumming. At first events appeared to follow a pattern familiar to me from my previous journeys into the lower world when the panther had paced alongside me down the spiral way and onwards deep into the lower world. On this occasion, however, the animal moved ahead, taking the lead and drawing me into the corner of a vast room. There he squatted beside my feet, his signal, by now familiar to me, that I should observe and take note of what I saw. The size of this unknown room, with its Victorian scale set off by golden walls and looming windows, discomforted me. I felt it become increasingly uncomfortable because it was visibly altering from moment to moment. After a while, I realised that I could no longer see out through the windows which now appeared to have clouded over mysteriously since the panther had led me into this room.

Presently, as time passed, something moving in the far corner of this bizarre space caught my eye. I thought I was gazing at a grotesque form and first perceived it to be a black witch. But, as I continued to gaze at this figure, I slowly became aware that a further transformation was underway, and the shape now differed from what I had first thought. The figure was still wearing black but, notwithstanding my former delusion, it no longer had a human form. The longer I stared, the more clearly could I see that it was two-dimensional: an object made from sticks and patches and waving black flags. As I began to understand its changing presence, it became clear to me that this grotesque gargoyle was expressing something symbolically. It dawned on me that I had been overwhelmed by fear for my future mental well-being, and that the fear had worsened during the decade of my mother's deepening dementia.

Claudia interrupted her drumming to ask what my panther was doing. Urged on by her, he led me out of the sinister room and along the underworld passage leading away from it. However, he soon stopped once again, becoming stubborn and grumpy when Claudia asked him to get a move on. She had to repeat her instructions more than once, ordering him to move. That triggered an almost mutinous response: moving forward a few steps, the panther soon squatted again. It was only after this part of the journey was over, that I had time to reflect that the panther was disconcerted, as if reckoning that Claudia had asked him to fulfil a role for which he had never been prepared. Of course, it being a power animal and purely a creature of my conscious or unconscious imagination, I had modelled my expectations on his previous behaviour which, of course, hitherto (and indeed later) had suited me well.

While Claudia continued to drum, I had no idea how I could connect with the panther until, unexpectedly, my thoughts clicked back to a distant memory from my adolescence in Central Africa. I recalled that I had long ago been familiar with another creature of my imagination, the housefly. I had never previously thought of the housefly as a power animal, but now recognised that it manifested many characteristics of that kind. Recognising this had so unexpected an impact on me that it felt as though Claudia had seen into my mind. Without ceremony, the fly lifted me instantaneously from the lower to the upper world. There I found myself sitting, apparently alone, in a meadow of rich grass where evening was beginning to close in. Not only did I notice that the fly had already disappeared but, in vanishing, it was doing exactly what the panther had done a moment earlier.

As this surprising moment demonstrated, the impact of a shaman's wisdom is wonderful. Claudia's insights extended and developed patterns of thought and behaviour into contexts previously unknown to me and which I could not otherwise have accessed unaided. I was to experience further visionary revelations before the session with her came to an end. These, together with the constant alternation of the scenes presenting themselves to my mind also brought on meditations (both conscious and unconscious) maturing in my head.

Philemon and Jung

After the fly had carried me up from the lower world, I became aware that a campfire was burning in the meadow near where I now found myself sitting. A pile of chopped wood lay within easy reach and, while Claudia continued drumming, other changes in the scene filtered into my conscious. I was not as isolated as I had thought at first, and now began to sense the presence of people around me. I could neither see nor hear them but knew with complete self-assurance that these must be the spirits of my ancestors. Soon I became aware of the figure of a tall, stately man. This was Philemon, a lone, visible spirit standing motionless behind the campfire. Whenever he has met with me, whether on this or the many occasions that followed, Philemon has let me know everything he wants me to understand without speaking a word. On this our first time together, he ordered me not to add more wood to the campfire. On the contrary, I should continue to sit silently in the meadow and let the fire burn until its last embers expired. By thus revealing himself as my spirit guide, he showed me that I was symbolically witnessing my own death before its time come. He let me know that the end of my life would be peaceful and there would be nothing for me to fear when the time came to step away from embodied, physical life. More than reassuring, this gave me what became a root stem of comfort and joyful insight for the remainder of my life.

This first meeting with Philemon, showed me that I was ready to explore the next in the sequence of steps that Twobirds teaches her students, namely, how to progress beyond visiting the lower world. Learning from the powerful connection between her guidance and Philemon's wisdom, I discovered how to engage my imagination in seeking out spirit figures in the upper world. As someone who had, with gathering enthusiasm, studied the writings of C. G. Jung since being introduced to them in secondary school by my teacher (and in later years close friend) the novelist William Rayner, it was clear to me that I must attempt a journey of the soul to meet the analytical psychologist in the spirit world.

There are plenty of well-known photographs of Jung working in his Bollingen tower in both his middle and late years. So, when in active imagination I entered his study, the room was recognisable. Equally familiar was a small black-and-white photograph of Philemon. This image had been painted by Jung himself, but only became widely known decades after his death when his family agreed to publication of his great work *Liber Novus* in full colour. Philemon's image now appears in *The Red Book* (2009: 154) and has reinforced my eagerness to make a journey of the soul to the spirit world and visit Jung. My intention was simple: to honour him and ask for his guidance. Thus, it delighted me that, when in imagination I reached Bollingen Tower, Jung looked up from his work and, foreknowing what I was coming to ask him, gave me a friendly nod and a wink, waving me forward to the door leading out from his study. There Philemon was waiting, ready to assist me in guiding souls to find their way in the upper world. Once again, I felt the authority of his presence as one of Jung's cherished spiritual associates and soon understood that he would become my spiritual guide, showing once more his ability to communicate with me wordlessly – sharing with me knowledge that I was to pass on to souls who had sought help to find their way in the world of spirits.

More than an introduction, this felt like a blessing. Not only did Philemon and I both understand that he had no need to speak to me, but his silent direction of my actions differed radically from his conversations with Jung. As recorded by Jung himself, his vigorous debates with Philemon centred on verbal contests between the analytical psychologist and his majestic visitor, the ghost recalled from ancient myth. For example, in Liber Secundus 148/149 Jung celebrates,

> You know, Oh Philemon, the wisdom of things to come; therefore, you are old, so very ancient, and just as you tower above me in years, so you tower above the present in futurity, and the length of your past is immeasurable. You are legendary and unreachable. You were and will be returning periodically.

Now in my mid-80s and the later stages of life, I can celebrate how passion for Jung and Film analysis have enriched my soul and taken me on directions of the psyche only outreached by shamanic journeying.

Notes

1 Eastwood, *Million Dollar Baby*.
2 Izod and Dovalis, *Cinema as Therapy*.
3 Mansfield, *Synchronicity, Science, and Soul-Making*.
4 Eliade, *Shamanism: Archaic Techniques of Ecstasy*.
5 *Initiation* is a descent into the underworld and an illumination by a principle of consciousness, which comes from the unconscious.
6 Jung, *Children's Dreams*, 299.
7 von Franz, *Archetypal Patterns in Fairy Tales*, 51.
8 Jung, *Visions*, 821.
9 von Franz, *Archetypal Patterns in Fairy Tales*, 160.
10 Gean is the term for a Scottish wild cherry tree.

Conclusion

If the following two segments on Jung and *Moonage Daydream* should be our swansong analyses, chosen for their mystical comments and views on death, dying, and the next stages of our individuation journey, then so be it.

In 2018 Tommaso Priviero updated our knowledge of the considerations informing Jung's writing. Priviero not only linked Dante's *Commedia* to the publication of *Liber Novus* but also to earlier writers who had influenced Jung's journey "on the service of the soul" (2009: 234). In the opening lines of *Liber Novus*, Jung recorded a sharp reversal in his passions when in the fortieth year of his life, "the desire for honour, power and every human happiness" suddenly ceased and "horror came over him" (Jung, 2009: 232), a crucial discovery in his spiritual development. Echoing Jung's theme, Priviero (2018: 32–3) cited Dante's opening of the *Commedia*.

> Half way along the road we have to go,
> I found myself obscured in a great forest,
> Bewildered, and I knew I had lost my way.
>
> Dante ([c.1308–1320]: 47, Inferno: 1–3)

By consciously echoing Dante's *Inferno*, Jung emphasised Hell's medieval appearance in also demonstrating his understanding of Hell not as an after-place of punishment and regret arbitrarily fixed in a dogmatic meaning, but as a transformative condition of psychic purification. He states,

> No one should deny the danger of the descent, but it *can* be risked. No one *need* risk it, but it is certain that someone will. And let those who go down the sunset way do so with open eyes, for it is a sacrifice which daunts even the gods.
>
> (*Symbols of Transformation*, 1956: §553)

In his interpretation of the *Black Books*, Jung had introduced a theme that he subsequently developed in *Liber Novus* (see Priviero, 2018: 43–5). This was Jung's encounter in his debates with the prophet Elijah, and more particularly with Philemon. These meetings with ghosts of the past were comparable to the multifaceted role played by Virgil in Dante's *Commedia* (see Shamdasani, 2009: 202). For just as Dante had conceived Virgil to his master and author,' so Jung thought of Philemon to be the "higher author" of his visionary material.

Priviero (2018: 42–3) summarised this aspect of Jung's argument in *Liber Novus* with the observation that

> to a large extent Jung's material resembles imagery and content of Dante's *Commedia:* the identity of the soul, the function of the guide, the function of shadows and ghosts, the devil and the integration of the evil counterpart, the ambivalence of fire symbolism (purification and transformation), the conical form of Hell, the guidance of the feminine principle, medieval imagery, Christianity, madness and divine folly. The blueprint on which all these themes rest in *Liber Novus* is in the first place a Dantesque inspiration for a psycho-cosmology of the opposites, where each element of regression (or *katabasis*, i.e. 'descent') is successfully counterbalanced and regenerated by an upward element of psychic progression (or *anabasis*, i.e. 'ascent').

Jung as Analyst and Shaman

Academic accounts of Jung's theories and practice usually focus on the architecture of his thought rather than his temperament. One of the more personal accounts of his teaching was published by Joseph Henderson (1975: 115) who eloquently described Jung's behaviour when analysing him.

> During most interviews he paced back and forth, gesturing as he talked, and he talked of everything that came to his mind, whether about a human problem, a dream, a personal reminiscence, an allegorical story or a joke. Yet he could become quiet, serious and extremely personal, sitting down almost too close for comfort and delivering a pointed interpretation of one's miserable personal problem so its bitter truth would really sink in. And yet he made some of his best life-changing observations indirectly, offhand, as if they were to be accepted lightly – even joyously.

Henderson's intimate account of Jung's approach to his clients celebrates the psychologist's personal characteristics, a feature of his intelligence which reinforces the sense of his humanity. He describes the man in language that we recognise intuitively.

Henderson's evocation of Jung's qualities is not the only description of his interaction with a patient. During the last decade of Jung's life (1951–1961), Sabi Tauber (both Jung's patient and his friend) sometimes told him her dreams and, on occasions, cited his response verbatim. She reported the following dream to Jung in the winter of 1951: "A timeless wanderer was walking with me through the ages. He showed me ancient carpets and marvels from all over the world, saying that they all belonged to me, for my great-grandfather on mother's side had been a vagabond." Jung reminded Tauber:

We all are pilgrims. We should not be all that attached to this world. A tramp is unbound; he is only a visitor on this earth; his home is in the beyond. The dream tells you: This is what you carry within – know and appreciate it!

(Gerber, 2021: 32)

Jung's words to Sabi Tauber reverberate with our understanding of Brett Morgen's and David Bowie's extraordinary film *Moonage Daydream* (2002). Thinking of the film's rich pairing of themes, *Facing Life and Foreseeing Death* seems deeply appropriate when it opens almost in silence and focuses on the printed words of its title sequence.

At the turn of the 20th Century, Friedrich Nietzsche declared that God was dead and that man had killed him. This created an arrogance within man that he himself was God.

But as God, all he could seem to produce was disaster.

That led to a terrifying conclusion: for if we could not take the place of God, how could we fill the place we had created within ourselves?

A sombre music opens like ethereal wind blowing across the universe to underpin Bowie's voices his thoughts during these opening titles:

Time! One of the most complex situations mainly made manifest. It's something that straddles past and future without ever grabbing present, or rather, it at first seems indifferent to the present. There's a tension of a most unfathomable nature. The world desires to be understood. You somehow feel that it's not you yourself that the world is addressing. It washes over you, holding a dialogue with something arcane that's maybe not mortal and you feel intrigued, captured even.

Here Bowie admits to doubt: "You're aware of a deeper existence, maybe a temporary assurance that there is no beginning, no end. And all at once, the outward appearance of meaning is transcended, and you find yourself struggling to comprehend a deep and formidable mystery. All is transient."

Here, at the very start of Brett Morgen's and his film, Bowie sets the question that the two of them meditate on during the next two hours: "Does it matter? Do I bother?"

Soon, the camera tilts up toward the heavens. Woven among the opening shots, Morgen introduces a landscape featuring a dark and mountainous terrain, a scene which steadily sweeps across a barren landscape imbued with mysterious voices-over but appears not to reveal a single human form. We cannot be sure that we have seen a human being even after noticing the figure of a young woman, prettily dressed in a long gown, but who, as she walks across this vast wilderness, passes the camera revealing her metre-long tail.

Two hours later, much the same scene will be repeated as in Morgen's and Bowie's imagining, the singer approaches death. As it happens, the latter's thoughts about his own mortality had already been expressed in a 1998 BBC programme about the British artist Richard Devereux. Bowie announced that he, like everybody else, was already confronting "a deep and formidable mystery. I'm dying. You're dying. Second by second, all is transient. Does it matter?" (see Kermode, 2022: 26–7).

Midway through *Moonage Daydream*, Bowie, having reflected further on significant alterations to both the form of his music and his life, left Los Angeles and moved to Berlin. There, he hired Brian Eno to work with him and announced his decision to seek chaos and random discovery in a new music which the players working with them set about creating, by undertaking minimal preparation before recording. Bowie justified his intention as being to embrace chaos, arguing that to fail to do so would be a great mistake because he reckoned that there had never been so rapid or exciting a change in music since the Industrial Revolution.

In reviewing the film, Corey Seymour (*Vogue*, May 24, 2022) introduced the resultant work as "a gloriously immersive kaleidoscopic examination not so much of Bowie's life here on earth, but of the life he lived inside his head and his heart, which led him to create his art." The key to recognising the genius of *Moonage Daydream* is as

> the first film to be officially sanctioned by Bowie's estate and the result of five years of painstaking research, writing, editing, sound mixing and deep dive immersion into the entirety of Bowie's archive of film, music, art and fashion (some 5 million assets) … astounding, bombastic, ground-breaking, electrifying, and among the best films about any artist or musician

seen by this critic. Seymour's eulogy also celebrates enthusiastically the work of writer-director-producer-editor Brett Morgen in taking those 5 million elements and assembling from them a mesmerising collage of sound and vision sure to entrance any Bowie fan. "Instead of telling you about Bowie, it puts you in the midst of his world; instead of teaching you things, it makes you *feel* the world he lived in." Morgen's intimate knowledge of Bowie's mind prepared viewers for the speculative vision of the life after death that was to round out their film.

Taking his cue from a film maker with intimate connections to Bowie, Kermode (2022) cites Bowie's son, the film director Duncan Jones, as having said that "It absolutely has the blessing of our family" because "I know it was made with love." Kermode added, "it is precisely that sense of love that shines through *Moonage Daydream*."

A sequence of hard cuts brings Bowie to Iman, whom he weds. Meanwhile his lyrics invest the richness of his imagining what with knowledge but also a tantalising sense of 'maybe' and 'should be' and, on the margins, 'the barely imaginable'. "Sweet angel born once again for me … Lord, I kneel and offer you my word on a wing… Lord, Lord, my prayer flies like a word on a wing … Does my prayer fit in with your scheme of things"?

Presently, he chants an upbeat invocation of chaos. "Moondust will cover you … Moondust will cover you …" then bright expanding light appears with a belt of nebulae across its equator, and Bowie sings:

> Something happened on the day he died.
> Spirit rose a meter and stepped aside.
> Somebody else took his place and bravely cried,
> I'm a black star ...

Bowie voices once more what we heard him say soon after the start of the film which now returns us steadily to traversing space, where raw conflict flares between brilliant light and blackest dark:

> And all at once, the outward appearance of meaning is transcended and you find yourself struggling to comprehend a deep and formidable mystery. I am dying. You are dying. Second by second. All is transient. Does it matter? Do I bother? Yes I do. Life is fantastic. It never ends. It only changes. Flesh to stone to flesh. And round and round. Best keep walking.

As he speaks, and as if to honour his words, a quiet choral humming is heard and once again there emerges (back lit by a black sun) the figure of the girl with a long tail, now seen in close up and moving forward. A countdown from ten begins as a voice announces, "The girl with the tail carries the astronaut's bejewelled skull in a glass box," and as her tail swishes against her skirts, lightning flashes behind mountain-top monoliths ... Presently, Bowie starts the chant that, as the lyrics are repeated, draws the film toward its close: "The sun machine is coming down and we're gonna have party!"

A number of young women gather round the girl while she displays the bejewelled skull to her fellow dancers who bow down to the ground to honour it. How could we refrain from asking whether the glittering skull is Bowie's in another life?

Here Joanna and John, as two celebrants of this extraordinary film, are driven to echo Jung when crucially in *Memories, Dreams, Reflections,* he asked his readers to consider the decisive question facing humanity, whether we are related to something infinite or not. That (to adapt Jung's question) should be the telling question of our lives.

Bibliography

Aspe, Bernard. "De l'origine radicale des choses." *Cahiers du Cinéma* (December 2011): 20–23.

Barnstone, Willis and Marvin Meyer, eds. and trans. *Essential Gnostic Scriptures*. Boston, MA: Shambhala, 2010.

Beebe, John. "The trickster in the arts." *The San Francisco Jung Institute Library Journal* 2, no. 2 (1981): 21–54.

Brody, Richard. "Terrence Malick's 'Knight of Cups' Challenges Hollywood to Do Better." *The New Yorker* (7 March 2016). https://www.newyorker.com/culture/richard-brody/terrence-malicks-knight-of-cups-challenges-hollywood-to-do-better

Bunyan, John. *The Pilgrim's Progress*. Harmondsworth: Penguin, 1965. First published 1768.

Cadwalladr, Carole. "The Great British Brexit Robbery: How Our Democracy Was Hijacked." *The Guardian* (7 May 2017). https://www.theguardian.com/technology/2017/may/07/the-great-british-brexit-robbery-hijacked-democracy

Campbell, Joseph. *The Inner Reaches of Outer Space: Metaphor as Myth and as Religion*. Novato, CA: New World Library, 1986.

Carotenuto, Aldo. *Eros and Pathos: Shades of Love and Suffering*. Toronto: Inner City Books, 1989.

Carotenuto, Aldo. *To Love to Betray: Life as Betrayal*. Asheville, NC: Chiron Publications, 1996.

Carotenuto, Aldo. *Rites and myths of seduction*. Wilmette, IL: Chiron Publications, 2002.

Eastwood, Clint, dir. *Million Dollar Baby*. Warner Bros., 2004.

Ebiri, Bilge. "Malick Goes L.A. in the Sumptuous 'Knight of Cups'." *The Village Voice* (1 March 2016). https://www.villagevoice.com/film/malick-goes-la-in-the-sumptuous-knight-of-cups-8336020

Edinger, Edward. *Anatomy of the Psyche: Alchemical Symbolism in Psychotherapy*. Chicago: Open Court, 1985.

Eliade, Mircea. *Images and Symbols: Studies in Religious Symbolism*. Princeton, NJ: Princeton University Press, 1991.

Eliade, Mircea. *The Myth of the Eternal Return*. Translated by W. Trask. New York: Pantheon, 1954.

Eliade, Mircea. *Shamanism: Archaic Techniques of Ecstasy*. Princeton: Princeton University Press, 2004.

Fairbairn, W. R. D. *Psychoanalytic Studies of the Personality*. London: Routledge, 1952.

Felsenthal, Julia. "Terrence Malick's *Song to Song* Is the Anti–*La La Land*." *Vogue* (17 March 2017). https://www.vogue.com/article/song-to-song-terrence-malick-review

Fleming, David H. "Cinema, Philosophy and Time." *Lecture at the University of Stirling* (17 October 2019).

Fleming, David H. and W. Brown. "Through a (First) Contact Lens Darkly: *Arrival*, Unreal Time and Chthulucinema." *Film-Philosophy* 22, 3 (2018): 340–363.

Gerber, Andreas and Irene Gerber, eds. *Encounters with C. G. Jung: The Journal of Sabi Tauber (1951–1961)*. Einsiedeln: Daimon Verlag, 2021.

Gilmour, Alison. "Ambitious, Beautiful Film Fails to Achieve the Transcendence Its Characters Seek." *Winnipeg Free Press* (31 March 2016). https://www.winnipegfreepress.com/arts-and-life/entertainment/movies/ambitious-beautiful-film-fails-to-achieve-the-transcendence-its-characters-seek-374188631.html

Goncalves, Claudia. *Shamanism as Medicine: An Initiation into the World of Shamanism.* Bloomington, IN: Balboa Press, 2022.

Greer, Mary K. "Carl Jung on the Major Arcana." *Mary K. Greer's Tarot Blog* (18 April 2008). https://marykgreer.com/2008/04/18/carl-jung-on-the-major-arcana

Greer, Mary K. *Tarot for Your Life*. North Hollywood, CA: Newcastle Publishing, 1984.

Hannah, Barbara. *The Animus: The Spirit of Inner Truth in Women.* Vol. 2. Asheville, NC: Chiron Publications, 2018.

Harding, Esther. *Woman's Mysteries: Ancient and Modern*. Boston, MA: Shambala, 1990. First published 1935.

Henderson, Joseph L. "C. G. Jung: A Reminiscent Picture of His Method" *Journal of Analytical Psychology* 20, 2 (1975): 115.

Henderson, Joseph L. and Dyane N. Sherwood. *Transformation of the Psyche: The Symbolic Alchemy of the Splendor Solis*. New York: Routledge, 2003.

Hillman, James. *Senex & Puer.* Uniform Edition 3. Dallas: Dallas Institute Publications, 2005.

Izod, John and Joanna Dovalis. *Cinema as Therapy: Grief and Transformational Film*. New York: Routledge, 2015.

Jenkins, David. "Song to Song." *Little White Lies: Truth & Movies* (7 July 2017). https://lwlies.com/reviews/song-to-song/

Jonas, Hans. *The Gnostic Religion: The Message of the Alien God and the Beginnings of Christianity*. 2nd ed., revised. Boston, MA: Beacon Press, 1963.

Jung, Carl G. "After the Catastrophe." In *Civilization in Transition: The Collected Works of C. G. Jung*. Vol. 10. Translated by Richard Hull. Edited by Herbert Read et al. pp. 194–217. London: Routledge & Kegan Paul, 1964. First published 1945.

Jung, Carl G. *Alchemical Studies: The Collected Works of C. G. Jung*. Vol. 13. Translated by Richard Hull. Edited by Herbert Read et al. Princeton, NJ: Princeton University Press, 1983.

Jung, Carl G. "Analytical Psychology and *Weltanshauung*." In *The Structure and Dynamics of the Psyche: The Collected Works of C. G. Jung*. Vol. 8, 2nd ed. Translated by Richard Hull. Edited by Herbert Read et al. pp. 358–381. London: Routledge & Kegan Paul, 1969. First published 1931.

Jung, Carl G. "Answer to Job." In *Psychology and Religion: West and East; Collected Works of C. G. Jung*. Vol. 11. Translated by Richard Hull. Edited by Herbert Read et al. pp. 355–474. London: Routledge and Kegan Paul, 1958. First published 1954.

Jung, Carl G. *The Archetypes and the Collective Unconscious: The Collected Works of C. G. Jung, Volume 9i.* Translated by Richard Hull. Edited by Herbert Read et al. Princeton: Princeton University Press, 1990.

Jung, Carl G. *Children's Dreams: Notes from the Seminar Given in 1936–1940*. Edited by Lorenz Jung and Maria Meyer-Grass. Translated by Ernst Falzeder and Tony Woolfson. Princeton: Princeton University Press, 2008.

Jung, Carl G. "Flying Saucers: A Modern Myth of Things Seen in the Skies." In *Civilization in Transition: The Collected Works of C. G. Jung.* Vol. 10. Translated by Richard Hull. Edited by Herbert Read et al. pp. 307–436. London: Routledge & Kegan Paul, 1964. First published 1959.

Jung, Carl G. *Memories, Dreams, Reflections.* Edited by Aniela Jaffé. Translated by Clara Winston and Richard Winston. New York: Random House, 1989. First published 1963.

Jung, Carl G. *Mysterium coniunctionis: The Collected Works of C. G. Jung.* Vol. 14. Translated by Richard Hull. Edited by Herbert Read et al. Princeton, NJ: Princeton University Press, 1970. First published 1954.

Jung, Carl G. "On the Psychology of the Unconscious." In *Two Essays on Analytical Psychology: The Collected Works of C. G. Jung.* Vol. 7. Translated by Richard Hull. Edited by Herbert Read et al. pp. 3–122. London: Routledge & Kegan Paul, 1981. First published 1943.

Jung, Carl G. "Picasso." In *The Spirit in Man, Art, and Literature: The Collected Works of C. G. Jung.* Vol. 15. Translated by Richard Hull. Edited by Herbert Read et al. pp. 135–142. London: Routledge & Kegan Paul, 1966. First published 1934.

Jung, Carl G. *The Practice of Psychotherapy: The Collected Works of C. G. Jung.* Vol. 16. Translated by Richard Hull. Edited by Herbert Read et al. Princeton, NJ: Princeton University Press, 1985.

Jung, Carl G. "Preface and Epilogue to 'Essays on Contemporary Events'." In *Civilization in Transition: Collected Works of C. G. Jung.* Vol. 10, 2nd ed. Translated by Richard Hull. Edited by Herbert Read et al. pp. 177–178. Hove: Routledge, 1970. First published 1946.

Jung, Carl G. "A Psychological Approach to the Dogma of the Trinity." In *Psychology and Religion: West and East; The Collected Works of C. G. Jung.* Vol. 11. Translated by Richard Hull. Edited by Herbert Read et al. pp. 107–200. London: Routledge & Kegan Paul, 1958. First published 1948.

Jung, Carl G. "Psychological Aspects of the Mother Archetype." In *The Archetypes and the Collective Unconscious: The Collected Works of* C. G. Jung. Vol. 9, pt. 1. Translated by Richard Hull. Edited by Herbert Read et al. pp. 75–112. London: Routledge & Kegan Paul, 1968. First published 1954.

Jung, Carl G. *Psychological Types: The Collected Works of C. G. Jung.* Vol. 6. Translated by Richard Hull. Edited by Herbert Read et al. Princeton, NJ: Princeton University Press, 1971.

Jung, C. G. "A Psychological View of Conscience." In *Civilization in transition: The Collected Works of C. G. Jung.* Vol. 10. Translated by Richard Hull. Edited by Herbert Read et al. pp. 437–455. London: Routledge & Kegan Paul, 1964. First published 1958.

Jung, Carl G. *Psychology and Alchemy: The Collected Works of C. G. Jung, Volume 12.* Translated by Richard Hull. Edited by Herbert Read et al. Princeton, NJ: Princeton University Press, 1980.

Jung, Carl G. "The Psychology of the Transference." In *The Practice of Psychotherapy: The Collected Works of C. G. Jung.* Vol. 16. 2nd ed. Translated by Richard Hull. Edited by Herbert Read et al. pp. 163–326. Princeton, NJ: Princeton University Press, 1985. First published 1945.

Jung, Carl G. *The Quotable Jung.* edited by Judith Harris. Princeton, NJ: Princeton University Press, 2018.

Jung, Carl G. *The Red Book: Liber Novus*. edited by Sonu Shamdasani. Translated by Mark Kyburz and John Peck. New York: W. W. Norton & Company, 2009.

Jung, Carl G. "The Role of the Unconscious." In *Civilization in Transition: The Collected Works of C. G. Jung*. Vol. 10. Translated by Richard Hull. Edited by Herbert Read et al. pp. 3–28. London: Routledge & Kegan Paul, 1964. First published 1918.

Jung, Carl G. "A Study in the Process of Individuation." In *The Archetypes and the Collective Unconscious: The Collected Works of C. G. Jung*. Vol. 9, pt. 1, 2nd ed. Translated by Richard Hull. Edited by Herbert Read et al. pp. 290–354. London: Routledge & Kegan Paul, 1959. First published 1950.

Jung, Carl G. *Symbols of Transformation*. Translated by Richard Hull. Edited by Herbert Read et al. London: Routledge and Kegan Paul, 1956.

Jung, Carl G. "Synchronicity: An Acausal Connecting Principle." In *The Structure and Dynamics of the Psyche: Collected Works of C. G. Jung*. Vol. 8, 2nd ed. Translated by Richard Hull. Edited by Herbert Read et al. pp. 417–519. Hove: Routledge, 1969. First published 1952.

Jung, Carl G. "Transformation Symbolism in the Mass." In *Psychology and Religion: East and West, Collected Works of C. G. Jung*. Vol. 11, 2nd ed. Translated by Richard Hull. Edited by Herbert Read et al. pp. 201–298. London: Routledge & Kegan Paul, 1969. First published 1954.

Jung, Carl G. *Visions: Notes of the Seminar Given in 1930–1934, Volume I*. Edited by Claire Douglas. Zürich: Spring Publications, 1976.

Jung, Carl G. *Visions: Notes of the Seminar Given in 1930–1934, Volume II*. Edited by Claire Douglas. Princeton, NJ: Princeton University Press, 1997.

Jung, Carl G. and Carl Kerényi. *Essays on a Science of Mythology*. Princeton, NJ: Princeton University Press, 1978.

Jung, Carl G. *Dream symbols of the individuation process: notes of CG Jung's seminars on Wolfgang Pauli's dreams*. Vol. 15. Princeton: Princeton University Press, 2019.

Kendrick, James. "Arrival." *QNetwork* (2017). https://www.qnetwork.com/review/3832

Kendrick, James. "Ex Machina." *QNetwork* (2015). https://www.qnetwork.com/index.php?page=review&id=3281

Kermode, Mark, "Stardust Memories." *The Observer* (18 September 2022): 26–27.

Language. *Wikipedia: The Free Encyclopedia*. San Francisco, CA: Wikimedia Foundation. https://en.wikipedia.org/wiki/Language

Lepp, Andrew and Heather Gibson. "Sensation Seeking and Tourism: Tourist Role, Perception of Risk and Destination Choice." *Tourism Management* 29, 4 (August 2008): 740–750.

Lidzbarski, Mark, trans. *Ginza. Der Schatz oder das Grosse Buch der Mandäer* [Ginza: The Treasure or Great Book of the Mandäer]. Göttingen: Vandenhoeck & Ruprecht, 1963. First published 1925.

Main, Roderick. "Synchronicity and the Limits of Re-enchantment." *International Journal of Jungian Studies* 3, 2 (September 2011): 144–158.

Malick, Terrence, dir. *Knight of Cups*. Nashville, TN: Dogwood Films, 2015.

Malick, Terrence, dir. *Song to Song*. Austin, TX: Buckeye Pictures, 2017.

Malick, Terrence, dir. *The Tree of Life*. Newhall, CA: Cottonwood Pictures, 2017.

Mansfield, Victor. *Head and Heart: A Personal Experience of Science and the Sacred*. Wheaton, IL: Quest Books, 2002.

Mansfield, Victor. *Synchronicity, Science, and Soulmaking: Understanding Jungian Synchronicity Through Physics, Buddhism, and Philosophy*. Chicago: Open Court Press, 1998.

Mathieson, Craig. "Arrival Review: Sci-fi Turned Inside Out as Alien Contact Gets Personal." *The Age* (8 November 2016). https://www.theage.com.au/entertainment/movies/

arrival-review-scifi-turned-inside-out-as-alien-contact-gets-personal-20161107-gsjokf. html

Mayward, Joel. "Arrival." *Cinemayward: A Montage of Film Criticism and Theology* (26 November 2016). https://cinemayward.com/review/arrival/

Meier, C. A. *Personality: The Individuation Process in the Light of C. G. Jung's Typology.* Einsiedeln: Daimon Verlag, 1977.

Nelson, Ryan. "The Beginner's Guide to the Gnostic Gospels." *Overview Bible* (21 September 2018). https://overviewbible.com/gnostic-gospels/

Neumann, Erich. *The Origins and History of Consciousness*, Princeton, NJ: Princeton University Press, 1954.

Neumann, Erich. *Fear of the Feminine*. Princeton, NJ: Princeton University Press, 1994.

Neumann, Erich. *The Great Mother*. Princeton, NJ: Princeton University Press, 1963.

Owens, Lance S. *Jung in Love: The* Mysterium *in* Liber Novus. Los Angeles, CA: Gnosis Archive Books, 2015.

Pinkerton, Nick. "*Knight of Cups*: Get Your Wings." *Reverse Shot* (4 March 2016). https:// reverseshot.org/reviews/entry/2185/knightofcups

Pride, Ray. "Time Regained: The Undertow of Terrence Malick's *Knight of Cups*." *NewCity Film* (9 March 2016). https://newcityfilm.com/2016/03/09/time-regained-the-undertow-of-terrence-malicks-knight-of-cups

Priviero, Tommaso A. "A Historical Study of Carl G. Jung's Understanding of Dante." *European Yearbook of the History of Psychology* 6, 2 (2020): 63–96. https://doi.org/10.1484/J. EYHP.5.121861

Priviero, Tommaso. "On the Service of the Soul: C. G. Jung's *Liber Novus* and Dante's *Commedia*." *Phanes* 1 (2018): 28–57.

Rithdee, Kong. "An Enigmatic, Carnal Pilgrimage." *Bangkok Post* (8 April 2016). https:// www.bangkokpost.com/lifestyle/film/925577/an-enigmatic-carnal-pilgrimage

Rothenberg, Rose-Emily. *The Jewel in the Wound*. Wilmette, IL: Chiron Publications, 2001.

Ruland, Martin. *Lexicon alchemiae, sive Dictionarium alchemisticum*. Frankfurt am Main, 1612.

Samuels, Andrew, Bani Shorter and Fred Plaut. *A Critical Dictionary of Jungian Analysis.* London: Routledge & Kegan Paul, 1986.

Schwartz-Salant, Nathan. *Narcissism and Character Transformation: The Psychology of Narcissistic Character Disorders*. Toronto: Inner City Books, 1982.

Seymour, Corey. "*Moonage Daydream* Pays Astounding, Electrifying Homage to the Genius of David Bowie." *Vogue* (24 May 2022).

Shamdasani, Sonu. *Introduction to The Red Book: Liber Novus by C. G. Jung*. New York: W. W. Norton & Company, 2009.

Sharrock, Roger, ed. *John Bunyan: The Pilgrim's Progress*. Harmondsworth: Penguin, 1965.

Shea, Peter. *Marie-Louise von Franz, On Dreams and Death: A Jungian Interpretation.* Boston: Shambhala Publications, 1987.

Sragow, Michael. "Deep Focus: 'Ex Machina'." *Film Comment* (22 April 2015). https:// www.filmcomment.com/blog/deep-focus-ex-machina/

Stein, Murray. *Solar Conscience / Lunar Conscience: Essay on the Psychological Foundations of Morality, Lawfulness and the Sense of Justice*. Wilmette, IL: Chiron, 1993.

Tisdall, Simon. "Weak, Divided, Incompetent … the West Is Unfit to Challenge Xi's Bid for Global Hegemony." *The Observer* (5 July 2020): 33.

Toppman, Lawrence. "'Ex Machina' Asks Where Humanity Begins." *The Charlotte Observer* (22 April 2015). https://www.charlotteobserver.com/entertainment/ent-columns-blogs/lawrence-toppman/article19235649.html

Vinterberg, Thomas, dir. *Far from the Madding Crowd*. Century City, CA: Fox Searchlight Pictures, 2015.

von Franz, Marie-Louise. *Alchemical Active Imagination*. Boston, MA: Shambhala, 1997.

von Franz, Marie-Louise. *Archetypal Dimensions of the Psyche*. Boston, MA: Shambhala, 1999.

von Franz, Marie-Louise. *Archetypal Patterns in Fairy Tales*. Toronto: Inner City Books, 1997.

von Franz, Marie-Louise . *The Cat: A Tale of Feminine Redemption*. Toronto: Inner City Books, 1999.

von Franz, Marie Louise. *Corpus Alchemicum Arabicum*. Vol. 1. Zürich: Living Human Heritage, 2006.

von Franz, Marie-Louise. *Creation Myths*. Boston, MA: Shambhala, 1995.

von Franz, Marie-Louise. *The Feminine in Fairy Tales*. Boston, MA: Shambhala, 1993.

von Franz, Marie-Louise. *Individuation in Fairy Tales*. Boston, MA: Shambhala, 1990.

von Franz, Marie-Louise. *The Interpretation of Fairy Tales*. Boston, MA: Shambhala, 1996.

von Franz, Marie-Louise. *The Problem of the Puer Aeturnus*. 3rd ed. Toronto: Inner City Books, 2000. First published 1959–1960.

von Franz, Marie-Louise. *The Way of the Dream: Conversations on Jungian Dream Interpretation*. Boston, MA: Shambhala, 1994.

Wang, Robert. *Tarot Psychology: A Practical Guide to the Jungian Tarot*. Neuhausen: Urania Verlags, 1990. 2nd printing.

Wang, Robert. *Tarot Psychology: Handbook for the Jungian Tarot*. Neuhausen: Urania Verlags, 1988.

Zuckerman, Marvin. *Sensation Seeking: Beyond the Optimal Level of Arousal*. Hillsdale, NJ: Lawrence Erlbaum Associates, 1979.

Index

Note: Page numbers followed by "n" denote endnotes.

3, 50, 56; patriarchal 44, 46; reflective 10; vague 35
creation mythology 2, 10, 26, 40, 43

Dan, Julia Scarlett 51
Dante Alighieri 5, 144–145; *Commedia* 105, 144, 145; *Inferno* 144; on love 104, 105
Days of Heaven 107
death 98–101
Dennehy, Brian 82
desirousness, frustration of 89
Devereux, Richard 146
Devs 41n7
discrimination 72, 108
distress 35, 125; collective 59
Dylan, Bob: "Rollin' and a Tumblin'" 114, 124
dystopia 20–23

Edinger, Edward 89
ego 11, 25, 26, 28, 36, 83; consciousness 1, 3, 50, 56, 71, 105; desires 79, 114; ego-Self relationship 26; personality 69
Eliade, Mircea 6, 43, 49, 56, 60n8, 134
Emond, Linda 119, 125
envy 69, 73, 118
Eros 15, 16, 20, 32, 35, 36, 60n5, 66, 76, 79, 81, 83, 94, 107, 108, 114, 117, 119, 123, 126, 127, 130, 135
eternal time 42–60
Ex Machina 1, 3–5, 24–41, 82; anima trapped in Eden 27–29; betrayal 36–40; exploitative orphan, exploiting 31–36; language 36–40; otherness 24; paradise owned 24–27; unconscious figures 24

Facing Life and Foreseeing Death 146
Fairbairn, W. R. D. 103n4
fairness 66
fantasy 2, 5, 29, 31, 75, 87, 88, 95–97, 110, 111, 135, 140; erotic 14; sexual 84; shared arousal of 33
Far from the Madding Crowd (Vinterberg) 4; and redemption of animus 61–79
Fassbender, Michael 106
Felsenthal, Julia 120, 129
feminine consciousness 3, 17–19, 56, 57

femininity 58, 97, 110
Fleming, David 51, 60
Franz, Marie-Louise von 2, 3, 6, 15, 27, 30, 41n3, 54, 67, 73, 94, 100, 105, 113, 114, 131, 136, 137; on marital relationship 77, 103n1; on neurosis 136; on *senex-puer* archetype 81
Frederickson, Don 133
freedom 5, 37, 39, 40, 47, 96, 101–102, 112, 116

Gielgud, John: *Pilgrim's Progress, The* 80
gift 63
Gleeson, Domhnall 24
Gosling, Ryan 107
grief 73, 75, 99, 113, 128, 133
Grieg, Edvard: 'Solveig's Song' 92, 94
guilt 40, 57, 76, 117

Hannah, Barbara 47, 49–51, 56, 57, 60n5, 60n6, 68, 69, 73
Harding, Esther 13, 96–97
Hardy, Thomas 61
Henderson, Joseph 145
herd instinct 79
heterosexuality 34
hierophanies 20–23
hierosgamos 112
Hillman, James 18, 20, 23, 81–83
humanity 2, 9, 18–20, 29, 36, 40, 43, 56, 58, 59, 85, 91, 99, 101, 145, 148
human suffering 4
humiliation 75, 90, 126
Hunter, Holly 117
Hymn of the Pearl, The 5, 81

Iggy Pop 117
individuation 1, 5, 6, 63, 64, 72, 73, 77, 82, 85, 87, 88, 95, 99, 100, 102, 113, 117, 133–137, 144; goal of 7; inner lawfulness of 116; mutual 104, 137; participation mystique and 18, 26; self-knowledge and 25, 79
Inferno (Dante) 144
inflation 26, 30, 32, 35, 74, 116, 125; egotistical 71; psychological 122
instinct 4, 11, 13–16, 18, 21, 22, 25, 32, 40, 50, 58, 64, 70, 71, 74, 85, 89, 95, 97, 108, 111, 121, 127; herd 79; masculine 28; of self-preservation 28; sexual 26, 112; unconscious 26

For Product Safety Concerns and Information please contact our EU
representative GPSR@taylorandfrancis.com
Taylor & Francis Verlag GmbH, Kaufingerstraße 24, 80331 München, Germany

www.ingramcontent.com/pod-product-compliance
Lightning Source LLC
Chambersburg PA
CBHW070343270326
41926CB00017B/3966

9 781032 899442